8a

LIFE ON THE RIM

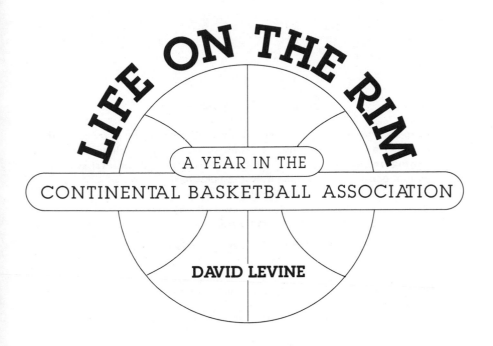

LIFE ON THE RIM

A YEAR IN THE
CONTINENTAL BASKETBALL ASSOCIATION

DAVID LEVINE

MACMILLAN PUBLISHING COMPANY
NEW YORK

Macmillan Publishing Company
866 Third Avenue, New York, NY 10022
Collier Macmillan Canada, Inc.

Photographs by Steven L. Twardzik

Library of Congress Cataloging-in-Publication Data
Levine, David, 1957–
    Life on the rim : a year in the Continental Basketball Association / by
David Levine.
        p.   cm.
    ISBN 0-02-570381-1
    1. Continental Basketball Association—History.   I. Title.
GV885.515.C66L48   1989
796.323'07'7—dc20   89-12317   CIP

Macmillan books are available at special discounts for bulk purchases for sales promotions, premiums, fund-raising, or educational use. For details, contact:
                    Special Sales Director
                    Macmillan Publishing Company
                    866 Third Avenue
                    New York, N.Y. 10022

10   9   8   7   6   5   4   3   2   1
PRINTED IN THE UNITED STATES OF AMERICA

FOR MOM AND DAD
FOR SUE

CONTENTS

ACKNOWLEDGMENTS

It is the nature of a book like this that the people who most helped me are the people about whom I have written; if your name is in here, I owe you many thanks, if only for letting me tell your story. Still, a few people need to be singled out.

First, my agent, David Black, who came up with the idea, helped me with the proposal, and sold it, plus offered continuous aid and constructive criticism—a bargain at 15 percent of the gross. Second, my editor at Macmillan, Rick Wolff, who bought the idea, encouraged the project, and always kept me on course. And to Rick's assistant, Jeanine Bucek, who fielded frantic phone calls from strange towns with a soothing voice and always accepted the charges.

Gary Holle was my first contact at the Patroons and the first to let me into this world; his entire front office staff, Beth Harbour and Kim Dickinson, made sure I got on the right planes and in the right hotels. Thanks to them, and to Patroons publicist Bill Heller and Doug Dickinson—aka Stat Man—for the numbers and the stories. Thanks also to the overworked and underpaid training staff, especially Jack Moser and, later on, Doc Nunnally. They both added more than they know to the material herein, and to the enjoyment with which it was collected. And to all the Armory staff and game-night volunteers who let me in the building.

Tim Wilkin was invaluable in offering advice, support, wonderful anecdotes, and friendship; he also bought many rounds above and beyond the call. Dan Levy, too, furnished stories and good cheer at home and on the road, and he always exhibited grace under pressure—he gave as good as he got.

Warmest personal regards to Barry Shapiro—Mr. B.—for being a strong and treasured friend, a fine journalist and, in my book, the Only Commissioner. And to Tom and Patty Smith—and Christopher and Andrew, too—who are simply great friends; you calmed us down when we were at the edge, you fed us and gave us aspirin and beer during our darkis (*sic*) hours, and we love you for it.

We, of course, is me and Sue, and Sue gets her own paragraph. My wife deserves special commendation for weathering long road trips, too many games, too many way-too-late nights (in the name of "research"), distracted and inattentive home life, crankiness, doubts, fears, poverty, and everything else that makes writing a book so pleasant. She lived with it all and only complained when it was needed to keep me in line. There is no way I can thank her enough.

Nor can I give sufficient thanks to Linda and Marshall Levine —aka Mom and Dad—for all their love and support (emotional, financial, and all that comes in between). I owe them just about everything.

To all the players, coaches, media relations directors, writers, radio announcers, team and league officials, van and bus drivers, cheerleaders, bartenders and waitresses, and fans around the league whom I met—in short, to all who *really* make up the CBA—my deepest appreciation.

It goes without saying—but I'll say it anyway: Without the cooperation of all nineteen men who wore Patroons uniforms this season this book would not have been possible. All of them were terrific and understanding, and they let me hang around and record their lives, which when you think of it is a remarkable thing to ask of someone. Some, of course, were more terrific than the rest, and were willing to share enough of themselves and their lives with me that I hope I can call them friends. I think they know who they are, and to them, a special thanks.

But the deepest bows must be directed toward the coaches, George Karl and Gerald Oliver. From the start they both embraced the idea for this book, gave me total access and never looked back, put up with my not so discreetly hidden tape recorder and my sneaking off to take notes (and trying to peek over my shoulder at them, don't think I didn't see you!), answered even my dumbest questions with patience, allowed my almost constant presence when they probably wished they didn't have to—all with style and grace and humor, and with nothing to gain except the (they hope) accurate depiction of an unlikely slice of sporting life. It is my greatest wish as well that they find this story accurate. For they have lived an extraordinary winter, and they let me share in it and tell about it. Thanks, GK. Thanks, Ollie. I hope this isn't clutter.

—David Levine

AUTHOR'S NOTE

On July 19, 1989, twelve weeks after this book was completed, Jay Ramsdell, the commissioner of the Continental Basketball Association, and Deputy Commissioner Jerry Schemmel boarded a flight from Denver to Chicago. They were on their way to oversee the 1989 CBA amateur draft in Columbus, Ohio. The aircraft—United Airlines Flight 232—developed serious mechanical problems en route, and crashed in Sioux City, Iowa. Jerry Schemmel survived the crash. Jay Ramsdell did not. He was twenty-five years old.

Ramsdell does figure prominently in this book; though I met Jay a couple of times, he is mentioned only when he and the Albany Patroons team cross paths. But Ramsdell was of course a vital and important part of the CBA. Much of the league's success in recent years is a result of his dedication and hard work. He started his CBA career as a team statistician in his home state of Maine at the age of fourteen, and worked his way to the league office, where he served in several positions before becoming commissioner in 1988. In essence, Ramsdell and the CBA came of age together. Despite his youth, he was respected by all who worked with him, and he was a good friend to many people throughout the league and with the Patroons' organization.

The loss of Jay is great. It is to his family and friends, and to his memory, that I offer this special dedication.

—D.L.
August 1, 1989

LIFE ON THE RIM

INTRODUCTION: BEFORE THE FLOOD

It's August already, and Gerald Oliver doesn't have a job.

By this time of the year, Gerald should have something lined up. He's fifty-three, and he's got a wife and a son, and he's been working steadily at his chosen profession for twenty-two years. He's good at it, too; well known and well liked, several real successes —and, sure, a couple of things that didn't pan out, but that happens when you work for a living, and it happens a lot in his field. But now it's August, and Gerald isn't working.

Gerald Oliver is a basketball coach. Not an NBA—Pat Riley—showtime type coach, though at one time Gerald worked in The League. Not a Bob Knight—cushy office on a pretty campus—all-powerful type, though he has also had positions in the college ranks. No, Gerald Oliver is a different kind of basketball coach. He is a coach in the little-known, little-followed, long-van-trips-through-snowstorms, small-towns-and-cold-empty-gyms mold. He has plied his trade the last several years in leagues with vaguely familiar acronyms, leagues like the USBL (the United States Basketball League), and mostly, for the last several years, anyway, the CBA— the Continental Basketball Association. He works at coaching; coaching is his work. And by August, with the CBA season only a few months away, a man should have a job. Gerald is a little worried.

But then, after all these years, maybe it's time to move on. Some security, a regular paycheck, living in the same city more than a

1

year or two. Maybe personnel, human resources; Gerald would be good at that. If there's one thing Gerald's good with, it's people. He likes everyone—not all the time, of course, not when they make his life difficult or don't hold to their word, but by nature he likes everyone—and everyone likes him. Coaching is kind of a human resources business, anyway, and as people say about him, if you can't work with Gerald you can't work with anyone.

Gerald Oliver is a big man in a lot of ways. When he stands tall—when fatigue hasn't hung his head or pulled at his shoulders—he is a little over six feet. No matter how he stands, he's a lot over his best weight. He has a round, full-moon face, and less hair and more chin than he'd like. Even in the most casual coaching garb—sweat suit, sneakers—he manages to look rumpled. In civilian clothes, his pants tend to hang low, and his shirttail is forever escaping the bonds of his waistband. If he looks a bit like Curly, of the Three Stooges (and he does, a fact not missed by opposing fans), it is unfortunate, because that implies a certain buffoonishness, and Gerald is not that. He is a thoughtful, intelligent man—he has a master's degree, and several hours toward a doctorate, in mathematics—and he knows a great deal about basketball, but his appearance (and his manner) sometimes cast a shadow over that intelligence, making him seem more clownish than he really is.

No, Gerald is no buffoon. But he is often somewhat befuddled. Gerald tends to do more than he should, take on more jobs and responsibility than he can easily handle. As a result he sleeps little, is often tired and therefore a little slow-moving. He seems confused, disorganized on occasion, but to him everything is under control. That's the way Gerald does things. He does them his way, and he gets them done his way. It's just that Gerald takes a winding, twisting path to get there, a path no one else can see. (He keeps his watch set one hour ahead of Eastern Standard Time, no matter what time zone he's in, and can't really explain why. "Ah'm on Greenwich Village time . . . Ah mean Greenwich Time," he jokes, but he's really on Gerald Oliver time.)

Gerald was once a proficient amateur boxer, and he has the gnarled hands and bent fingers to prove it. His left leg gives him trouble—an old knee injury—and when he's tired he walks with a pronounced limp. At other times the limp is less obvious; he just sort of lumbers. A native of Tennessee, Gerald has a voice that is as big and round as his body, a rich, rolling, barbecue voice that sometimes sounds more like a parody of a southern accent than a southern accent. He tends to talk loud when he gets excited, tends to repeat things once or twice with a laugh when telling a story. He talks a lot, too—"Ah do go on sometahmes," he admits—using thirty-five words where three will do, and sometimes he gets lost on the way to whatever point he's trying to make, a trait that adds to the overall impression that Gerald is more than a few steps out of the base path. But mostly, he is pure joy to listen to. His voice fills a room and envelops everyone in it like a thick, sweet-smelling fog. His eyes sparkle when he's happy, and his favored greeting is a delighted "Hey, buddy." When things go right, or when people do him right, he holds his hand close to his cheek, points a stubby finger like a gun barrel at his target, and gives a firm thumbs-up.

He is known as Coach Oliver to most. Coaches are among the few professionals, along with doctors, reverends, rabbis, professors (but, of course, not attorneys), whose work is respected enough to become his title, and Coach Oliver has earned the honorific. When he's not Coach Oliver, he is simply Gerald. Or, to hear him, he is "*JRRR*-ld," long and hard on the first syllable, quick and low on the second, no vowels necessary, the way they say it in Tennessee.

Gerald—Coach Oliver—has a long, distinguished résumé in the basketball world. He has coached nearly everywhere from college to the NBA. He began his career in 1966 at Carson-Newman College in Tennessee, and from there went to the University of Tennessee, where he was Ray Mears's assistant for eight years. In 1975 he got his first job in the professional ranks, going to the ABA as an assistant for Bill Musselman in San Diego. After a year there he returned to college, first at Jacksonville and later at Marquette, working under Hank Raymonds. In 1980 Musselman, who was then coaching the NBA Cleveland Cavaliers, called him once again to be his assistant.

Cavaliers owner Ted Stepien sold his club in 1983 and bought the CBA Toronto Tornados (the franchise has since moved to Pensacola). He named Oliver coach and general manager. Oliver stayed with Stepien until 1984–85, but in the end life with the contro-versial owner became too much. During Oliver's last days with the Tornados in 1985, Toronto won 17 of 21 games and made the final playoff spot on the last day of the season. Stepien rewarded Oliver by firing him just before the playoffs began. Oliver likes to say he was fired "due to illness. Ted was sick of me." In reality, Oliver was happy to go. Years of second guessing, bizarre moves, and irrational interference—Stepien was known to force player transactions sug-gested by his chauffeur—had worn Oliver out.

In 1985–86 he coached the Maine franchise in the CBA, then went to Charleston, West Virginia, the following year. He also coached summers in the United States Basketball League, in Spring-field, Massachusetts, and Staten Island. Gerald Oliver is the classic journeyman coach, a man happy to be working in basketball, making a decent living, so what if it isn't the big time.

But Charleston decided not to bring him back for the 1988–89 season. As of August 1988, Oliver had no job.

○   ○   ○

Neither did George Karl. Unlike Oliver, though, Karl wasn't looking for one.

George Karl, a former All-American basketball player at North Carolina, a five-year ABA-NBA veteran with the San Antonio Spurs, and for four years an NBA head coach, offers a stunning contrast to Oliver. At thirty-seven, he is tall and strong and athletic, despite the persistent paunch that now stretches at his shirts. Where Gerald moves kind of slowly, hindered by various aches and pains, Karl is an active, competitive man, always challenging someone at something—sports, video games, basketball shooting contests, card tricks, Jeopardy! He finds it hard to sit still. His mind is sharp, quick, and active, too; his eyes seem to study, to look for the edge, where Oliver's drink in. Karl has brown hair—in full retreat on top, a little long at the sides and back—and a droopy mustache. His face—his nose and chin—is all angles and points (softened a bit by a few excess pounds that round out his cheeks). A pronounced, heavy eyebrow ridge can give him, when he's angry, a primitively men-acing look. And he can get angry. His temper is quick, sarcastic, and biting. Some find him caustic, and his wit, which is usually just locker-room sarcasm—ribbing, busting chops—sometimes goes too far. Some might wonder what he's after, why he's getting on them so. But he is, at heart and on first impression, a friendly, fun-loving man, a Pittsburgh native at home in divey bars, drinking beers—one in each hand—out of the bottle (two more, miss, thank you), eating greasy food, chatting with strangers, joking with friends, flirting with waitresses. He is direct, honest to a fault, clear in his opinions. If he comes across as confident, cocky, a bit arrogant, he knows it—"I've been this way since I was nine," he admits—but he is also self-conscious enough to know that the act can sometimes be inappropriate and smart enough to back off when needed. To those who don't know him, he can appear the stereotypical con-ceited jock, the performer, the center of attention, but where that archetype is often offensive, Karl manages to pull it off with a likable grace. Karl, even when he's in a bad mood, is fun to be around. He has an unmistakable charisma, a kind of charming fuck-you aloofness that men gravitate toward (it's rare indeed that he isn't at the center of some small group, at bars, ball games, or the like) and women often find attractive (even when he's heaping friendly abuse on them). He pulls it off mainly because his arrogance is not the whole story. Underneath, Karl is a complex and thoughtful man, and it comes across even when he's at his most biting.

When knee injuries forced his retirement, he moved on to coaching, first as an assistant at San Antonio—his former team—under Doug Moe, starting in 1978. In 1980 Moe was fired, and Karl, whose personality almost demands he be a head coach anyway (he likes to be in charge, to "have the hammer," as he puts it), took a gamble and a job in the CBA. From 1980 to 1983 he coached the Montana Golden Nuggets, and in two of his three seasons he was named CBA coach of the year. Success followed success; when he moved up to the NBA Cavaliers as director of player personnel in 1983 and, the next season, became the Cavs head coach (at the age of thirty-three, the youngest head coach in NBA history), he became the first CBA coach to become a head coach in the NBA. As such Karl was something of a CBA poster boy prior to the '88–89 season. He was given a three-page spread in the official CBA guide, complete with pictures and quotes and solemn prose ("George Karl was somewhat of a pioneer in pro basketball coaching circles," his documentary begins). In the same way that such CBA graduates as Rickey Green and Brad Davis and, more recently, Michael Brooks and Tony Campbell make CBA players believe that the NBA is not an impossible dream, Karl served notice that coaches, too, can prepare for the big leagues in the CBA.

And they can do well. His initial season, Karl led the Cavs to their first playoff appearance in seven years, and finished third in the balloting for NBA Coach of the Year honors. He was released the following year, with Cleveland at 25–42, but was hired by Golden State in 1986–87. Again Karl had success. The Warriors made the playoffs for the first time in ten years. In the first round of the playoffs that year, Golden State rallied from an 0–2 deficit against the Utah Jazz to win three straight and capture the best-of-five series, the first team to come back from 0–2 to win since 1956. This time Karl finished second in coach of the year voting. But once again, the second-year jinx struck. In March of 1988, with Golden State at 16–48, and pressure coming from the front office and rumors that general manager Don Nelson would soon take over as coach, Karl resigned.

The Warriors continued to pay Karl, however; his contract with them reportedly paid him $300,000 for the remaining three years, and in fact would keep him comfortable for some time after that. So Karl was content to sit out a year, calm down from the NBA wars and regroup.

○   ○   ○

Gerald Oliver didn't have that luxury. When he heard that the Albany Patroons, the defending champions of the CBA coming off the most successful season in the history of professional basketball, were looking for a new coach for the upcoming 1988–89 season, he applied for the job. And waited.

The 1988–89 season of the Albany Patroons actually began four months earlier—on April 30, 1988. On that date the '87–88 Patroons capped an extraordinary season with a 105–96 seventh-game victory over the Wyoming Wildcatters, giving the Pats the league championship. Albany's record over that season, 48–6, established a record for CBA and NBA regular season marks; no club in either league has ever had a better winning percentage than the

Patroons' .889 standard. Remarkably, Albany lost only one game at home all year.

The coach of that team was Bill Musselman, Oliver's old friend, a severe, intense, mad genius with close-cropped hair and locked jaw who stormed into Albany that year after winning three straight CBA titles in Rapid City. He assembled a team that would send four players to the NBA before the season ended—Tony Campbell to the Lakers, Michael Brooks to Denver, Scott Roth to Utah, and Rick Carlisle to the Knicks. It also had a spot for a former NBA star not wanted in the big leagues: Micheal Ray Richardson, the former all-star banned from the league for drug use. Musselman's legendary knowledge of players and agents throughout the country allowed him to fill roster spots quickly, and fill them with talent. And that was his greatest gift as a coach. On the court he was, by the description of players, fans, and referees, a lunatic. He told his players he expected to win every game, to go 54–0, and he meant it. His maniacal presence and screaming hysteria on the sidelines endeared him to the Albany fans; his was the greatest presence on a great team, his was the strongest personality among many characters. The players hated him; Richardson would tell people he only had two things to say to Musselman at the end of the season: "Thank you, and fuck you." "That year was a living hell," center Greg Grissom, a central target of Musselman's who would be the lone player to come back from that season, would say. But the fans loved his act, and loved what it brought them: their second league title in four years. It was an act and a personality so strong that its ghost would haunt whatever and whoever was to follow.

Few expected Musselman to come back to the CBA. The NBA was expanding, and by August it was official. Musselman was to become the first head coach of the new franchise in Minnesota, the Timberwolves, who were to begin play in the '89–90 NBA season. The Patroons were left without a coach and without any players. The new season was only three months away.

Musselman had planned to return to Albany had the NBA job fallen through. It didn't, but the announcement was delayed until August, just before the annual CBA college draft. By that time the Patroons were interviewing several candidates who had applied for the job. One of the candidates was Gerald Oliver.

The 1988 CBA draft, held August 24–25, was televised by ESPN. By coincidence, George Karl was working as an analyst, television being one of the first options any "former"—former player, former coach—might naturally consider, especially one as articulate and basketball-smart as Karl. He was at the draft on something of a tryout of his own. Patroons general manager Gary Holle (he pronounces his last name like holly) was also at the draft, and on a whim Holle introduced himself to Karl and asked, "Would you consider coaching in Albany?" It was a long shot; Holle never really expected Karl to accept. Why would an NBA coach come back to the CBA? Besides, there were other potential problems. If Karl were to accept, how long would he last before being called back to the NBA? Karl would claim, then and all season long, that his intention was always to remain in the CBA the entire season. He wanted to get back to the NBA, but only under the right circumstances—only if he had the hammer—and midseason coaching changes are rarely the right circumstances. Still, even he would have admitted privately that, should the call come during the year, he couldn't be sure how he'd react.

Holle and Jim Coyne, the Albany County Executive and the founding father and guiding light of the Patroons, came up with a plan: hire Gerald Oliver as a personnel director. Gerald has been in the league, they reasoned, he knows the players and can put a team together. Oliver had always done well in Albany whenever he brought his teams in, his was a familiar face to the Albany fans, and his reputation was that of a popular, hardworking, caring coach. If Karl accepted the job, fine; if not, they would make another choice. Maybe Oliver, maybe not. The important thing was to get someone working on personnel. Only one player from the previous season, Greg Grissom, was still under contract. And by now, the other teams in the league were well under way stocking their larders with players. In the CBA, every slate essentially is wiped clean every year, and a late start can be suicidal.

Oliver was happy; this was where he wanted to be. It wasn't clear whether he would travel with the team—league rules had been changed recently, allowing assistant coaches to travel (although in the past assistants often traveled under the guise of "trainer," legitimate or otherwise), but the decision was up to the owners and the depth of their pockets. Upon returning from the draft, Holle, Coyne, and Oliver talked, and Oliver was hired. "At that point I had my basketball things packed, and was probably going to go into something else," Gerald says. Thus, basketball retained one of its true characters, at least for one more year.

Karl, meanwhile, wasn't so sure. The circumstances under which he had left the NBA were not pleasant; his reputation, he felt, was soiled. He had been criticized for being too young, for being volatile and immature and emotional. In the NBA, players—not coaches—often have the hammer, and it was said that Karl couldn't handle the NBA superstar with the NBA super contract. One writer called him the Billy Martin of basketball, and the description, though not entirely accurate, was close enough to stick. Karl had fought often and publicly with one player in particular at Golden State, Joe Barry Carroll. And while he wasn't the first coach to have trouble with Carroll—also known as Joe Barely Cares to fans around the league—his handling of the situation was messy, and he knew it. But Karl also knows he is a good coach, not just from his natural self-confidence but because he *is* a good coach, and he knows talent when he sees it. After his quick rise and early success, he wondered what went wrong. He was having a hard time figuring out why talent wasn't enough, why simply being a good coach didn't necessarily allow you to coach. George Karl sees things in black and white: Either you're good or you aren't, either you're honest and truthful or you aren't, either you're a man or you aren't. In some ways he is a throwback; "When I was in Montana," he says with admiration, "I loved it because two guys could be arguing in a bar, go outside and kick the shit out of each other, then come in with their arms around each other and buy each other a beer. I loved that." He is like that, too, and wants the world to work like that, wants it to be all right to drink a beer and flirt with a pretty woman and punch a guy in the nose if he deserves it. He understands subtlety and shading, but he doesn't always like it. Though he'd be loath to admit it, the politics and the nuances—the shadings—of the NBA may have overwhelmed him; after years as a player, where talent is all that counts, and as a CBA coach, where surviving is all that counts, Karl found himself in the big leagues in more than one way. And perhaps the critics were right. Perhaps he *wasn't* ready.

Karl was set to turn down Holle's offer, but he thought about it some, called his basketball friends, talked with his family (he is married, with two children), and decided to take the job. "It was not a year for George Karl not to be coaching," he would say in a rare slip into third-person jockspeak. So he called Gary Holle, negotiated a contract—the salary cap in the CBA for coaches is $55,000, but certain perks can still be arranged—and accepted. He didn't quite know what to expect; the CBA changed in the five years he was in the NBA, but it is still *this* league" to Karl, where the NBA is *"The* League."

For Oliver, this league is fine, and he also accepted. He would be director of player personnel and assistant coach. They agreed on his salary (there is no cap for his position). A handshake squared the deal—he didn't ask for a contract and didn't receive one—and then he got to work. He had a team to put together, and not much time to do it.

In the NBA, the preseason runs through a number of rookie and free agent camps over the summer, then a month of official training camp with a full ten- to fifteen-game exhibition schedule. In the CBA, training camp would begin at 5 P.M. November 2 and run all of two weeks. No official exhibitions; you want a real game, you set it up. In that time, a continually changing number of players from all over the country and with all manner of basketball skills must be brought to Albany, evaluated, signed to contracts, housed, fed, transported, and trained by a coaching staff of two, a front office staff of three, and a training staff of a couple of part-timers, volunteers really, until a final ten players, the maximum allowed on a CBA roster, are selected. These ten, with occasional additions and subtractions, will then begin a five and one-half month, fifty-four game odyssey known as the CBA season.

The Continental Basketball Association has been known as such for ten years, but in actuality it is the oldest professional basketball league in the country. It was originally the Eastern Basketball League, est. 1946, a circuit of dingy gyms, broken-down buses, and few fans. For the first several years of the new CBA (the name changed when the league went continental, stretching from Alaska to Maine, in 1978) that reality persisted. Even today, the CBA image is of long van rides through snowstorms, even though teams fly nearly everywhere; of empty high school gyms, even though the league features fine modern auditoriums seating many thousands; and of small crowds, even though the CBA gate has increased rapidly, topping one million in total attendance during the 1987–88 season. The league has its own TV contract with ESPN to televise several regular season and playoff games.

Most important, it has a three-year, $1.8 million contract with the NBA. Unlike baseball, basketball has no official minor league system; the CBA has become, over time, basketball's equivalent of Triple A baseball. It is filled with players good enough to be an eleventh or twelfth man on an NBA roster (occasionally even better—approximately 90 percent of CBA players were drafted by NBA teams, many of them in the first three rounds) but who are not in the league for a variety of reasons: no openings at the appropriate position, guaranteed contracts keeping rosters closed, being the wrong height (the 5' 11" guard, the 6' 9" center, the 6' 7" power forward), personality clashes. The league offers a good number of familiar names and faces: recent college players who didn't make their NBA clubs; former NBA players looking to make comebacks; the fringe talented who shuffle from league to league and country to country, just to stay in the game or because they don't know what else to do. And there are still the anonymous local players who can stick in the CBA on the strength of a killer jump shot. Most of them are here only to make a last stab at getting an NBA callup; short of that, they might get a chance to play in Europe, where the money can be huge and the benefits are more than enough to compensate the lost dream of the NBA.

Still, it's the dream that is the primary motivation here. Over the course of a season, CBA players are called up to fill NBA rosters. Under the NBA-CBA agreement, an NBA team can choose any CBA player for either a ten-day tryout (a maximum of two such tryouts per player) or for the season. In the '87–88 season there were fifty-four former CBA players in the NBA, and that number grows each year. Scouts take the CBA seriously, coaches take it seriously, players take it seriously.

But in the middle of it all, it's hard to take it seriously. It's a league devoid of defense and bereft of quality referees, a league that worships the three-pointer, a league where no one ever fouls out (when a player commits his seventh foul, a technical foul is called and an extra shot is awarded). League standings are determined by points, not wins; it's a seven-point system, in which teams get a point for every quarter won (tied quarters earn each team one-half standing point) and three for winning the game. That way, each quarter becomes a minigame to entice fans to stay and watch, even in a blowout ("So what if it's 140–85; we can still win the fourth quarter"). It's the league that brought basketball the collapsible rim, the Million Dollar Supershot fan promotion, sudden death overtime (first team to lead by three points wins; much hated and since retired, mercifully), PROgressive Basketball, and assorted other bizarre gimmicks and rules which George Karl calls Druckerisms, after the CBA's first commissioner and chief promoter, Jim Drucker. And if it is no longer a league where, as described by CBA coach and noted writer Charley Rosen, "a dissatisfied benchwarmer tried to drown his coach in a toilet bowl" and where "a center with bad hands was traded for a sex act to be consummated later," it is still a league where anything might happen, and character, in all its forms, rings true.

It is a league where ten Albany Patroons players, two coaches, and a couple of extras will live cheaply and travel cheaply. They will visit the towns—for this is a league of towns, not cities—of Cedar Rapids, Iowa; La Crosse, Wisconsin; Rapid City, South Dakota; Rochester, Minnesota; Pensacola, Florida; Charleston, West Virginia; Rockford, Illinois; Wichita Falls, Texas; Topeka, Kansas; Tulsa, Oklahoma; and Quad City, Illinois. They will play against teams whose nicknames sound like they come from sports fiction—the kind of inspirational sports books you read as a kid—or modern-day beer commercials, names that approximate real sports teams' names but somehow don't seem quite right: the Thrillers, the Catbirds, the Tornados, the Gunners, the Sizzlers. They will travel by bus and plane, by car and van. They will know Holiday Inns and Howard Johnsons, McDonald's and Popeye's and Dunkin' Donuts. They will play hundreds of dollars' worth of video games and walk hundreds of miles' worth of shopping mall aisles. They will carry their own luggage. They will fight and complain, they will be traded and released. Some will get called to play in Europe, or the NBA; some will end their careers. Most will simply play the season. Their wives and girlfriends—those with wives and girlfriends—will look for jobs and they will look for apartments. Or maybe they'll stay in a hotel. For their time and trouble, they will divide $80,000—the CBA per-team salary cap—among ten players over sixteen weeks and five days; that will come to an average of $480 per week per player. Before taxes.

And sometime in March or April, depending on the success in the playoffs, it will all be over. They will go home—those players who are still here, Gerald Oliver and George Karl—and decide what to do next.

As they say up here, often and with good humor:

Welcome to the CBA.

1

WELCOME TO THE CBA

"Albany *Times Union*. Can I help you?"

"Yeah, I need to talk to the guy in sports."

"One moment please."

"Hello, this is sports . . ."

"Yeah, I'm gonna play for da fuckin' Patroons. I gotta know how ta get to da fuckin' stadium."

"Who's this?"

"John."

"John who?"

"John from Queens."

"Okay. Take the Thruway north and get off at exit 24. Then take I-90 to Everett Road. Make a right off the exit and go to the bottom of the hill, that's Central Avenue. Make a left and stay on Central and it will merge with Washington Avenue. The Armory is right after that, on your left. It's an old brick building at the corner of Lark Street."

"Lahk?"

"Lark, like the bird."

"What the fuck . . ."

"L-A-R-K. Lark."

"Oh."

"Once you get on Central you can ask people. They can direct you."

"So who's on the team?"

"Well, Clint Smith, he played in the NBA for the Warriors. Ozell Jones, he played for San Anto—"

"Oh, them. I'm a guard. I'm really fuckin' good."

"Did you play anyplace last year?"

"Yeah, in Wilkes Barre."

"Where in Wilkes Barre?"

"All over. So, when does practice start?"

"In two days."

"What time?"

"Listen, why don't you call the Patroons office. The number is—"

"Yeah, I know. I called some guy Gerry Oliver and I don't wanna call him again. I already called him a coupla times. I don't want him to think I'm a fuckin' asshole or somethin'."

○　○　○

If John from Queens doesn't make it abundantly clear that things are different in the Continental Basketball Association, then George Bell will. That's because George Bell is the tallest human being anyone is ever likely to encounter.

George Bell would tower over Kareem Abdul-Jabbar—that is, if Jabbar were somehow, on this frosty fall morning, to set foot into the Washington Avenue Armory in Albany, New York, in the next few moments. He could spot Patrick Ewing six inches and still look down at the Knicks' massive center. He is the only professional basketball player who can, with some justice, call Manute Bol "shorty." Of course, Bell would never do that. When you are seven feet eight inches tall and a long shot to make the roster of the Albany Patroons, you don't go around calling people names.

Besides that, George Bell is the nicest 92″ person in basketball. He knows that only in the CBA would he even be in sweats and sneakers on the last weekend of October 1988, trying out for a paying job in basketball. The same hormonal disorder—a tumor on his pituitary gland developed when he was eleven—that propelled Bell to his lofty height prevented him from playing sports as a youngster in North Carolina. From the age of eleven to the age of eighteen, Bell grew from 5' 9" to 7' 6", lost 50 percent of his eyesight (he has since regained it), suffered knee and headache problems, and was overall too ill to compete. He did play some at various colleges, and averaged 5 points a game at Biola University in California. He also toured with the Harlem Magicians, a lesser version of the Globetrotters. He then sat out for three years. Now, at the age of twenty-eight, having just been cut by the NBA Los Angeles Clippers after a short stay in that club's training camp, George Bell is in Albany.

Bell is but one (well, nearly two) of seventeen basketball players attending the free agent camp of the Albany Patroons, the defending champions of the Continental Basketball Association, as October segues into November. (The uninvited John from Queens has yet to make his way north.) Getting these seventeen players here begins as soon as George Karl accepts the head coaching job; that day, Gerald Oliver makes the first of several thousand phone calls.

Karl lets Oliver make the personnel decisions, partly because that is Gerald's job, but mainly because Karl doesn't know this league or the players available, and doesn't much want to know. The two talk often, of course, during this recruiting process, but Gerald works the phones, makes the trades, drives the miles and cajoles the players into coming, establishing the working relationship that will serve them well all season. Gerald does the grunt work, the detail work, with honor and dedication, leaving Karl free to concentrate on coaching.

At this point Gerald also begins the Herculean task of keeping his records. His notebooks—first a blue, three-ring, schoolboy type, and later a brown vinyl number with clear acetate sleeves—will be his constant companions and security blankets, and in them will be lists, notes, and reminders of all he has to do, all he has done, all he wants to get done. His lists of players (Albany's and those of every other team in the CBA) are updated almost hourly: who is where, which team is trading what for what, what players are at which positions. For Gerald it's a seemingly losing struggle to keep himself under control. "Ah gotta get myself organized," he will mutter under his breath several times daily as he slips a pair of reading glasses down on the end of his nose and begins shuffling through all his papers. This one act is as much a perfect symbol of Gerald's character as it is a central necessity of his working mission.

Gerald's first phone call is to Clinton Smith, a 6' 6" forward who had played in the NBA (for Karl in Golden State) after his college days at Cleveland State. Smith had played only twelve games the previous season, five with Oliver at Charleston and seven in Albany under Musselman. Albany still holds his rights. Oliver drives up to Cleveland to see him play. Smith is scrimmaging at Cleveland State; to Oliver's experienced eye, he is in the best shape of his life.

"Clinton, you're ready," Gerald says.

"Yes I am," Clinton tells him.

"You want to wait a while or will you sign a contract?"

"I want to come play for George."

Oliver would find over the next days that that was a common response. "It is a lot easier signing players for George than it was for myself," Oliver will admit. Even with Oliver's considerable contacts and influence, NBA clout—which Karl obviously has—is a powerful bump in the CBA. When the rewards are delayed, as they are in the CBA, the future enticements need to be palpable. No one is playing for money or fame or glamour here, at least no one with the right sense of perspective; each one is playing to get The Call. With Karl on hand every day, that call seems a lot more possible.

It also makes the less-than-luxurius life of CBA preseason worth living. Players sign standard CBA contracts before camp, mostly to ensure that they will be able to collect workmen's compensation if they get injured. Actual compensation: During the preseason, teams are required to supply only a hotel room and $15 a day meal money. Some teams don't even go that far. But then, some go further.

"A coach tried to trade us a player," Gerald remembers. "Ah said, Coach, tell me his contract. Saw his contract and said, well, we can pay that, it's within our salary cap. So I talked to the player and he says, Coach, I get a free apartment. I find out he also got a free car. I said, son, you don't get either one of those here. Another begged me to trade him to another team one year. He said, Coach, I cain't take the loss. So I did trade him.

"I wish we could get 'em all free apartments and cars. But if you're playing here for money you're playing for the wrong reason. You could be further on in your career if you're out there working at something else. But some players come for the life-style. They're here not to move on but to live this life-style, which is pretty high class for a short period of time. For them, the money is important.

"One player was getting part of his team's concession money last year. He's not this year. The joke around the league is that's why he's not playing so well.

"We are trying to help the player with a good basketball environment, which is Albany and George Karl," Gerald goes on to say. "If that's not worth living within the rules then your priorities aren't in going to the NBA. This is the closest place to the NBA in the CBA. George Karl has the most credibility, the most direct contacts. This is the place. That's what I sell. That's the extras."

Besides selling George Karl, Oliver can sell Albany. And selling Albany to prospective players is easier than one might think.

Albany offers a small but wonderful gym in the Washington Avenue Armory. The Armory, in its shortened form, was built about a hundred years ago; it looks like something out of the Middle Ages, more castle than gymnasium, a massive, city-block-filling brick and stone behemoth. Running down its dark, dirty sides are rounded towers that are topped with pointed copper turrets, now oxydized to a pale green. Inside it is dimly lit through a series of tall thin windows—they look like mail slots stood on end—that are covered by iron bars. It is actually a working armory of the U.S. armed services. The government bills the Patroons for the space and the utilities (which makes for some chilly practices as the franchise tries to keep its costs down). The army stores live ammo in the basement, in a room that also serves as the referee's locker room. The Armory is one of the few gyms left that jibes with the old CBA image.

As you enter from Washington Avenue, through its fourteen-foot brick archway now filled with heavy metal doors with heavy bolt-locks, you travel through a short vestibule—first signing in, so the government knows what's going on—and pass staircases on both sides that go down to the locker rooms. Past the stairs is the arena. It feels like an airport hangar; the ceiling is high and vaulted, hung with acoustic tiles that do little to improve the acoustics and crossed with steel beams that look like the ribs of a great whale as viewed by Jonah from within. The basketball floor in the middle is a super-slick surface. It is embossed with the Patroons logo, a Dutch wooden shoe with a basketball in it. (The team's nickname comes from the Dutch landowners, called patroons, who settled the area three hundred years ago; the Albany region is still rich in Dutch heritage.) The basket at the north end of the court is a bit higher than the one at the south end; that southern basket, on the other hand, is not quite parallel to the baseline. The court is surrounded by wood risers about seven levels high. Circling the risers is an indoor track for the public's use; during afternoon practices, joggers pound along the floor, while in the corner exercisers ride stationary bikes and aerobics classes fill the gym with bouncy pop music.

Downstairs is the locker room, maybe fifteen by twenty feet, a dingy, dank, musty storage closet lined with government-issue lockers—olive drab, stenciled numbers—and covered with several layers of chipped white paint. Steam pipes hang low from the ceiling, offering extra options for coat hangers. A chalkboard leans against the far wall, under a filthy window that looks onto nothing. A stained mold-green carpet covers the cement floor. No benches, just folding aluminum chairs. A table fills the center of the room. The only showers are out the door and to the right, through the men's room. The public men's room.

It's a creaky, cold, drafty, poorly lit place, but its character is unmistakable; it's the Boston Garden of the CBA, and when 3,000-plus fans—the Patroons of '87–88 averaged over 3,800 fans per game, 700 more than the arena's official capacity of 3,106, by far the smallest in the league—fill the bleachers that sit only inches from the court, it's a daunting place to play.

The franchise, now in its seventh season—nearly eternity in the CBA—has played here since its inception in 1982. It is on fairly stable, solid financial footing (which is not to be undervalued in a league where franchises come and go like benchwarmers, and teams have moved midseason). It was originally started as a not-for-profit organization by a group of investors headed by Albany County Executive Jim Coyne. The idea was to bring a team into Albany as part of Coyne's effort to rejuvenate downtown. Albany at night, like many old eastern cities, was a ghost town in the early '80s. The Patroons, it was hoped, would bring people into the city, generate support services like restaurants and bars, and give the area a psychological as well as financial boost. It's worked well; downtown Albany, while no great metropolis, is nevertheless a far livelier, more pleasant place to live and play, and the Patroons have played a part, however small, in that.

The Albany metropolitan region, which includes the larger cities of Albany, Schenectady, and Troy, and stretches approximately to Saratoga and Glens Falls to the north, western Massachusetts and southern Vermont to the east, the mid-Hudson River Valley to the south and Cooperstown to the west, is a fast-growing area, one of the few regions in New York State to experience significant population growth recently. And while the region is still struggling to deal with its quick growth (it doesn't even know what to call itself, being known by various marketing names such as the Capital District, the Capital Region, Capitaland, the Tri-City region, and the Albany Metro region, or how to promote itself to prospective businesses, much less deal with the horrible parking problem downtown), it has become an attractive place to live and work.

The CBA's franchise fee, which back then was $100,000—it was only $8,000 in 1978; it's now $500,000, an indication of the league's growth—was raised quickly, deposits were placed for season tickets, and the club was born and has survived.

Things are changing though, in Albany as through the rest of the league. In 1988 the club was sold to a private owner, a businessman and board member named Ben Fernandez, to inject new capital after the club was declared ineligible for not-for-profit status in a legal snafu. Coyne, now affectionately called the founder by Patroons staffers, still plays an active role, as do a couple of other investor friends. And in 1990 the new Albany Civic Center—to be called the Knickerbocker Arena—is scheduled to open, and the Patroons are expected to move into a large, modern arena. Like the rest of the CBA, the Patroons are at a cusp, a transition point in history. The Patroons and the CBA are inexorably becoming more professional, more reputable, more financially sound, more . . . responsible. They are beginning to talk around the league of the good old days, the crazy days of the not so distant past, the days before there were big-time sponsors like AT&T and Minolta and Wilson, the days that are becoming increasingly numbered.

But it's not over yet. The CBA still can be, and is, the Crazy

Basketball Association. For now, they are still the old Patroons in the old Armory.

Along with the gym and the city, the Patroons have a league-wide reputation for the most vocal and caring fans in the league. The winters may be bad, but they're no better in Minnesota or Kansas. Knowing that the franchise will last, that the gym will be filled, and that the team will be competitive helps Gerald get players to Albany.

So too does Albany's proximity to New York and Boston. Three hours, more or less, from two NBA cities (three, counting the New Jersey Nets), Albany has a solid advantage in drawing scouts to the Armory. Often, NBA teams will come to New York or Boston and send a representative to have a look. Or else they'll simply have an eastern-based scout drive in on a slow NBA night. The NBA has scouted the CBA much more actively the past few years, and it's a rare night that some NBA rep isn't seated at the courtside table taking notes. All things added together, Albany is an attractive place for a basketball player to spend his winter. It's not New York or Boston or Los Angeles, but it might be one very small step below.

○ ○ ○

Another early acquistion by the Patroons is center Ozell Jones; he comes to Albany in a September trade with Quad City for a third-round draft choice. With only Grissom back, Albany is clearly short of big men. League-wide, the CBA is weakest at center; good guards are plentiful, but good big men are harder to find. Jones is big— listed at 6′ 11″—and has NBA experience with San Antonio and the L.A. Clippers. But that NBA talent is often lost, as is Ozell; he has a habit of disappearing in games, and his head is more of a concern than his body. He is twenty-eight years old, out of Cal-Fullerton, an unlikely prospect with little chance of making it back to the NBA. But to Karl and Oliver, Ozell is a gamble worth taking; if he isn't ready to play, he won't stay. If he is, and if Karl can get him to play at a level somewhere approaching his potential, he could be a force.

With Ozell and Grissom and Smith in place—George Bell, too—the search goes on. Several players will come from the Washington Bullets. Under the NBA-CBA agreement, each CBA team is officially affiliated with two NBA clubs. That affiliation is really a one-way street, in that the CBA team gets the rights to any player cut from its NBA parent, but once in the CBA, that player can be called up by any NBA team. The Patroons' affiliates are the Knicks and the Bullets, and from Washington Albany gets four of the Bullets' cuts: Ken Johnson, a 6' 9" power forward/center; Vincent Askew, 6' 6", a natural shooting guard in the NBA but a forward in the CBA; Danny Pearson, a 6' 6" shooter and defensive talent; and Doug Lee, also 6' 6", all hustle with a sweet shot, particularly from three-point range.

Oliver is at the Bullets camp when Askew is cut. Vincent is a special case. He is only twenty, perhaps the youngest professional basketball player in the country. (Although there are some who think he's really older.) He is from Memphis, and had a troubled college career at Memphis State, the results of which will explode around him in the first week of camp. But he is a gifted player, with what basketball people call an NBA body: thick, powerful legs, a natural grace, a commanding athletic presence. Strong and solid at 6' 6", 210, he can leap high and far. But his career in college ended too soon—he came out after his junior year at Memphis State—and played only fourteen games for the Philadelphia 76ers (the team that drafted him in the second round of the 1987 draft) in '87–88. Now cut by Washington, Askew is at a critical point in his career. Oliver gets him at the right time.

"Vince, you're too young to quit basketball," Oliver will say. "There's time. You oughta come to the CBA and develop. You've got to look at your age. You're young. This is the place you should be. This is the year." Vince signs.

Gerald continues to work the phones and drive the countryside looking for players. Clint Smith will recommend his friend Vince Johnson, a guard, and Johnson gets invited. Some local players will file in. Keith Smith, a 6' 4" guard cut by La Crosse last season, is signed. Othell Wilson, the former Virginia star and teammate of Ralph Sampson, comes over in a trade. And in a move that could happen only in the CBA, a retired player is traded for the rights to a point guard playing in Mexico. Sidney Lowe, who had announced he wouldn't play in the CBA this season (except in the playoffs, when he would), is sent to Rapid City for Kelvin Upshaw, a 6' 2" guard and former CBA all-star now, as far as can be determined, south of the border.

While George Bell is the sight of the free agent camp, which is held the weekend before the official training camp begins, the find would be Steve Shurina, a 6' 4" guard who played at St. John's. Actually, Shurina watched more than played, averaging all of 1.6 points a game over four years as he enjoyed Chris Mullin and Ron Rowan from the bench. He was not drafted by either the NBA or CBA. Shurina is recommended to Karl and Oliver by his agent and by his summer league coach; he spent the summer playing in the USBL, in Long Island. A friendly, talkative twenty-two-year-old from Queens, New York, with big ears, a crooked smile, and dark, wavy hair, Shurina is not very quick, not very strong. He can jump some. He can shoot well. More than that, he runs. He runs the offense at point guard, in a way that makes other players enjoy playing with him. His game is built on hustle, intelligence, fearlessness, and hard work, which compensate for his limited and underdeveloped natural talents.

Karl had never heard of him before free agent camp (he'd never heard of a lot of players here and throughout the league). Shurina is just starting out on his professional career; unhappy with his time at St. John's, he wants to see how far his basketball can take him. He just wants a chance to build a basketball résumé, make a name for himself, maybe make some money before getting on with life. The USBL was his first stop, he wants the CBA to be his next. Making the Patroons is a critical step in his career.

Karl takes the recommendation and skeptically brings Shurina in; Shurina responds by earning a longer look. He is invited to attend the regular training camp. By the first game of the season, Karl would be telling everyone how much Shurina reminds him of Brad Davis, and could be heard reciting Shurina's name to the heavens and smiling. "Steeeeve Shurina," he would say musically, enjoying the sound of it. "Steeeeve Shurina." "I don't know," Shurina tells Karl, when asked where he's been hiding all these years. "Sometime this past summer, I just started kicking ass."

Then there are the players who don't make it to Albany. The Patroons own the rights to several players "on the bubble"—that is, players in NBA camps who are close to making their teams. John

Stroeder, a 6′ 10″ center with NBA experience whom the Patroons covet, is cut by Golden State and then picked up by San Antonio. Wayne Engelstad, the Pats' first pick in the CBA draft, is expected to get cut, but injuries to other players allow him to stick with Denver. Dave Popson, a fellow Tarheel enticed by Karl to come to Albany, is released by Detroit, only to get picked up by the Clippers. Rick Carlisle is kept by the Knicks, and Scott Brooks, a member of last year's championship team, is a surprise stick with Philadelphia.

What it all means is, when the official Albany Patroons preseason training camp starts, Karl and Oliver aren't really sure exactly who will show up.

2

NOVEMBER

"Hi, this is John again, ya know, from fuckin' Queens."

"Hey John, where are you? You should be up here now if you want to make the team. They're having a tryout for free agents."

"Yeah, I know, but that's for fuckin' scrubs. I'm not a fuckin' scrub. I'm fuckin' *good*."

NOVEMBER 2–8

Over the preceding weekend, free agent camp was held. Sixteen players showed (John from Queens not being one of them), and six are invited to stay: Shurina, Bell, Norman Taylor, Kevin Brown, Gerald Jackson, and Kevin Strickland. They are joined by a dozen others, including Keith Smith, Ozell Jones, Cliff Pruitt, Vince Askew, Ken Johnson, Anthony Teachey, and Clinton Smith. Doug Lee and Danny Pearson come later in the week. So does Othell Wilson. Greg Grissom drives his Mercedes up from Texas, and appears opening day. A player named Oscar Taylor never shows. In fact, players come and go so fast, the Patroons roster seems to change almost hourly.

Training camp officially opens Wednesday, November 2, with eighteen players in all in the Armory, and controversy hits. On Tuesday, November 1, the NCAA announces that the University of Kansas is being put on probation for three years for recruiting violations. Vince Askew is the recruit at the center of the violations.

After completing his sophomore year at Memphis State, Askew spent the summer at Kansas, looking to transfer there. He admits to Tim Wilkin, who is covering the Patroons for the Albany *Times Union*, that while there he had in fact accepted a $364 round-trip airline ticket to visit his ailing grandmother, another ticket to fly from Memphis to Kansas City, money to pay for unpaid electric bills and for clothing, and "at least" $297.12 for a no-show job in Kansas.

In the end, Askew decided not to transfer, but during his junior year at Memphis State "the NCAA people came around and started asking me questions." Partly because of the investigation (and partly because of his ability: he scored in double figures in a record-tying thirty-three straight games at Memphis State), Askew decided to come out early and was drafted by Philadelphia in the second round.

For Vince it may have been an unwise move. He played little in Philadelphia that year. And when he was cut by the Bullets this season, his career seemed at a standstill. Askew is trying to get a grip on himself and his basketball future. By nature a quiet, shy, somewhat naive young man, Askew, it seems apparent from the start, will need careful handling. The distractions caused by the Kansas allegations, thankfully, come and go quickly.

For the others, it's the beginning of a difficult two weeks. They are living at a down-at-the-heels Howard Johnson Motor Inn several miles from the Armory (an establishment best known for a murder committed there several years earlier) and are bussed to and fro by Tony D'Amato, the Patroons' underpaid and inconsistent assistant, and by Gerald, who is also situated at the HoJo. George Karl is settled into a town house in the suburbs with his wife, Cathy, and two kids, conveniently above the fray.

Karl had been watching the preseason camp, and though by league rule he wasn't allowed to coach then, he was certainly taking notes. And if, during the free agent look-see, he slipped off a stationary bike to make a comment or two now and then (which he didn't, of course, that being against CBA rules), he has the opportunity to say a lot now. He establishes his presence from the outset. Karl is not an inventive curser—his repertoire consists almost exclusively of using the F-word with an -ing suffix as an adjective— but he shows a fine ability for screaming when things aren't done his way. Seated on a rickety folding chair or standing in his signature pose—feet planted wide, arms crossed over his expanded chest, head cocked back, eyes glaring down the scope of his nose—he makes his authority known immediately and his limited patience for mistakes apparent. He has only one weak spot in his armor; being nearly addicted to diet Coke, he sucks them down at a rapid clip. The result is a frequent need to relieve himself, sometimes, unfortunately, just when he's at his most animated.

With only two weeks to pick ten players, develop a team, and set up a system, the CBA makes its members work fast. The first several days are crammed with two- and sometimes three-a-day practices; chalk talks and films are occasionally thrown in to break it up. But the players have it comparatively easy. Gerald Oliver is working overtime. He calls himself the assistant coach without title, the assistant general manager without title, the assistant travel agent without title; to those he could add assistant financier, housing authority, transportation expert, and a few others. Gerald's duties —his "bidness"—include coordinating with the Armory in getting practice time, organizing the van, supervising Tony (which takes more time than it should, Tony being difficult to locate, depend upon, or otherwise handle), distributing the players' per diem money, coordinating contracts, keeping up with the rest of the league, tracking down players, updating his notebook—and even coaching a little, whenever he gets a chance.

Tracking players is critical. When camp opens, the coaches don't really know who will even attend. Much is dependent on the NBA; those last cuts are being made, and the Patroons are waiting on three important people. Within days all three will be lost. Scott Roth, a key member of the championship team of '87–88, is cut by the Utah Jazz on Tuesday the second, the day training camp opens. But Karl doesn't expect him, and proves to be right; the Jazz re-sign him on Thursday. By cutting and re-signing Roth, the Jazz avoid committing to a guaranteed contract; if they cut him again later, they don't need to pay him. It's likely he will be cut again—only injuries to two other Jazz players allow Roth to make the team— but even then he will not play for Albany. He was here last season only to play for Musselman, to whose family he has always been close. Eric Musselman, Bill's son, is a close friend, and Eric is also general manager of the CBA's Rapid City Thrillers. That's where Roth wants to play if and when he returns to the CBA. Karl and Oliver begin negotiating with the younger Musselman on trading his rights. "Let's do it now," Karl says. "It'll only get more difficult later when he's cut again." But nothing comes together, and Karl will be proven right again when it does get more difficult—and nasty. But that is still to come.

Also lost is Wayne Engelstad, Albany's top pick in the CBA draft, who makes Denver's roster. Gone, too, is Dave Popson, a 6' 10" forward cut by the Pistons. Popson, a former Tarheel, has committed to Karl to play for him. But after a few days of waiting, Popson is picked up by the Clippers.

The most curious case is that of John Stroeder, a 6' 10" center cut by Golden State. Stroeder played for Karl at Montana, and Karl, still closely connected with his old NBA team, hears from the Warriors that they are trying to trade backup Jerome Whitehead, and re-sign Stroeder. It appears Stroeder will be lost as well, but in fact it will take two weeks before this situation plays itself out.

The first days of camp are full days. Players van in from the Howard Johnson's in their sweats. Many have brought nothing but sweats, since there will be little time for anything else but basketball, to be followed most likely by a quick flight home. They change their shoes on the long flat risers that surround the court. Those who know each other from earlier playing situations reacquaint themselves, others are getting to know each other for the first time. For the first few days, though, its mainly business.

Karl is clearly in charge, the chief screamer and chief bullshitter. He is serious on the court, loose and jokey off it. Yet even his needling often carries an edge. When he gets on a player, it is almost always with an underlying purpose in mind.

"Hey Gris," he yells to Greg Grissom before one practice, "what's the fattest you ever played at?"

Grissom smiles; at 6' 11" and listed at 260 pounds (though 290 looks more likely), his weight is not his greatest ally. Gris is not in possession of an athletic-looking body; his legs and arms and chest are skinny in comparison to his midsection, and his messy blond hair, goofy/charming grin, and Texas drawl give him the air of a Sunday hacker more than a professional player. Musselman rode

Grissom hard last season, calling him a loser, a beer-truck driver, and assorted other meannesses. But Karl intends more than just to convince Grissom to get into shape.

"Suppose some NBA coach calls me and says, 'I hear Grissom is overweight.' Now, what am I supposed to tell him?" Karl asks, smiling but with sincere concern.

Grissom nods. The point is made. Getting to the NBA is the goal here. Coasting on the CBA status quo is not what Karl is interested in, and it is an attitude he will continually try to impart. He also lets them know, subtly but unambiguously, that his recommendations, his connections, will play a large part in getting players up to The League. Karl throws his NBA weight around often; to the uninitiated, it might sound like name dropping, but in fact Karl really is more in touch with the NBA than he is with the CBA. While Gerald is constantly on the phone with CBA coaches and players, Karl is more likely talking with NBA insiders. And he isn't shy in letting his players know that.

Cuts come quickly. On the second day of camp center Kevin Brown is sent packing. He leaves without paying his phone bill at the Howard Johnson's, which burns Gerald: "As far as ah'm concerned, he is an asshole. His agent says he'll pay it; if he does, fine. Until then he's an asshole." His spot is filled by Danny Pearson, the Bullets' cut.

Two days later, George Bell, who hasn't played much after hurting his back and his knee, is released. Everyone is impressed with his attitude and desire. "He did everything we asked of him," Oliver says. The gamble cost maybe $1,000 to fly him in, put him up, and feed him (if $15 a day can feed a man 7' 8" tall). But in the end, Karl says, "He's a CBA project. I'm not sure I'm ready for a CBA project."

Bell takes it well. "There are other things in life besides basketball," he tells the *Times Union*'s Tim Wilkin. "Tall people can do a lot of other things, you know."

Forward Cliff Pruitt doesn't take it so well. After coming to camp out of shape and performing poorly, he gets the news from Oliver. "But Coach, I was saving myself for the games," he explains. "I was saving my energy. I'll be your leading rebounder once the season starts." Oliver is not swayed.

Strickland is also sent packing; the roster is quickly down to fifteen, one under the maximum sixteen allowed on Tuesday, November 8. By Friday the 11th, rosters will be down to twelve, and the final two will go by the following Tuesday. The season opens two days after that. The Patroons haven't played a game yet.

And they are still waiting on Stroeder and Kelvin Upshaw. Stroeder is home in Washington State waiting to hear from other NBA clubs. Upshaw, it's been confirmed, is still in Mexico. Gerald is on the phone constantly, talking to Stroeder, his agent, his father. Upshaw is harder to reach.

Karl is concentrating on running the practices. To help he has brought in his former assistant, Gene Espeland, from Montana. Espeland is a tall, quiet, handsome man, a native Montanan with a distinctly western feel about him and a dry sense of humor. "I was home bussing tables at my restaurant, so I'm thrilled to be here," he reports with a soft smile. He is here at Karl's, and not the Patroons', expense, and therefore is not getting much money for his trouble. The players call him Coach Gene, and he is a good fit here. He complements the intensity and swagger of Karl, and the self-inflicted confusion and brash southern good humor of Gerald, with a stolid, intelligent presence. Together, the three work well, laugh often, and serve as a strong coaching staff.

Karl is fighting to establish his identity both with the club and with the community. During practice on the seventh, he is coaching his club through "legal zones" and some of the arcana of his defensive schemes, which is based on colors—there is a red defense, a blue, a black, and so on. (His offense runs primarily on numbered series.) A fan watching practice—the Armory is open by day to joggers, aerobics classes, and basketball fans—is impressed, even while being a bit confused. "He was a three-time all-American for Dean Smith," he tells his friend about Karl, with some innaccuracy but genuine admiration. "A *three-time all-American*. Why don't I remember him?"

On the eighth, the pressure of two-a-days boils over. Rodney Martin, an overly aggressive guard out of Acadia University in Canada, is defending Othell Wilson, when Wilson throws a punch. Martin takes it over the eye; he's cut, and is taken to a hospital. Wilson, acquired in a trade before camp, has been disappointing in practice. Though he had a strong chance of making the club, his play and demeanor have reduced his chances considerably. The fight is quickly forgotten—one of those things that happen in training camp—but the incident is a further sign that Wilson isn't quite right.

NOVEMBER 9

It's finally time to get out of the gym.

"Game tonight, guys," Karl says after practice. "Dress nice. I'm not a tie guy, but look good. A nice sweater is OK."

The edict is poorly received. "I didn't bring no good clothes to Albany, Coach," comes an anonymous complaint. And it sets off a flurry of trading activity. "Who's got a sweater I can borrow?"

Two scrimmage games have been set up against a group called the Tri-City All Stars, one tonight, one tomorrow. Tonight's game is at Hudson Valley Community College, a school across the Hudson River in the city of Troy. The van leaves the Howard Johnson's at 6:30.

Before leaving, Gerald works the phones. His room at the HoJo is a mess. Unread newspapers are stacked high atop the television set. Boxes, clothes, uniforms, and papers are scattered about his bed, the dresser, the floor. Gerald seems at home. He makes a call, to John Stroeder's dad. Stroeder has been lost again; yesterday he was signed by San Antonio, one day after agreeing to play in Albany.

"That's great news for John," Gerald says into the phone. "Great news. You tell him we all are as happy as can be for him. Great news. Just do me one favor if you would. Ask John to send back those airline tickets we sent him. He don't need 'em now, does he. Just tell him we wish him the best of luck down there."

That makes four big men lost to the NBA—Popson, Roth, Stroeder, and Engelstad. The only possibility left is Upshaw—not a big man, to be sure, but a big addition if he can be located. Oliver is still tracking him down. Karl says sarcastically that he'll probably be picked up by the NBA, too. The Patroons are looking like an average to below-average team now, small and fairly quick, but not particularly powerful. Losing Stroeder is a big blow.

To compensate, Oliver accepts some advice from Rockford

coach Charley Rosen, who recommends a player on his club, a 6' 7" forward named Mike Yeost. Rosen says he's got a chance. He can shoot and pass. Oliver agrees to try him out. Officially the trade is for a player to be named later. Really, it's essentially a free tryout for a player likely to be cut anyway. Yeost appears in time for tonight's game, but remains in street clothes, looking lost.

Two vans head to the game, driving through a light snow, and pull up in front of a typical small college gym. When the teams take the court, a crucial error in communication is realized: Both clubs are wearing green jerseys. Quick negotiations ensue; the Patroons have reversible jerseys, so it is agreed they will switch.

"Go white, guys," Karl yells, and then, realizing what he's said, grins a wide grin. The black members of the team dance with laughter. All flip their jerseys inside out. And the game begins.

What should be a rout, especially when such expected All Stars as former NBA players Eric Fernsten and Hollis Copeland don't show, is a difficult struggle at first. The Patroons' big men aren't playing big. The defense is lax. Small local college players are taking it to the hoop or popping from outside.

Eventually, the Patroons pull away and win 126–74, in what becomes a boring, mindless exhibition. At the end, the game seems interminable; the gym is nearly empty, and even the cheerleaders have gone home. And yet, down by 45 with a minute to go, the coach of the All Stars calls a time out. Karl can only roll his eyes toward the ceiling. It takes moments like this to realize just how far it is, in the basketball sense, from Madison Square Garden or the L.A. Forum to an empty juco gym on a cold Wednesday night in upstate New York.

"We did some good things tonight, guys," Karl says in the locker room. "Big people, you gotta be bigger."

"Everybody mark your shorts," Oliver yells.

"Hey Gerald. They gonna have any better players tomorrow night?" Karl asks.

"Only if I go out and get some. Don't make me do that, Coach. I got too much to do as it is."

With that, the players are vanned back to the hotel. Coaches, referees, and assorted personnel repair for beers and pizza. "Gerald, you're coming with us," Karl orders.

"But Coach, I got a million—"

"*Gerald!* Come on."

And off they go. Karl smiles as he enters the bar and orders two Lite beers for himself, his standard request.

"I win a game by 50"—he laughs—"and I'm pissed off. That's what coaching does to you."

NOVEMBER 10

A cold, rainy, windy night to drive to Pittsfield, Massachusetts, for tonight's game. Gerald drives one van, Tony the other. Neither prospect is heartening.

The windows are fogged, the wipers squeaking across the windshield. Quiet fills Gerald's van. Darkness envelops the countryside as Route 20 snakes through the Berkshire mountains, past lonely homes and through one-stoplight towns. In the back, Ozell Jones and Anthony Teachey are mimicking the whispery sound effect noises from *Friday the 13th* movies. "SHHH-shhh-shhh-shhh. KILL-kill-kill-kill."

"I bet ol' Jason in these hills somewhere." Teachey giggles.

Gerald is weaving all over the road, eliciting muffled groans from the back. "Ah remember one time, driving a van from Louisville, Kentucky, through a driving snowstorm," Gerald tells of the days when van trips were the only way to travel in the CBA. "There on the side of the road were three bodies. Dead. Sheets over 'em, covered with blood."

"Musta been the Klan," comes from the back.

The van continues on. Dark and quiet.

"SHHH-shhh-shhh-shhh. KILL-kill-kill-kill."

○ ○ ○

The game is at the Pittsfield YMCA, a benefit for the Pittsfield Boys Club. The Patroons change in locker rooms 1 and 4, next to a group of eight-year-olds putting on swim trunks.

The person who helped organize these games is Tom Mc-Andrews, a big, friendly fellow who also serves as the All Stars' coach. He introduces himself as a local coach and agent. His business card, which he happily distributes, is headlined BASKETBALL CON-

NECTIONS, and lists as his domain CBA, USBL, Europe; All-Star Teams; Guest Speakers; Clinics; Scouting Service; Franchise Consultant; Booking Agent; and Player Agent.

"Who do you represent?" he is asked.

"No one," he says proudly. "But I just got accredited." He promises to keep tonight's game moving. No time-outs if he's down by, say, 30 or more.

Before the game, Gerald is at his customary position, on the phone, still looking for Upshaw. "I gotta call this number to see if he got on this plane. If he didn't I call this number and find out why not." Out on the court, George and Gene pick sides for an intersquad scrimmage when the All Stars show up late.

Eventually the All Stars field a team; again Albany struggles. At the half—actually, the quarter; the teams are playing only two Q's after the intersquad game—it's 31–27. The Patroons head downstairs to the locker room. Tony starts to go with them. "Stay and guard the balls," Karl says. Tony keeps larcenous boys away from the inviting loot.

Tony has worked for the team since 1983, he says. He's a small, slim young man, soon to turn twenty-five, with thick black hair and the hint of a mustache. His main duties are as team chauffeur, working with both the Patroons players and, during the season, the visiting teams (in the CBA, it's the home team's duty to get the visitors from airport to hotel, from hotel to gym, from gym back to hotel and back to the airport). He also services the Patroons bench during home games, distributing towels and water, fetching whatever needs fetching, and offering unheeded coaching advice. His greatest talent is not being around when needed; his second greatest is furnishing excuses for not being around when needed. Still, he serves an invaluable function in the understaffed CBA organizational chart. And all for a pittance (which is the main reason the front office puts up with his unreliability). During the season, he says, he gets $25 for a day's work, $15 for a half day. "I do this 'cause I love sports," he says. "I don't get hardly no money or nothing. I got five bucks for driving last night." Just now, the PA announcer comes on. "Would the owner of a red van, license number . . ." Tony doesn't need to wait to hear the actual numbers. He jumps up and dashes out of the gym.

Albany is better in the second Q. Karl likes the fluidity of the offense. But quickness is a problem. The All Stars have a former Patroon and CBA veteran named Lowes Moore on their team, and Moore, now retired to coach the Hudson Valley College team, looks better than anyone on the Patroons. After the game, Karl asks—only half-joking—if he'd like to come back. It won't be the last time he asks.

Gerald is in the lobby, on a pay phone.

"Gerald, we're going to a party," Karl barks. "Get off the phone."

"Coach, I got problems, I need just one more minute . . ."

"*Gerald!* We're going."

"Coach, why don't you ever let me do what I'm supposed to do? You never let me do what I'm supposed to do. Then the next day, when it isn't done, you go an' ask me why it isn't done. Now, why is that, Coach?"

"Gerald—" Karl laughs. "Get in the van."

"All right, Coach. I'll be right there."

Standing by Karl is his wife, Cathy, their two children, nine-year-old daughter Kelci and son Coby, who is five, and Warren LeGarie, an agent and friend of Karl's, who have driven over for the game. Cathy Karl is an attractive, bright-eyed woman, slim and athletic-looking, with short, curly brown hair. And she is a strong match for George and his biting, sharp-tongued humor. Upon being introduced to a local writer, the first thing she asks, with a wide smile and mischief in her eyes, is, "Has he told you yet about the time he split his pants while coaching? And he doesn't wear underwear."

o   o   o

McAndrews has set up a reception and party at a restaurant near Pittsfield. It's been a long period of practices and games, and the players are tired. They eat quietly, but would rather be elsewhere. The coaches and Cathy Karl are at a table off to one side. Kelci and Coby Karl are asleep on chairs. Gerald limps over from the pay phone and sits down, beaming.

"Coach, I have got good news. And it's a story. I have got to tell you about a young man who has overcome adversity, shown some character, paid the price, gone the extra mile to get the job done."

"Is this gonna take long, Gerald?" Karl says with a laugh.

"Coach. I just been on the phone with US Airlines—USAir. Excuse me. And they have informed me that this young man got on his plane in Chicago, made a difficult connection in Pittsburgh, a difficult connection because his plane was late. He had eighteen minutes to make that flight, and we all know the Pittsburgh airport is a difficult airport. He ran—*he ran!*—through the airport and made that connection and is in the Albany area as we speak. He is at the hotel as we speak."

"Kelvin?"

"Kelvin. I think we should buy him breakfast tomorrow morning."

"Well"—Karl smiles—"let's see how he plays first. I hope he's as good as you say he is, Gerald. Or he isn't worth the trouble."

"No trouble at all, Coach." Gerald smiles. "Now, I believe I'll have a taste of that spaghetti."

NOVEMBER 11

Rosters need to be down to twelve today, a Friday. With Upshaw, whom Karl sees for the first time today in practice and is impressed—"he has NBA quickness," Karl says, almost surprised to find anything resembling the NBA here—the Patroons have seventeen in camp, one over the limit. Ozell Jones will be placed on the injured list to make the limit. Jones had his cheekbone fractured in a Los Angeles street gang fight over the summer. "I was wearing the wrong colors in the wrong neighborhood," he says. "Probably chasing down some girl," comes a comment from the back.

The cuts are to be Anthony Teachey, Norman Taylor, Rodney Martin, and Gerald Jackson; that's what Karl tells the local press. Teachey, the former Wake Forest star, never impressed and wasn't in good shape. Taylor, Jackson, and Martin were simply beaten out. That brings the roster to twelve.

Until sometime after practice. That night, Karl suspends Othell Wilson. A source at the league office tells Tim Wilkin that Wilson failed his drug test. No one will confirm it: not Karl, not Oliver, not even the league. On Saturday, Wilson is officially cut. (Ozell is not injured, keeping the roster at twelve.) Karl and Oliver say it is a "basketball decision." They say that Steve Shurina has been playing so well that they have decided not to wait; they will cut Wilson now. To be fair, Othell has not played well. And the league, which has just this year begun its mandatory drug-testing policy and perhaps hasn't gotten the procedures in place, never officially confirms Wilson failed his test. Nevertheless, in lightning speed, Wilson is gone.

NOVEMBER 12–13

At Saturday's practice, no one is talking about Wilson. It's business as usual. If this were an NBA city, especially a media-intensive city like New York or Boston or L.A., the story would be covered by a horde of press people. But this is the CBA, and the Wilson issue slides through. Tim Wilkin, the only local reporter, print or electronic, to cover the beat thoroughly, tries to get more out of the team. Karl will only say, "I think we made the right cuts." And then, patting his heart, "The next two are gonna hurt."

The season is drawing close. Armory workers are setting up the folding aluminum chairs—red on one side, green for the other three—on the wood risers. (Folding chairs will also serve as the players' bench.) And the cold has infiltrated. Gerald, who loves playing here, says with real southern charm, "The cold of Albany winters won't diminish the heat of this Armory." And, liking the sound of that, he says it again. Jim Coyne, who has stopped by to watch practice, complains how the army "creams us" with charges for the heat. The U.S. government bills the Patroons for everything from heat to lights to security. Since it would take a full day of heating to warm up the drafty expanse of the Armory for two hours' practice, the Patroons make the sound fiscal decision to keep it chilly.

Gerald is organizing, to no one's surprise. His blue notebook is open and pages are scattered around the press table set up at courtside. He moves sheets from one clear sleeve to another, organizing and reorganizing. "Doin' mah job," he calls it, and whenever he gets a moment's peace he attacks his book. He has a list of calls to make, players to find apartments for, money he owes and is owed, and a general to-do list that would humble an ordinary man.

He flips to his league-wide rosters, which he has just today brought up to date. He looks the other teams over. "You know something? I'm gonna tell you what. [Gerald never tells you what without first telling you he's about to tell you what, never asks you a question without first saying he's gonna ask you a question.] When we started this thing I thought we were fifth or sixth best. We managed to move up to fourth, then not too long ago we moved up to third. Right now, right this very minute, I think we're tied for second. And we're not far from first." He closes his book. "Not far from first."

Scrimmage is in full swing. When Grissom misses a play, Karl fairly hisses at him. "Shitty decision, Greg. Wrong, wrong, wrong." Grissom kicks a chair, then sits in another. "Sorry, Coach."

Clinton Smith gets set to inbound when Karl starts waving his arms. He's trying to call a play, but Clinton doesn't get it. "My boy, George Karl. It's hard enough remembering all those numbers and colors," Clinton jokes. "Now you want us to learn sign language too? That's my boy, Coach Karl."

Afterward, Gerald dispenses per diem money. Players line up for their $15 (once the season begins the figure jumps to a still paltry $22), which Gerald distributes, notes down, collects signatures for, and generally makes a large production out of. Gerald likes to do things this way, and if it takes a little longer than some might like, well, that's just the way it is. The players wait patiently, only grumbling a little.

Karl, in a fit of energy while waiting for Gerald to finish, has begun heaving full-court shots at the opposite basket. Kelvin feeds him balls off the ball rack whenever he yells for help.

"Help." Zing. Off the backboard.

"Help." Zing. Knocks over a folding chair.

"Help." Zing. Another chair is sent flying.

"Help." Zing. Off the rim. "Ooooooo I thought I had that one."

Ten balls later, seven chairs are toppled, Karl is panting, Upshaw is laughing. Gerald is counting up his receipts. "I'm short fifteen dollars," he says, not at all amused. "I believe I been taken to the cleaners, dad gamit."

O O O

The next day, chairs lie flattened and folded; the end court bleachers look like a smile with missing teeth.

Practice is at five o'clock. It's raining again, and a cold mist hangs in the Armory. Karl's manic mood continues.

"Ozell, you're gonna play every minute tonight. We're gonna get that skinny body in shape."

"Clinton Smith, what's our number-one priority? Stop the fucking penetration. Don't be trying for the steal."

"Ozell Jones! You got to learn to get that shot off legally."

"*Ozell Jones!* I want you in the paint, bumpin' and buttin', elbows and assholes. You're out here playing like Magic Johnson. Don't do it. Be *big!*"

"Clinton Smith, find your man! Vince Askew, cheat up! *Cheat up!*"

"Ozell! Whywhywhy? Why try to make a steal on Ken Johnson? He's a mediocre offensive player, at best. You're not a guard! Be fuckin' *big!*"

"*Doug Lee Doug Lee!* Don't let that man cut in front of you like that."

"Kelvin, don't back up. Don't back up."

"Ozell Jones Greg Grissom. When a guy starts pump fakin' like that stand tall. Arms up. *Be big!*"

"*Ozell! . . .*"

The scrimmage ends in a huddle. "Thanks, guys. That was good intensity," Karl says. "I know the bodies are sore after two-a-days and some games."

As the players file out, Karl yells once more to Ozell. "Hey Ozell. Whatever you been eatin' the last few days, keep eatin' it." Ozell might not be considered a special project, but he does get a lot of Karl's attention. Those who know Ozell's history say he's playing better than ever.

"OK, gentlemen," Karl announces to Gene and Gerald. "Let's go get some dinner and decide who we're gonna cut."

Over hamburgers and beers, the three cast their votes. It's a pure democracy, as Gerald will point out. "I have one vote. Gene has one vote. George has three votes. We'll let anyone vote, so long as George gets one more than all of us." The first decision is easy. Yeost will go. Karl was looking for another big man, but the 6' 7" Yeost plays more like a small forward. And Danny Pearson and Clinton Smith have played better at that spot. Yeost is released on Monday the fourteenth, exactly five days after arriving.

Five days might seem quick, but in the CBA it's hardly even worth mentioning. Teams have been known to call a player in, only to meet him at the airport with tickets back home. Consider the Patroons' favorite such story. It's 1984, and former Knick Phil Jackson is the head coach. The Patroons are in desperate need of a big man. Word comes of a Californian, name of Louis Brown. Money is tight, of course, so Jackson calls Brown at 10:30 at night California time and tells him to get on the red-eye to the East Coast. Brown does, and appears at practice at 9:00 the next morning. He hasn't slept much and doesn't even have his own equipment. The Patroons supply him with ill-fitting gear and throw him on the court. The other members of the Patroons, feeling threatened that this Brown fellow will take one of their jobs, start hammering him. Elbows are thrown, and Brown is receiving most of them. Jackson can see that Brown isn't the answer; rather than keep him over the weekend— or even for the next practice session—Brown is sent home. Within three hours of his arrival, he's back in the van and off to the airport for a flight back to California.

"Man, you guys are crazy," Brown tells Gary Holle on the way to the airport. "I can't believe you're doing this to me. You fly me in all night long for a three-hour tryout, you don't even want me, and now you're sending me back?" Holle tries to apologize. "Well," says Brown philosophically, "I wasn't doing anything this weekend anyway."

The final cut is the hardest. It will be one of two players: Ken Johnson or Vince Johnson. (They are not related.) Vince Johnson, a 6' 5" guard, is a hustler, the kind of player who can change a game's tempo and direction, a wild, aggressive guard who can ignite the team and the crowd with the spark of his energy. He has played very well all camp, well enough to make the team. He is also well liked by his teammates, and appears to have the right attitude toward the difficulties of CBA life. Ken Johnson is a bull, a 6' 9", 260-pounder from Michigan State who has not played all that well. He came into camp with extra baggage; he is twenty-five, married with two kids, and his family is in California. He has been cut from the NBA, mainly—and admittedly—because of his poor work habits. He tried to play in Albany last season, but was thirty pounds overweight and terribly out of shape; and he is not yet in proper condition. He also comes across as a complainer; he's an articulate, intelligent man who speaks his mind, sometimes speaking too often, and he can rub some as arrogant. He wants to play, because he wants to get back to the NBA. But when he asks for more playing time—which he does often—it seems more like "bitching and moaning" than the reasoned request that Johnson thinks he's making.

Gerald calls it a philosophical cut: "Do leopards change their spots or not?" he asks rhetorically. Vince, it is clear, would have the better attitude all year long. Ken will more likely have a harder time, being away from his family while trying to support them on the meager CBA salary, having to work hard to get back to the NBA. Moreover, Ken is a potential rather than a reality. Right now, he is not an NBA player (and barely a CBA player), not in attitude or effort or skills. But he has the potential to be one. Vince has proven himself in camp to be a certifiable CBA talent, and he gives Albany something that perhaps no one else on the roster can. On the other hand, Ken is one of the few big men in camp; if nothing else, he can go in to a game, bang some bodies, grab some rebounds (his one true talent), pick up a few fouls, and come out. Vince is one of several 6' 5" and 6' 6" guard/forward types on the roster, and his role might be filled by one of the others, someone like Steve Shurina or Doug Lee.

The discussion goes on; Karl listens passively as Gene and Gerald argue to keep Vince. Gene sees a look in George's eye, a look he recognizes. "You've already made up your mind, haven't you, Coach?" Gene smiles.

Karl smiles back, and calls for the check.

NOVEMBER 15–16

John Stroeder is cut, again. On Tuesday he is let go by the Spurs; if he clears waivers, he could join the Patroons. But the 76ers have a spot to fill, and the word is they're considering picking Stroeder up. By now, Gerald is skeptical. "I'll believe he's here when I see him walk through the door," he says.

He will walk through the door of the Howard Johnson's Tuesday night. Stroeder is the big man Albany needs; the addition of Upshaw and Stroeder make the Patroons a vastly improved team. Where Upshaw adds quickness, court sense, and CBA experience, Stroeder is the force. He can rebound, of course, but at 6′ 11″ he can also run the floor, he can make the pass, and he has a surprisingly soft shooting touch. Stroeder is an intense red-haired giant with a high forehead, a square jaw, and a piercing gaze that, in conversation, seems to cut straight through his opposite's eyes to the back of his head. Stroeder doesn't talk so much as bark, especially during games, where he howls, screams, and shouts in short, bone-rattling bursts. He looks like a Marine drill instructor, and plays like one. He is also the only player Gerald will consider bringing into camp this late. A lesser player, without Stroeder's NBA experience and reputation, might be resented by the other players. Stroeder, everyone knows, is needed.

But no one knows how long Stroeder will stay; it could be all season, but then again it might be one day. Stroeder, out of the University of Montana, hasn't played much in two years; he was a backup in Milwaukee last season, playing in forty-one games, and the year before he played seventeen CBA games in Rapid City. He spent much of his career in Europe (except for one CBA season with Karl at Montana). At the age of thirty, he needs to work out the rust to get another chance at the NBA.

First, the Pats make their last cut. Karl's three votes win: Vince Johnson goes, Ken Johnson stays. On Wednesday, November 16, Karl and Oliver have their final lineup. Ten players are given their W-2 forms, gainfully employed by the Albany Patroons.

At the guards: Steve Shurina, Keith Smith, and Kelvin Upshaw.

Shurina, twenty-two, 6′ 4″, 200 pounds, from New York City, out of St. John's, undrafted. Hard working ... loves the game ...

makes the other players better because they enjoy playing with him ... intelligent, honest, direct, funny, with a voice that is pure Queens ... Enjoys an evening out, but so concerned about making the team he spent training camp nights in his motel room, "working over my rosary beads, freaking out every time the phone rang or there was a knock on the door." His talents: shooting, passing, hustle ... his limits are unknown: If he improves, a long shot at the NBA. If he slips, might not last in the CBA.

Keith Smith, twenty-four, 6' 4", 190 pounds, from California, out of Loyola Marymount, second round pick of Milwaukee (1986). Fine athlete ... all-around player ... best defensive player on team. An up-and-down career: played forty-two games with Bucks in '86–87, then cut by CBA team in '87–88 ... left-handed shot ... sharp dresser, sharp with the ladies ... early nickname: "clothes and ho's" ... no stranger to a good time.

Upshaw, twenty-five, 6' 2", 180 pounds, from Chicago, out of the University of Utah, second round CBA draft pick (1986). Streets-of-Chicago tough, with eyes full of suspicion and a cocky, sometimes distant air, but also has impish sense of humor and a wide, toothy grin. Has letters "LV" carved into his haircut, for Louis Vuitton ... cat-quick; runs with a loose-jointed bounce of confidence; shoots ugly—uses a pigeon-toed launching stance—but effectively ... CBA all-star last season with Rapid City ... can be selfish player: likes the ball, likes to run the offense ... three-year veteran, was once highly competitive, may be burning out by now. Questions: Will he work? Will he take Karl's needling? ... Could be team catalyst; key pickup. Known as Shaw.

Swing man, guard/forward: Doug Lee, twenty-four, 6' 6", 218 pounds, from Peoria, Illinois, out of Purdue, second round draft pick of Houston (1987). Spent last season as non-roster player with Rockets ... always hustles, always full blast, always on the floor after loose balls (Purdue practice shorts have Play Hard written across butt) ... was team MVP for Purdue his senior year ... top three-point threat and free-throw expert. Curly dark hair, mustache, Roman nose (told Shurina, "with my nose and your ears we'd make the all-time Mr. Potato Head"). Married (wife Becky will join him in Albany), family-oriented, mature in his manner, but given to verbal practical jokes. Can turn a game around with his shooting.

Forwards: Danny Pearson, Clinton Smith, Vince Askew, Ken Johnson.

Pearson, twenty-three, 6' 6", 180 pounds, out of Jacksonville, third round draft pick of Washington (1987). A pure shooter . . . quick, but doesn't show energy . . . silent, almost invisible player whose talents show up on film. Coaches appreciate Pearson more than fans. Quiet on and off court, but driven, internally motivated, and supremely competitive . . . adds what Karl calls "the glue"; can be mean, dirty if needed, on the court, willing to do the dirty work that wins games. Lives exclusively on junk food; favorite restaurants are McDonald's, 7-Elevens, and vending machines . . . as a result, possesses most interesting metabolism on team—sleeps a lot, except at night.

Clinton Smith, twenty-four, 6' 6", 210 pounds, from Cleveland, out of Cleveland State, fifth round draft pick of Golden State (1986). Great defensive player, plays hard, lousy shooter . . . emotional player, a bit rusty; played only twelve games in CBA last year. Jive talker, a practiced con man, friendly and persuasive, one of the usual suspects (though rarely caught). "Don't call me Clinton, it's Clint." . . . Everyone is "my boy." One of best players in camp.

Vince Askew, twenty, 6' 6", 210 pounds, from Memphis, out of Memphis State (three years; did not finish), second round draft pick of Philadelphia (1987). Best talent, best body, most potential, needs most work . . . a definite NBA prospect, if Karl can keep him on course . . . started slowly, almost cut in camp . . . so strong, will play some power forward, even though he's only 6' 6" . . . very shy, quiet off court, almost childlike innocence, but a potential for getting into trouble . . . has a lot to learn, in many areas.

Ken Johnson, twenty-five, 6' 9", 260, from California, out of Michigan State, second round draft pick of Chicago (1985). Body of a linebacker . . . can rebound strongly, and score if needed . . . will also see time at center. Married, two children, family will stay back in California. Smart, articulate, talkative (perhaps to a fault), can pontificate like a college professor or rap with the home boys . . . at a turning point in his career . . . will take extra effort to pull him through to next level.

Centers: Ozell Jones, Greg Grissom.

Jones, twenty-eight, 6' 11", 240 pounds, from Long Beach, California, out of Cal State-Fullerton, fourth round draft pick of San Antonio (1984). Earned spot on the roster, needs help to reach next level of ability. Playing better than has in years, or so people say; still inconsistent, erratic, moody ... says one coach, "I think he was the kind of player who was always going to be great. Somewhere along the line he reached a point where coaches were always angry at him because they wanted more than what he gave." ... Honest, direct, says what he thinks. Will be one of Karl's main projects.

Grissom, twenty-five, 6' 11", 260 pounds, from Longview, Texas, out of TCU, third round CBA draft pick (1986). Big and friendly, more athletic than he looks, competitive nature on the court, fun-loving off it ... has a good-old-boy, laid-back demeanor, likes a beer or two (or thirty-six, his one-sitting record, though he says "they were only light beers") ... good rebounder, excellent passer, inconsistent shooter ... little chance of NBA callup ... only player back from championship team, on which he played little.

At the Howard Johnson's: John Stroeder, thirty, 6' 10", 260 pounds, from Bremerton, Washington, out of Montana, eighth round draft pick of Portland (1980). Might be the best center in the CBA ... played in forty-one games with Milwaukee last season ... needs to play. At times, he tends to coast, lose concentration, can be stripped of the ball. Could be in the lineup for the home opener. But that's not until Friday.

The flight for Charleston, West Virginia, leaves at seven o'clock in the morning on Wednesday, November 16. The Albany Patroons, with no big names, no stars, no marquee value—indeed, with no chance of impressing anyone on paper—are a team. The season opens tomorrow, two weeks after it all began, right on schedule.

Preseason Epilogue

Gerald leaves practice that afternoon to be approached by an unknown fellow.

"You Gerry Oliver? Yeah, it's me, John from Queens. I wanna tryout."

"I'm real sorry, son, but we already picked our team."

"But you have ta give me a fuckin' tryout! I drove up here, slept in my car all night. Your friend said you know basketball an' can tell if someone's good or not. Ya gotta gimme a tryout. Just let me on the fuckin' court an' show ya what I can do."

"No, son, I'm sorry, I can't help you."

And John from Queens gets back in his car and points it south, to New York, never to get his fuckin' tryout with the fuckin' Patroons.

NOVEMBER 17

The theme is restated in the heavy-footed prose of the *Times Union*.

PATROONS: TOUGH ACT TO FOLLOW

By Tim Wilkin.

Battle No. 1 for the Albany Patroons is tonight's opener with the Charleston Gunners. This one they can win.

But there's a war they'll fight throughout the Continental Basketball Association season they can never win.

The Pats will struggle to rid every city—especially their home city—of the ghost of CBA championships past and the ghost of Bill Musselman.

Last year Musselman made Albany the Shangri-La of the CBA, assembling a team the likes of which will probably never be seen again. The Pats of a year ago went 48–6 in the regular season, 12–4 in the playoffs. Sixty wins in 70 games. Now comes the new era. Before it starts, remember:

George Karl is not Bill Musselman.

Clinton Smith is not Derrick Rowland.

Ken Johnson is not Tony Campbell.

The list could go on and on.

Down in Charleston, it's Just Say No To Drugs Night. The timing is a bit unfortunate, since Charleston's Skip Henderson has just tested positive for cocaine and been suspended by the league. The Gunners will therefore play with just nine players in front of a club-record crowd of 4,765. All of them, it appears, are just saying no.

Those nine are enough, however, to edge the Albany ten, 104–103. Albany is sloppy, committing twenty-three turnovers. There are moments, such as the second quarter, when Albany is in control; the Pats take that Q 32–17 after losing the first by 6. And there are moments when Albany is completely out of control, losing the third quarter 36–20. A 9-point halftime lead is a 7-point deficit after three quarters. That deficit grows to 12 until Shurina, off the bench, scores 6 points in a 10–2 spurt to cut the Charleston lead to 2. And when Charleston misses two free throws with 10 seconds left, the Pats trail by only 1.

Karl draws up a play; he has more plays in his head than anyone in the CBA, a league not known for structured offenses. This is Karl's forte, it's where he feels he can beat anyone here. Other coaches let them play. George Karl *coaches*. This play calls for Shurina to come off the pick, take the pass on the left wing, and shoot. It works perfectly, Shurina is open, accepts the pass from Upshaw, and fires. It hits the rim and bounces away.

"I shoulda pump faked, drawn the foul," Shurina says later.

For Karl it is an early lesson. Throughout the season, his plays will work, at least as they are drawn on the board. The X's and O's become real on the court. Only the results will be in doubt. Karl can get them the shot. He can't make it for them. The talent on this team is not NBA talent, and no amount of NBA coaching can change that. It is a frustration George Karl will come to know very well.

Despite the loss, Albany wins two quarter points. And that's the CBA maxim: Take two on the road. The Patroons leave for home tomorrow morning.

NOVEMBER 18

"We're on a break now, George," the cameraman tells Karl. "We'll be back soon."

Karl is standing before a lone television camera in the midst of pregame chaos. It is two hours before gametime—which in Albany is 8:05 P.M.—and the Armory has been transformed: Concession stands are set up, and the first smells of popcorn and hotdogs are wafting through the chilly air. The early smatterings of a crowd wander the track while a couple of players in warmup suits shoot baskets with the ballboys. The Green Coats, Albany's legion of volunteers who monitor the clocks, keep stats, and generally try to bring order to this chaos, march in; they all wear blazers in an unnatural shade of green (the Patroons colors are green and gold) to distinguish them from the crowd. Gary Holle, properly green-coated, is running around like a madman, now stopping a moment to instruct his crew of interns where to let people stand. "No one between these red lines. I tell ya it's a bitch keeping this area clear."

Karl stands among all this; there is no media room here, no enclave of safety for the coaches. It's all in the open. Karl looks up into the monitor, earphone in place, microphone hooked to his sweater.

"Hi, Ed . . . No, I don't think so. We shot poorly last night, only forty percent from the floor, seventy percent from the line and we were still in a position to win the ball game. . . . Just early season jitters, I think. . . . No, we haven't found the right combination yet, we're still working on that. . . . Thanks, Ed." Karl quickly unhooks his earpiece and microphone and heads downstairs to the locker room. Before leaving he leans into team publicist Bill Heller. "Don't tell anyone, but I've never beaten Panaggio. I think I'm 0–8 against him."

"Don't worry, Coach. He's never won here," Heller says.

Mauro Panaggio is in his eighth season as a CBA coach, and Quad City, tonight's visitor, is his fourth team. A fan wanders over to the bench and asks politely, "Where is Quad City?" He is told it is mostly in Illinois, and a little bit in Iowa.

Comes the game: A full house, over 3,000, stand and cheer as Jay Silverman, the public address announcer, booms: "Ladies and Gentlemen [pause]. Let's get up and greet [another pause] your defending CBA champion [longest pause yet] Albany Patroons!" With great flourish Silverman makes "Albany" sound like uh-AL-BANY, as if he's getting a running start into the word, and the crowd leaps up. The Patroons take the court. Each player is introduced, first the reserves and then the starters—Ozell Jones at center, Keith Smith and Kelvin Upshaw the guards, Clint Smith and Vince Askew up front. John Stroeder, in suit coat and tie, sits alongside on the bench.

"Don't forget," the PA reminds the crowd, "the corner score-boards keep totals for the quarter scores. The big board overhead is the running score." The fans need no reminder; when Shurina goes end to end and lays in an off-balance, out-of-control finger roll with 10 seconds left to give the Pats the first quarter, the crowd acts as though they've won another championship.

The next two quarters come easily. Ozell dunks off the fast break to put Albany up by 6, which is the margin at the half, and Askew's two free throws at the end of the third give Albany the Q 27–25. The game lead is 94–86. Upshaw's three-pointer from the wing with less than 4 minutes left brings the lead to 11, but the Patroons slow down the tempo. A couple of Quad City threes and a three-point play later, and the lead is down to 4. That's how it ends, 121–117. Albany takes six of seven standings points.

And the season feels officially under way. The tiny locker room is jammed with the TV reporters who will only occasionally be back, and Karl, changed back from his coaching uniform—coat and tie—to sweater, sips a beer and introduces himself to the Albany viewing audience. Players, their nakedness covered only by towels gripped tightly around their waists, push past the fans and through the men's room to shower.

Thirsty's, the official saloon of the Albany Patroons, awaits.

NOVEMBER 19–21

Gerald continues his off-court activities, helping find apartments, organizing practices, coordinating travel, talking up the league. Karl continues coaching.

The main decision is what to do with the roster. Stroeder makes eleven Patroons where only ten are allowed. But there are still rumblings he may be called up at any moment. Until that happens, he'll play. Who will go?

Steve Shurina has been bothered by a bad back. He played through it in camp; "I had to play to make the team," he says. It is bothering him still (though he thinks he can still play) and with more small men to spare than big, he's the one to go. There are a couple of ways to do it. One is to waive him; it's unlikely he'd be picked up by another team, and the Patroons could reclaim him when a spot opens. They can also put him on injured reserve, which will keep him out of the lineup a minimum of five games or ten days. The coaches let Shurina make the decision, and Gerald calls him over to explain the choices.

That night Karl gets a call from both Shurina and Shurina's agent, confused about what is being done. George assures both everything is all right and promises to talk to Steve before the game on Tuesday.

NOVEMBER 22

Karl and Shurina head up to the top row of seats. "Steve," Karl says, "we want you to know we're happy with you here. We want you to stay with the club. We think injured reserve is the best way to do it."

Shurina is relieved. "That's what I thought Gerald was telling me, but you know how he gets. I was real confused. You know, sometimes Gerald talks in tongues."

○   ○   ○

Stroeder is in uniform for the first time; will it be the last? Philadelphia, New Jersey, and Boston have all inquired; the Nets, who have lost three players to injury—Chris Morris, Keith Lee, and Joe Barry Carroll—called yesterday. And Houston has a scout at tonight's game.

The Lacrosse Catbirds are in town. The coach is Ron Ekker, a CBA veteran; the roster includes some veterans as well, like Perry Moss and a balding, well-traveled Ron Brewer.

Karl tabs the same five starters. "I'm too dumb to change" is his glib line. "People put way too much importance on who starts" is his real reason.

Stroeder quickly proves him right. Coming off the bench, Stroeder scores the first 6 points of the second Q to turn a 3-point lead into a near rout. In 27 minutes, the most playing time he's gotten in two years, Stroeder finishes with 16 points and 4 rebounds, and runs the floor with grace and power. The rust doesn't show; at times he seems a man among boys.

The halftime lead is 59–45 when the Patroons return to the floor. Before the second half begins, the PA announcer calls for a moment of silence. Today is the twenty-fifth anniversary of the assassination of John F. Kennedy. Some quick mental computations reveal that, on November 22, 1963, Ken Johnson had just turned one year old. Ozell Jones was three. John Stroeder was five. Kelvin

Upshaw and Greg Grissom were in their first year of life. None of the other Patroons had yet been born.

Stroeder's presence clearly helps the rest of the club. As La Crosse is forced to double-team Stroeder, Ken Johnson has room to move; Johnson capitalizes with 12 points and 12 rebounds. And as the game progresses, the Patroons, still largely nameless, faceless unknowns, vagrants who have landed in Albany and inhabited the Armory for only three weeks, become known. The Armory grows loud for the first time. For a time, at least, Musselman's Patroons are forgotten.

But only for a time.

In all, seven Patroons score in double figures, and Albany dominates the boards, 44–26. The final is 110–92, but at one point in the second half Albany's lead is 26. Only the fourth quarter point is lost.

In the locker room Karl keeps a promise: no practice Thursday—Thanksgiving Day—for a win tonight.

"I am a bribe coach," he says. "I believe in bribes."

NOVEMBER 23

Wednesday comes first, and practice is still on. Coffee and donuts sit on the scorer's table. Everyone tries to get warm.

Gerald is flipping through his notebook. "Gotta get organized." He is repeating his mantra when a soldier in full camouflage and heavy boots wanders by. The army has been unloading supplies from two government issue vehicles parked out front. The soldier hands Gerald a small box. "Compliments of the U.S. Army." He smiles. Inside, a couple of ballpoint pens, in regulation camouflage pattern. Gerald is touched.

George Karl, a CBA coach's duties never done, is sweeping the floor. Ozell is asking about his apartment. Gerald is thinking basketball. "The next team we play"—which is his former employer, Charleston—"scored 147 and 146 points its last two games. We don't wanna get in a shootin' match. We're gonna work hard today," he says, and then, nodding toward the sluggish, sleepy players stretching on the sidelines, "even though the bodies aren't really here today."

"OK, Gerald," Karl yells. "Let's get these boys, I mean men, running." A tough practice, working on position play; Askew moves from the 4 (the power forward spot) to the 3 spot, (the shooting forward) his more natural position, Pearson tries out at 2 (shooting guard), Lee works at 3. Grissom volunteers to try his 6' 11" body at the 1, making him the largest point guard in history. Karl declines the offer.

Stopping by to watch the workout, as he does nearly every day, is Jim Laverty. Laverty is not a player. He is not a coach. But he is an important part of this team. There is a Jim Laverty for every pro team, really, and especially in this league; without the Lavertys, CBA teams would have a hard time functioning.

Jim Laverty is a native of Albany. He grew up "poor as dirt" a few blocks from the Armory. Now in his forties, with a successful insurance business, he spends a good part of his time both helping out and hanging around the Patroons. Laverty is on the Patroons' board of directors and was an initial investor in the team. "Me and Coyne and a few guys were sitting in a bar talking about getting a team here, and it happened," he likes to say. But Laverty is one of the few actively involved. (Another is John DiNuzzo, the proprietor of the aforementioned Thirsty's. DiNuzzo supplies Patroons players with discount coupons to eat at his place after games.) Laverty helps find apartments and cars, sets up housing (last year, he even boarded a player at his home), and generally greases the wheels between the team and the community. "I know everybody in this town, I can get things done," he says without boasting, and he does get things done.

Which earns him the privilege of coming to practices, going to lunch and dinner with the coaches, having cocktails—he's been known to enjoy a cocktail—after games. Laverty, silver-haired and rubber-faced, is a fun and funny booster; his nose is often red, and his formidable belly, which seems a later addition to his thin-legged, slim-shouldered body (like a new wing on an old house), cuts a recognizable profile on the sidelines. Some part of his wardrobe is usually Patroons—or is it Irish?—green, and his smoky, street-harsh voice is often in mid-story or joke. He is the link between teams past and present, too, often telling the old stories while the new ones develop around him. Laverty is as much a part of the team as

George Karl or Greg Grissom. Maybe more so. They will be gone in five months. He will always be here.

"Stroeder makes this team awful goddamn good," he says while watching practice.

Karl is discussing the team's progress with Wilkin. He says the team hasn't yet found that belief that it can find a way to win in any situation; the first game's loss is an example. But the togetherness is developing, and Karl is happy. "We're not there yet, but it's getting better." And Stroeder's presence should open things up for everyone else, especially the other big men.

"Everybody in," he suddenly yells. "Gerald's gotta talk to us."

"Listen up," Gerald says, his accent resonating off the empty Armory walls. "At fahve forty-fahve at the Quality Inn, Clinton, Kelvin, Stroeder, Ken, Ozell will be picked up. Doug Lee will take Vince. And his wife. Greg and Steve, you gonna get there on your own. It's at the Lexington Grille. It's called Meet the Patroons night. And it's a buffet meal. The minute you walk in you kin start eatin'.

"Ozell and Danny. I'm workin' on your rooms. I'll know more later. Stroeder, I'm workin' on the things we talked about.

"Now, who needs somethin' else worked on?"

"Gerald, why don't you relax?" Karl laughs.

" 'Cause I got assholes for players." He laughs back, his voice rising in volume and pitch. "If ah didn't have assholes for players I wouldn't be cleanin' up shit all the time.

"Oh, ah forgot. I don't curse anymore. That's mah last curse."

○   ○   ○

The Lexington Grille offers Patroons and Miller Lite for $1.25. Ozell starts eating right away, pausing only at the pasta primavera. "None of them round things," he says, pointing at a zucchini.

Gene is giving Tony a hard time. "Tony, how'd you like to come to Montana and be my driver?"

"I'll go anywhere if the money's right, Coach."

"You know, there are no paved roads in Montana."

"Don't matter to me, Coach. Paved, no paved, don't matter to me."

Tony dashes off.

"He'd fit right in in Montana," Gene says dryly.

And that sets off a flood of memories about coaching in Montana, and the odd culture shock that results when mostly black, city ball players are stuck in the wild west. Karl comes by with a plate of food. "Hey Gene. Remember the time in Montana. We're in the seventh game of the finals. Before the game we can't find one of our players. We find out he's got a plane ticket home that day; he didn't think the series would last this long. So he's got a ticket, and he's gonna use it. He's going home."

Gene laughs. "The owner had to go to the airport and drag him off the plane. Brought him back, and he played that night."

"Another time," Karl goes on, "we're driving through Montana or somewhere, out west, a couple of players in the back. And there's a bald eagle, sitting along the roadside. So I say, 'Look, there's a bald eagle.' These guys get all excited. They think it's *the* bald eagle, our national symbol, like there's only one. That's it."

Gene: "Another time we're driving along and we pass these big bales of hay. The guys had never seen such a thing. Had no idea what they were or how they got there. They thought they grew like that or something. I had to explain that they let the grass grow, then it's cut and rolled up by a big baling machine . . . the damnedest conversation I think I ever had."

Karl laughs. "We're driving one time, and I'm telling some wild grizzly bear stories. Guys getting mauled by grizzlies, all kinds of gruesome stuff. I pull over along the road to take a leak, and one of the guys yells, 'Don't stop, don't stop. Don't get out of the van.' He was terrified a grizzly would attack us while we peed."

"How about the time I got that technical," Gene says. "The only technical I ever got. After the game it's a six-hour drive back to Great Falls. George makes me ride back with the refs. In the back of their mini, six hours. I never said a word the whole trip."

George gets up to talk to the players. "Before you guys leave, stroll through the bar. Mingle. Shake some hands. Watch the game on TV."

At the bar they chat with patrons, sign some autographs. Kelvin is standing quietly by the door, an uncomfortable shadow, his sweatshirt hood tied tightly around his head, holding two shopping bags, looking for a ride home. Tony has disappeared once again.

At the bar, Gary Holle is agitated. He's ordered name plates to put on the players' jerseys, but he can't remember if he ordered the right color.

"Are our numbers green or gold? Gold, right? Or green? Jeez, I hope I ordered the right color."

NOVEMBER 24

Thanksgiving. As promised, a day off, the first since camp began. Everyone is invited to a Thanksgiving dinner at Pat Riley's. Not *that* Pat Riley; although the Lakers coach happens to be a native of Schenectady; this Pat Riley is a local referee and Patroons booster. Greg Grissom lives with the Rileys during the season. Every Thanksgiving Riley throws a dinner for the team, some friends, and family. The Karls, Gene and his wife, and Doug Lee and his wife show up. No one else makes it for dinner."We've had too many team outings recently," Karl theorizes. "Too much togetherness."

After dinner, Shurina and his girlfriend, who is in Albany for a visit, stop by. So do Gerald and Jim Laverty; Gerald had dinner with the Lavertys. That is, after the police called.

"I get this call from the cops," Laverty tells. " 'There's some guy named Gerald here, he says he's looking for your house.' "

"Ah got pulled over," Gerald confirms. "The officer asks why I'm speeding. I say, 'Well, officer, I'm lost. I don't know where I'm supposed to be and I don't know where I'm going.' "

He comes bearing the scouting report for Charleston, which he and Karl study at Riley's home bar. Gerald sits in his snow parka.

"Coach, I got a call from Rochester," Gerald reports. "They want to trade Gerald Paddio."

Karl listens. "Gerald, I like this team. I like my team."

"Don't I know it, Coach?" Gerald howls, banging on the bar laughing. "I didn't even bother to call you. I didn't even waste your time, did I? I didn't even waste your time."

"Gerald, will you take that coat off. You look like an Eskimo."

"I'm leaving, Coach. I'm going to the office."

"Gerald, it's Thanksgiving," Karl says, devouring a turkey sandwich. "Relax. Have a beer."

But Gerald leaves. He will spend Thanksgiving night alone at the Patroons office. Gerald is looking to define his role on the club.

He has a deep respect, almost an awe, for Karl's coaching abilities. On the way to the office, Gerald calls Karl one of the five best coaches in the world, and he means it. He is amazed at Karl's ability to see the whole game and all ten players at once, to know instantly when a player isn't running a play correctly or is out of position ever so slightly. He loves to hear Karl teach, loves how he motivates, respects his desire to make these players the best they can be. A coach's responsibility in the CBA, Gerald says, is only to win; beyond that, a coach has a responsibility to himself and his players. Gerald has seen a lot of things in the CBA, and it hurts him when people don't take these responsibilities seriously. Seeing that Karl does gladdens his heart, and it is one of the reasons he pushes himself so hard. It is why he drives off from the party to go to work.

"I don't know if he uses this stuff," he says getting into his car, "this stuff" meaning his reports. "I don't know if he wants it. He don't ask for it. But I do it for me. I do it so we can win. And I wanna win. I've lost before. I wanna win."

NOVEMBER 25

The name plates match the numbers, both are green. Gary Holle is saved.

As Charleston, in navy with gold trim, takes the floor, Karl gets a kiss at the bench from Coby and Kelci, and the game begins.

The strategy is to get the ball inside more; in the loss in Charleston, this didn't happen enough, a tactical mistake considering Charleston's biggest player is 6′ 8″. Tonight will be different. Stroeder and Johnson combine for 32 points and 25 rebounds, and Clint Smith pumps in 31. At the half, the lead is 16. Laverty tells Cathy Karl, "George oughta be happy with this one."

She knows better. "I bet he's pretty pissed."

Late in the half, Albany's discipline breaks down. Karl runs the most sophisticated, most NBA-like program in the CBA. In part it's to get his players ready for the NBA. The main reason, though, is that he knows it's a better brand of basketball, an intellectual, strategic, demanding game. CBA ball tends toward the free form of street ball: long-range shots, few set plays, run and gun (what Karl calls "shake and bake"). Karl hates it with deep passion. To him, basketball is a thinking man's game, a chess game to be played move by move, strategy by strategy. That's where coaching is fun, in the challenge of making order out of chaos, of giving his players the best plan under which to win. When they don't stick to the plan is when he is most angry.

In the locker room he launches into his season-long theme about "CBA bullshit." Too much finesse, too many behind-the-back passes, too much individual play. Karl tries to stop it immediately. "They are a fucking awful basketball team. If we're worse for playing 'em, then we're a dumb fucking team." Karl buries his face in his hands: "They are so fuckin' bad," he cries as if he can't believe what he's seeing. He recovers, and predicts that Charleston will come out playing selfish, CBA-style ball. "If we're any good we'll kick their ass big-time. If we're any fuckin' good we bury 'em. We bury 'em early, and it's over."

Karl gathers himself. "Now we can play around with the crazy game. That is not the kind of basketball team that you want to become. You want to get better. You don't want this CBA bullshit to drag your games down. These guys have nothing that's gonna get them to the NBA. I'm judging on the way I'm gonna judge you, not by CBA standards. And I saw a little selfishness on this team tonight. I guarantee, that's the quickest way to the bench."

They respond by losing the third quarter; the shooting touch disappears, and the lead is down to 4. But Karl remains calm in the huddles, and Stroeder is a fury on the court, growling, howling, barking, leering. The game comes back to them, as Karl says it will, and the Pats take the fourth quarter by 10. The final is 125–107. Six more points in the standings, and at 3–1, second place in the Eastern Division.

Greg Grissom doesn't play a minute. At Thirsty's, trainer Jack Moser finds Karl. "Grissom's been spotted over at the Sports Bar. And he wasn't drinking. He must be really down."

NOVEMBER 26

CBA play rules once again. After attempting twenty-one three-pointers last night, a record even for the three-intensive CBA, Charleston comes back in the second game gunning even more furiously. Karl is beside himself, but implores his troops to relax. "Take your time, the game will come to you," he reassures. And, "Doug, have patience," when Lee throws up an ugly J that misses. And more: "Don't let frustration fuck up your mind," he says as the Pats fall behind late in the second quarter.

Tonight's crowd is small—only about 2,300—and quiet. Assistant trainer Rich Sill, a beefy, slope-headed man who sits just behind the bench, is the loudest fan in the gym. He emits a low-pitched, throaty "Hohhhhhh, Hohhhhhh," whenever opponents shoot foul shots, followed by a diabolical, horror-movie laugh—HAW-haw-haw—whenever his howling causes them to miss. He also tries to stir up the crowd to chant "dee-fense, dee-fense." Tonight he's a human sound machine.

"Hohhhhh-*Hohhhhhh*. Hohhhhh-*Hohhhhhh*. *Dee*-fense. *Dee*-fense. Hohhhhh . . ."

When that doesn't work, he simply cheers. "Let's go, Kevin," he yells. "Let's go, Calvin." Kelvin looks at him, confused.

The Patroons take a 64–59 lead into the half. Karl is upset at the poor concentration—he calls it brain-lock—but not as angry as last night. He's more subdued, more patient. "The game will come to us," he repeats, "if we establish our game, and not let this fuckin' shit happen." As the players file out into the hallway, Gerald and George confer quietly in the locker room.

"I don't know if we kin afford to start a center who isn't ready," Gerald says. "And I cain't tell you if Ozell is ready. I say we go with Stroeder." Karl sits silent.

Stroeder starts the second half. But the third quarter is still trouble; the lead is 4 after three quarters, and the Patroons have won only one quarter point.

"C'mon, fellas," Upshaw cheers on the bench. "This is our house." Rich Sill is howling. *"Hohhhhhh."*

Then Doug Lee takes charge. He hits a jumper, tosses in a couple of free throws, then sticks a three-pointer. "Threeeeee for Doug Leeeeee," screams Jay Silverman over the PA. Lee scores 14 points in the fourth Q and the Patroons pull away, 130–113. Five more standings points, and Albany takes the lead in the division. After winning from the inside yesterday, it's outside shooting—Lee and Keith Smith each score 23, and Upshaw adds 16—that wins it tonight. The Patroons are showing the ability to win even when not playing well, and against a style of play Karl truly hates and sincerely believes he can overcome. In his heart, he knows his style is the best. And the best will always win; that's the idea. Karl is pleased.

"Day off tomorrow," he announces.

"I love you, Coach," Kelvin cries.

For the second night in a row, Grissom hasn't played. In the quiet of the Armory tonight, a few fans had gotten on the situation, yelling "Put Gris in," and "Gris is getting cold, Coach." Grissom had vowed he would never go through another season like last season, when he played little and took heaps of abuse. But now it seems like it's happening all over.

He dresses quickly and walks quietly up the stairs.

NOVEMBER 27

Gerald doesn't take a day off. After the game, he stays up till 2:30 trying to get a film of the Tulsa team—the next opponent—to scout. Films are acquired by trades with other teams; it's an I'll-help-you, you-help-me world. But Gerald is having trouble getting the film in on time.

He naps a few hours, then heads to the Patroons office downtown, a spare, unattractive couple of rooms furnished with standard office-supply furniture—plain metal desks, squeaky chairs—and some photos and posters of teams past. Last year's team photo hangs on one wall, and a poster of an ad featuring Bill Musselman hangs on another—Musselman and his team continuing to look down on this year's Patroons. A fish tank holds the office's pets, two goldfish named Gerald and George. Actually, only one remains; in what is hoped not to be an omen, Gerald or George (no one is sure which) has recently passed away.

It's a rainy Sunday evening. Gerald takes a few calls, makes a few calls, organizes his notebook. At 6:30 Karl calls to see if the film came in.

"I tell you what," Gerald says, tired but proud. "If I have time I can think of solutions. It's when I don't have time to be sittin' and thinkin' of solutions that I cain't solve problems. I finally figured how we could get these films. I suddenly remembered you can get something called PDQ. That's Package Delivery Quick. I think. It cost us forty-nine dollars. It cost my American Express card forty-nine dollars. They put 'em right in the pilots' compartment. And I got 'em. Yes sir. Ah'll call you back after I watch 'em."

At 10 p.m., Gerald calls Karl. "Coach, if we play hard, I promise you, we will kick Tulsa's butt."

"That's fine, Gerald. Tell me about it in the morning."

"We're gonna be a winning ball club," he goes on. "I think we'll win this division. If we can keep first after these next four games at home. If we go out of here in first place I think we'll come home in first place. If we come home in first place we're gonna be all right. We will have survived the road and the home. And that's good. The road's hard. That's why I'm working so late tonight."

"Gerald, you're talking in tongues again. Good night."

Gerald switches off the VCR and the television, extinguishes the lights, locks the office door, and places the key in its special hiding place. He rides the elevator down eleven floors, pulling a blue wool stocking cap low over his head, nearly covering his eyes. And then he limps gently out into a warm, sad Sunday night rain.

NOVEMBER 28

Hanging around practice, a smattering of conversation:

"So I figured, Cordero hadn't won in two or three days, I figured, geez, he's gotta win soon," says Gene.

"How much longer, Coach? Coach said he'd be done by twelve," says Tony.

"Last year the guys would all be hanging out together all the time. They'd be in September's every night chasing pussy. Those guys chased pussy big time. These guys are boring. They all brought their wives, their girlfriends," says Laverty.

"White, you're up. Passing game," yells Karl.

"Stroeder hasn't played well lately," says Laverty.

"Not as well as he can. He's shown some signs of coming to life today. He hasn't played much the last two years," says Espeland.

"Doug Lee's apartment will be ready Friday. Hey Gerald, do I get things done or what," says Laverty.

"You know, I have recurring dreams. I dream the same thing over and over. And that's the way I get when I read Tim Wilkin's stories about last year's team and last year's record," says Karl.

"Who do you like tonight? I'll give you the Knicks and four," says Wilkin.

"Coach, I have a problem. You said we should come and see you whenever we have a problem," says Clint Smith.

"Gerald! Clinton Smith needs twenty dollars," says Karl.

"What am I doing here?" says Karl, slapping his head.

NOVEMBER 29

It's payday, and Oliver hands out the paychecks. He also settles some scores. "Now, son, I want you to go across that street to that bank and take out fifty-six dollars and come right back here and pay me what you owe. Or else I'll butter your nose."

Later, Gerald is shining his shoes at the scorer's table before tonight's first of two games with Tulsa. He's fired up—when he says it, it sounds like he's fahr'd up.

In front of him lies the league scoring list. On top, at 31.5 points per game, is Tulsa's Dexter Shouse; Shouse was part of the trade that brought Othell Wilson to Albany. Gerald knows Shouse well. "He may not play tonight. He didn't feel like practicing today. Tired or something. Shouse is a knucklehead. He does what he wants."

From there, he's off. "Was talkin' to one team last night about a trade. They are titanium heads. Y'know what titanium is? Hardest steel in the world. Need nuke-u-lar fission to get through. *Titanium heads!* And I ain't usin' nuke-u-lar fission. Assholes, too, if I was still cursin', which I'm not.

"Ahm fahr'd up about this game. Ahm talkin' full force!

"Hey, *Alton! Alton Lee Gipson!* Now what you doin' on top o' that blocked shots list. You're on top of this here blocked shots list. You leave our boys alone, Alton Lee Gipson."

George Karl grabs a seat and a roster. "OK, Gerald. Who are these guys?"

"Coach, Ahm three days from gettin' my bidness done. Three days from just basketball. And I ain't cussin' no more."

Henry Bibby, the Fast Breakers head coach, walks in. He's sporting a loud purple tie. Karl awards him the first point of the night, for dressing the part. When Bibby leaves, Gerald gets on Karl. "Coach, if you're gonna leave, win me some quarter points. You won't call a time-out to win a quarter point." Karl hates the point system; to him, a game is a game, not five games, and a win should be a win. He finds it hard to conduct strategy to win a quarter when the game is—or should be—what matters. To Karl, the point system is just another example of CBA bullshit. Gerald, though, is more of the CBA, and considers it important. He is often bickering with Karl over CBA-isms. "I asked him about winning me a quarter point, asked him what he thought about that," Oliver says. "He said, 'I don't think about that.'" Karl sits by quietly. *If you're gonna leave...*

The Indiana Pacers called today. Jack Ramsey quit as head coach. They want to talk to Karl.

"Ah tell you what. We kin beat this here team by 35," Gerald shouts. "Ah am fahr'd up."

○   ○   ○

Stroeder starts in place of Ozell, and rejects a Tulsa hook shot first thing. Albany goes up by 4. Kelvin screams, "We bury 'em right now. We bury 'em right now." The crowd stirs. It buzzes. But not from the game. The word spreads. Tyson's here. It's Tyson.

Mike Tyson makes Albany one of his homes. He trains in Catskill, not far down the road, and can be found at watering holes around Albany on occasion. Dressed all in black, he takes a seat courtside with a box of popcorn and his entourage, a male friend and a female friend who, a press table pundit loudly notes, is definitely not Robin Givens. (Tyson is just now in the middle of a noisy separation from his actress-wife; his divorce is still a few months away.) But with Tyson here, a full house, a 4-game winning streak, a 4-point lead, the Armory is the place to be in Albany, New York, on a cool November evening.

Then it falls apart. Stroeder scores 19 and grabs 14 rebounds, but also turns the ball over six times, four at key moments in the fourth quarter when the game is still within reach. Stroeder looks tentative, confused. Tulsa gets big nights from Shouse, who decides he will indeed play and scores 32, and Eric Newsome, an alleged

5' 9" guard who looks closer to 5' 5", who hits for 28. Overall, Albany turns the ball over twenty-eight times and loses 131–125. It's back in second place.

Karl is quiet, understanding. He sees an opportunity to teach, not scream, in this particular loss. He preaches his litany sternly— defense, hustle, position play, rebounding. "The game was lost because we never put a polished act together. We have a lot of work to do, a lot of polish to put on the game. I will not tolerate individualism. I will not tolerate CBA basketball. And tonight we got close to CBA basketball. I will not play that way.

"But the great thing is, we got these same motherfuckers tomorrow night."

NOVEMBER 30

The first big game of the season. The standings read Wichita Falls, 28 points; Albany, 27; Tulsa, 26 1/2. Wichita is off tonight, so the winner here takes over first. And after the guest trumpeter blows a squeaky "Star-Spangled Banner" (then takes his spot behind the Patroons' bench as waterboy), the game begins.

Pearson starts in place of Clint Smith, to balance the starting/ bench scoring. But the tempo carries over from last night; turnovers hurt, and Tulsa takes the opening Q 34–22. The only excitement for Patroons fans comes when a two-year-old boy in a Syracuse baseball hat toddles onto the court—while the ball is in play. Head trainer Jack Moser sweeps the child up and whisks him to the bench, and hands him to Tony, who holds the boy stiff-armed and awkwardly, not quite sure what to do with him.

The second quarter is better—Albany takes it by 8—but the Pats trail 63–59 at the half. The third Q is Albany's by 9; only tiny Eric Newsome keeps it that close. During a three-minute spurt, Newsome knocks down consecutive threes, is fouled on a third attempt and makes all three free throws (in the CBA, a foul on a three-point attempt awards three shots), then sticks another three He also tosses in a jumper and another free throw: 15 points in three minutes. Newsome brings Tulsa back in, takes the crowd out, and has Karl rubbing his forehead.

Karl—and maybe the game—is saved as the clock ticks down

in the third quarter. Five ... four ... three ... Clint Smith grabs a loose ball, stands, looks down three-quarters of the court at the basket, and fires. A sixty-footer. Off the glass and in. The buzzer sounds. The crowd is frenzied. The lead jumps from 2 to 5. The Fast Breakers hang their heads. And Smith, taking a seat at the bench, looks to the first row of seats behind him and winks to his girlfriend.

The shot seems to energize Albany and deflate Tulsa. The fourth quarter is easy. Keith Smith adds a couple of three-pointers to set a team record of four in one game. But Newsome continues to fire away, too. He finishes with five threes—and misses four others, not including the two he is fouled on. Albany wins, though, by 16, and takes six points. Back in first.

For Karl, the victory is draining. Everything he believes in— patience, defensive control, sound fundamentals—keeps being tested by lousy refs, selfish play, and outrageous threes. As he sits on a folding chair, beer in hand, suffering from the flu, just outside the locker room in the basement of the Armory, amid reporters and fans and players and friends, Newsome walks out of his locker room. He is still in uniform, carrying his game shoes in one hand, ready to board the van back to the hotel. He limps gingerly up the stairs, alone, looking like a lost child.

Karl watches him go. He sips at his beer and leans back in his chair. And he shakes his head and says softly, "A different world."

3

DECEMBER 1

Gerald Oliver turns to George Karl and says, "I'll tell you what, I think we had a great practice today."

"I think it sucked," says Karl.

Oliver is taken aback, but recovers quickly, as always. "Well, I guess we were looking at different things, Coach."

There is an edge to today's practice; after back-to-back games the players are tired, and Karl promises that if they "bust their asses," practice will be only half an hour. But an hour and fifteen minutes later, they are still going at it. Oliver asks Karl about his promise.

"I don't count warmups," Karl says. He is only partly kidding.

Much of the work today is on the passing game offense, in which the players spread out and move the ball quickly around the perimeter. Karl feels that the defenses in the CBA are as suspect as some of the offenses; individual efforts outnumber solid team defense, and with opponents constantly looking for steals, quick ball movement should open some lanes and generate easy baskets.

That's the theory, anyway; in practice, the Pats haven't been moving the ball as Karl wants it moved. Today, passes are flying. So are bodies. Johnson and Lee lock up underneath for the second time in a week and exchange angry words. But things cool down quickly, and Karl calls an end to things.

The players shoot their free throws. Oliver wanders over. "Coach, I'd really like to hear why you think practice sucked."

"Bullshit attitudes," Karl says angrily. "I'm pissed at Vincent's attitude. Stroeder gave a bullshit effort...."

"Well, yes, that's true," Oliver says, "and Gris was ready to pack it in. But Clinton played hard. Real hard. Big Ken, he gave us a great effort. A great effort. Keith and Kelvin ..." Oliver goes on, getting more and more animated. Karl can only shrug. It's impossible not to be affected by Gerald's loud optimism. But George is still concerned.

"Maybe it's time for Vincent to get my 'collision' speech." He smiles. "That's the one where I say, 'Vincent, you and me are on a collision course. And you're gonna lose.' "

"Coach, we got problems. I gotta have a short meeting with the players," Gerald interrupts. "It's time I got outta the housing bidness. I'm almost out, but I'm not out yet."

"Gerald, you've already done ten times what you should be doing." Karl laughs.

"Well, this is eleven. And I'm through with it."

Karl jumps up and heads to the bleachers where the players are changing their shoes. "Gentlemen, Gerald's gotta talk to you. He promises to keep it short. He says it's time he got out of the housing business."

Gerald is fussing with his notebook and chatting with Jim Laverty, who reports casually that he has gotten jobs for Doug Lee's and John Stroeder's wives.

"You have?" Gerald hollers. "You have? Why, you just crossed out half of my to-do list." He turns to the empty gym and hollers again. "He just crossed out half of my to-do list! Jim Laverty, you are a wonderful person. *A wonderful person!* I could just kiss you. And that's what I'm gonna do." And that's what he does, rolling his hefty body across the scorer's table, planting two shaky legs on the floor and one wet smooch on Laverty's cheek. Laverty seems unmoved.

"Gentlemen! Let's talk," Gerald says, limping toward the stairs to the locker room. "I'm gettin' outta the housing bidness." Players follow reluctantly. Bets are placed as to how long Gerald's "short" meeting will take. The over-under seems to be thirty-five minutes.

Then follows the now traditional postpractice wind-down, feet-up bullshit session:

LAVERTY: "Good thing you're a good coach, George, or you would've lost by 30 points last night."

TIM WILKIN: "You should've heard Shouse last night, talking to Bibby. 'Get me outta this shitty game. I'm not playing in this shitty game anymore.' "

KARL: "He could say that to me. Once."

WILKIN: "When Phil Jackson was coaching, he'd make the players run a mile on the track in here. Thought it was a quarter-mile track, so he'd tell 'em to run four laps. Except it's eight laps to a mile."

LAVERTY: "No wonder those teams were always out of shape."

KARL: "Clinton played good off the bench last night, didn't he? He liked that, coming off the bench. He told me, 'Good move, Coach. Good move.' "

The meeting continues downstairs, to no one's surprise. Karl hassles Tony for another diet Coke—"I'm still waiting, Tony. Still waiting"—then turns to Gene: "We've got a decision to make." Steve Shurina is eligible to come off the injured list, and Karl wants him for the game tomorrow night. Someone will have to go to make room on the roster. The two most likely candidates are Ozell Jones and Greg Grissom; neither has played much, if at all, the last three games as Johnson and Stroeder continue to be the better big men. So while the decision on Shurina was whether to place him on the injured or waived list, tomorrow's decision will be complicated by determining which player to injure or waive. During today's practice, Ozell was the dominant player, clearly outperforming Grissom, which leads Espeland to respond, "I thought the decision was already made."

But further discussion will have to wait. Gerald emerges from the meeting, briefcase bulging under his arm.

"I'm outta the real estate bidness," he bellows. "Outta the real estate bidness.

"Now I'm in the transportation bidness."

"Forget about it, Gerald," says Laverty with a laugh. "I'm buying lunch."

DECEMBER 2

Ozell Jones's jaw injury has mysteriously worsened, by decree of the coaching staff, and he is put on injured reserve. Shurina is back in the lineup.

It is a fairly easy decision. Grissom needs more playing time to be evaluated, and Jones has a legitimate injury (the CBA will call team physicians to verify any reported injury and will occasionally ask for second opinions to be sure all is on the up-and-up). And with Stroeder and Johnson, the center position is well filled. So Jones sits for five games or ten days.

As with Shurina, Jones gets to choose his options. He asks to be injured, and he asks the coaches to look at trades. Before the game, Karl sits down at the table next to Oliver. Gerald reports that Ron Ekker has called from La Crosse. "He interested?" Karl asks. "I think so," says Oliver.

"I gave Ozell my commitment speech," Karl says. "I told him, 'Ozell, people tell me you're playing two hundred percent better than you've ever played. I think you're playing well. I consider you fun to coach. There's some things about you I really like, and some things I really hate. But you have got to trust me as a coach. You have to commit to me. When I sit you down or get on you, don't start bitchin' and mopin' around. Commit to my knowledge and experience as a coach.'" Ozell understood; whether he responds is the ongoing question.

Both Karl and Oliver had talked to Jones—not necessarily to avoid the chance of his not understanding Oliver's labyrinthine explanations, but possibly so. Gerald has had another busy day, picking up tickets at the airport for the upcoming road trip ("You gotta get them tickets early or you get stuck with a lot of middle seats. You should hear the bitchin' and moanin' then," Oliver says with the voice of experience); organizing housing ("I am getting out of the housing bidness," he says again, "and am getting in the transportation and money-lending bidness. Basketball is what I want to be into, and I'm getting close"); and agreeing to participate in a promotional scheme for tomorrow night's game: The Pats are sponsoring a donation drive for Christmas toys for needy children, and if three hundred toys are donated, Oliver will allow his head to be shaved. "George'll buy three hundred himself, just to see that," Gerald says laughing.

The big news of the day comes from league headquarters, where it is announced that Rockford coach Charley Rosen has been suspended for four games (along with one of his players, Jim Lampley, for one game), stemming from an incident the previous Saturday. Rosen, one of the league's more vocal coaches (he's a writer; words are his life), was ejected in the fourth quarter of a game against Rapid City, and reportedly proceeded to knock over a 24-second clock, refused to leave the playing area, and "verbally abused" the officials. It's the latter charge that raises curiosity. As Gary Holle walks by, a chorus rises from the table: "What did Charley say?"

"It was bad," Holle says smiling. "It was really bad. Jay Ramsdell [the CBA's twenty-four-year-old commissioner] told me that, even by CBA standards, it was bad. He called the refs faggots, said they were fucking each other up the ass. He was screaming it at them, in front of the fans and everybody. It was bad."

"Hey Gary, if I get suspended I still get paid, don't I?" Karl asks. Doug Dickinson, the Patroons' official statistician, stops by with the updated stats, including a new column: combined field goal percentage, adding both 2- and 3-point shots for a total percentage. Karl has been needling Dickinson about this every day—"If you don't add 'em together it's a worthless stat"—and Dickinson happily complies.

He also remembers a story. The discussion has turned to CBA travel. Oliver has complained about complaining among the players concerning this subject, and says that today's CBA is a picnic compared to the old days. He tells of stopping the van he was driving one day to confront a player who was questioning Gerald's skills as a driver—and Gerald, to give the players credit, is not a confidence-inspiring driver—and taking him out to fight. Which sets Dickinson off.

"One time when Phil Jackson was coach he was driving the van to Toronto. Here's one white guy driving nine black guys in a van. The border guard asked Phil what his business in Canada was; he says, 'Bringing in slaves.' Frankie J. Sanders was laughing so hard he fell off his seat."

○ ○ ○

Tonight's opponent is Pensacola. The Tornados boast a strong starting unit, including some familiar CBA/NBA names like Mark Wade,
Jerome Henderson, and Brooke Steppe ("a good solid player," Karl
says in the pregame meeting, "but crazy. He's a legend in several
NBA cities. If his head is in the game, he'll be a factor"), but no
bench. One of their reserves is best known for having flunked out
of UNLV.

Ozell, in silk suit and turtleneck, but no socks, takes Shurina's
spot at the end of the bench, next to Gerald. The other big change:
water bottles, with players' names taped to them, replace the small
paper cups. Tony is very proud of them. By the end of the game,
the players will demand a return to the old system.

On the court, things break down a bit. CBA-style play rules;
Steppe is a mass of nervous energy, talking to himself, to teammates,
to Karl, to fans; pointing and laughing, tugging at his shirt, grimacing
and shaking his blond hair. He is also red hot, scoring 22 of his 39
points in the first half. Karl continually cries to his players to wake
up; they respond by complaining about playing time. At the half,
down by 2 points, Karl blows up.

"This is city-league shit. I make the decisions on who plays and
who doesn't. I don't need any attitudes. I'm not gonna name names,
Kelvin—all right, I'll name names, Kelvin and Kenny. I don't want
to hear a thing. None. If you guys were playing great, maybe. No
one played fuckin' great that half." No one is spared, either. Johnson's attitude. Upshaw's attitude. Askew's concentration, Stroeder's
concentration ... it's all-encompassing. And it is hard. But Karl
always manages to turn ugly to pretty. He typically ends all locker
room talks, even the angry ones, on a positive note. Once the anger
is out, strategy is discussed. When angry, Karl spits out his com-
mands in short phrases, a staccato burst of instruction. "Don't over-
react to Steppe knocking that long-range shit down. Don't fall asleep.
Stop the penetration. Get your minds back in the game. Wake up.
Get aggressive. Be smart. Move the ball. Stay together."

Within 2 minutes the Pats have the lead, and by the end of the
quarter they are up by 7. And when a nine-year-old boy hits a three

pointer to take $3,500 in the Bombs for Bucks contest between quarters, the Armory crowd explodes. The boy accepts a high-five from Kelvin and a hug from his mom. All seems right with the game.

But Pensacola fights back, regaining the lead with 6 minutes to go. Which is an opportune time for the Patroons to play their best defense of the season; they go on a 13–3 run over the next 4 minutes. Askew, who is responding to Karl's methods and slowly becoming a star in the CBA, is a force at both ends of the court.

Albany wins 104–99, but loses the last quarter point. And for the first time, Karl tries to win a quarter. In fact, he goes overboard, screaming instructions, drawing plays, calling time-outs. He even pulls off his tie. He hates coaching like this, but, when in the CBA.... Despite his efforts, they lose the Q by 2.

Afterwards, he apologizes: "I'm sorry I went a little crazy trying to win the quarter point." He compliments the effort over the last several minutes but adds, "We still need a hell of a lot of polish."

And then, the usual postgame chaos. Tony walks in to announce there is no hot water for showers. Gerald passes out meal tickets to Thirsty's. Steppe, still in uniform, wanders in, grabs two beers from the tray on the table, and talks with a reporter. Pearson washes off out of the water jug.

Just another night. "My boy, Danny Pearson. Welcome to the CBA," Clinton Smith says with a toothy smile and heads upstairs, where players, wives, girlfriends, green coats, and the last of the hangers-on look over the final box scores.

DECEMBER 3

Some fine stories are told today. Doug Dickinson has been promising his story from last season for two days. It turns out to be a you-had-to-be-there story, about a sixteen-hour trip from Wyoming to Albany, via Newark, New Jersey. The punch line is using Gary Holle's American Express card—Holle isn't on the trip, but his card is—to treat the travelers to an $800 dinner at a restaurant in New Jersey known to Micheal Ray Richardson. Cute, but not as funny as the memory it triggers in Tim Wilkin.

"We're in Wyoming a few days before this," Wilkin says. "We're driving back to the hotel from practice and Micheal Ray says [here Wilkin mimicks Richardson's stutter], 'I w-w-wanna ride w-w-with the press,' meaning me. So I give him a ride back to the hotel.

"On the way, we're driving along, and right next to the highway is a herd of antelopes. I mean right there. Richardson freaks. 'S-s-stop the car! S-s-stop the car!' So I stop the car, and he jumps out and takes off after these antelopes, screaming and waving his arms. A 6'5" black guy in gray sweats tearing after antelopes in the middle of nowhere, Wyoming. He chases them down this hill, and he's gone.

"After a while he comes back, and gets in the car. I ask him, 'What did you do that for?' He looks at me and says, 'I just wanted to f-f-f-fuck up some antelopes.'"

When everyone stops laughing, Oliver says, "We still got Richardson's rights, Coach."

"Trade 'em," says Karl.

○ ○ ○

The locker room is upbeat; Karl outlines the adjustments, reiterates the importance of stopping the penetration, focuses the defense's attention on Steppe.

"Gentlemen, it's been a good homestand," he finishes. "If we go 7–2, that's a helluva start, a lot of things to be proud of. If we go 6–3, it's not that great. Let's go get it done."

The players clap their hands together and head out the door. Except Kelvin. "Hold on, guys. I gotta go wee-wee."

As usual the coaches sit in the locker room for a few minutes more. Karl changes out of his sweater and into his coat and tie. Gerald is fired up. "I'm more excited about this game than any so far. It's a great challenge. A great challenge. You got 'em ready, Coach. It's all there on the blackboard. If it's in their hearts and in their heads, we're gonna kick some ass tonight."

Karl smiles. "So, Gerald. You won't be here at the half?"

"I saw they brought the hair cutter in. Some girl. Saw the clippers, too," says Gene.

"Gerald," Karl says, "do you know how ugly you might be without hair?"

The Patroons open up with their best quarter of the season,

taking a 33–18 lead. The second Q is more of the same, until halfway through. The referee gets bumped on an inbounding play and cuts his chin. It takes 10 minutes to track down a Band-aid. There is none in the cardboard medical kit, but one is finally located in the orange backpack/first-aid kit downstairs.

More significantly, a fight breaks out between Pearson and the Tornados' Eric Laird. Doug Lee has been furious with Laird since last night; Laird elbows, pushes, and grabs all over the court, and is never called. When he grabs Pearson's jersey, Danny swats his hand away. Laird answers with a right to the cheek, sending Pearson down. Pearson, up quickly, counters with three quick, powerful shots of his own. Both are ejected.

Karl tries to keep the team calm in the huddle, reminding them that it's a common trick to try to start fights when you're losing. "It gets guys thrown out, gets the refs confused. Keep your cool. Let them play the crazy basketball." The team finishes the Q strong, and leads 62–41 at the half.

Gerald storms into the locker room, plants his feet wide and his hands on the table. His accent is thick as smoke in his anger. "Gentlemen, I've played this team a lot of times for a lot of years. They're not gonna get us to play their kind of game. We're gonna play our kinda game. We're gonna play clean basketball. We're gonna play solid basketball. And we're gonna kick their fuckin' asses!"

"Coach. They want you upstairs," says Tony.

Gerald straightens. He pats his hair down on the sides. He smiles. "I'm ready."

In seconds, he is seated at center court. A leather-skirted young woman named Linda takes out her electric shears. And Gerald's head is shaved. One fan, about twelve, offers that "this is better than the fight."

Karl is finishing his speech when Gerald walks back in. "Gentlemen, it's gonna take a solid twenty-four minutes of . . ." and then he looks up, sees Gerald's round slick head, and cracks up. Gerald grins sheepishly.

The third Q degenerates into lousy calls and CBA-style ball: Karl's nightmare. "Remember, all this bullshit can steal a basketball game," he pleads. But the Q goes to Pensacola. And even though

Albany dominates the fourth Q, Karl is eating himself up. "I'm tired of this bullshit basketball," he mutters to no one. Even when it's not all bullshit. Ken Johnson, who has been everything Karl hoped, rebounding with the best in the league, gets the ball in the paint, guarded only by the little-used David Willard, right in front of the Albany bench. "Take him, Ken," Kelvin and Keith yell in unison. "Take him, Big Daddy." Johnson clearly hears them and goes to work. He fakes left, spins right, leaves Willard lunging at air and lays one in. Upshaw and Smith leap off the bench—"Yeah! Big Daddy!" For the first time this season, a huge lead is developing, and lightness appears on the bench. Smith towels up some water that Karl spills like a good waterboy and laughs. Karl tries to teach some subtlety to certain plays. "Learn how to finesse it, to fake it. Make them think it's going here, then take it there." The Tornados, exhausted, disappear in the Q 38–15. Albany takes the game by 41.

And Gerald takes a new nickname. Elmer Fudd. A Patroons baseball cap covers the damage. "It don't look too bad, does it?"

DECEMBER 4–5

Practice is optional, with three exceptions: Shurina and the two Smiths are invited for individual work. Karl wants to do more of this as the season progresses, to concentrate on certain parts of each player's game. Lee and Grissom also show for a little three-on-three.

That night, a pre-road trip feast at Thirsty's. Steaks, salads, fruit—"real fruit," Oliver notes—with Karl manning the grill.

○   ○   ○

Overnight, Albany gets its first real snow; one to two inches dust the streets, and the air snaps with the first taste of winter.

The Armory is colder than ever. All the players are practicing in full sweats. During breaks Upshaw pulls on a wool ski cap. In quiet moments, breath forms steam around an individual's ears.

Tony is arranging the road uniforms. Shorts and jersey, covered by jacket and pants, on a hanger. Uniform number, written on a piece of paper, attached to hanger hook. Each package is laid on a seat in the first row. Assistant trainer Bob Shaffer, still in his fireman's jacket (his full-time job), is not impressed.

"Why don't you put the fuckin' jersey on the outside with the fuckin' number showin'? If they can't read their own fuckin' number they shouldn't be goin' on the fuckin' trip. That paper shit is stupid." Tony considers it. Then he forgets it as Bob walks out.

Which leaves Karl as acting trainer; when Shurina twists an ankle, Karl has to pull his diet Cokes out of the cooler and set up an ice bath for Shurina's foot. And with Shurina out, and Grissom still limping from a knee injury suffered in warmups the night before, Karl switches from trainer to player, patrolling the wing looking for a J in the scrimmage.

After the game, Karl calls a huddle. Despite a 7–1 homestand, a 7–2 record, and an eight-point lead in the Eastern Division standings, Karl is not happy. He uses the Utah Jazz as an example of a good NBA team that has always struggled away from home. He tells them the attitude is bad, the intensity level is too low, there is too much talking back, there is too much bitching and moaning. He warns them to be strong in the face of the CBA Blues. He reminds them that, by his standards, "We're not that good yet."

He calls Kelvin and Keith over; Karl likes his point guards to be leaders, on and off the court, and he tells them so. He is especially rough on Kelvin, whose city-tough, distanced cool is bringing him more and more into conflict with the coach. Both Kelvin and Karl are strong-willed; both look for an edge. Neither sees the other completely clearly.

After practice, an emotional moment. Coach Espeland is returning to Montana. The players liked Gene; his kind-hearted, quiet strength served as a balance between Karl and Gerald. Good-byes and thanks all around.

Back home—wherever home may be—to pack. Those now staying at the Quality Inn—Ken Johnson, Ozell, and Kelvin—are told by hotel management that they will be locked out of their rooms for unpaid incidentals if not paid immediately. Last year the hotel was stuck with an unpaid phone bill of several thousand dollars from one player. Arguments ensue. Another thing to worry about.

In three hours, they begin the longest road trip of the season.

DECEMBER 6

Karl gets a jab in on the players in the Albany paper. "I think a lot of our guys are a little too cocky going out on this trip," he is quoted by Wilkin as saying. "When you get a lot of wins at home, sometimes it changes your work ethic. Too many players get the idea that if you win, you don't have to work as hard in practice. Those players are wrong."

Those players have gotten the message personally. When the story comes out, the Patroons are already settled in at Rapid City, South Dakota. The team arrived last night at 9 P.M. via Chicago and Sioux Falls. NBA players travel first class. In the CBA, it's coach. On the flight, Clinton Smith, Lee, Askew, and Johnson discuss which NBA team they'd like to play for, and why.

The coaches assign roommates: Johnson and Kelvin, Shurina and Keith Smith, Lee and Clinton Smith, Stroeder and Grissom, Pearson and Askew. Johnson is supposed to keep Kelvin in check (Upshaw played here last season). Shurina, who is still new here and, for now, tends to go to sleep early, complements Keith, a veteran performer who tends not to sleep at all.

○ ○ ○

Life on the road: After morning shootaround, radio announcer Dan Levy accompanies Doug Lee and Greg Grissom to Mt. Rushmore. They are underwhelmed. The tape narration by Tom Brokaw comes under considerable criticism. Vince and Ken go shopping; 6'6" and 6'9" black men don't often shop in Rapid City, and curious shoppers take note. Especially when Vince comes strolling down the aisle with an armful of Fruit of the Loom underwear. "How much for these drawers?" he asks the cashier.

Rapid City offers some interesting angles tonight. Their point guard, Clinton Wheeler, who had been averaging 26 points and nearly 9 assists per game, became the first CBA player called up to the NBA two days earlier. Now with the Miami Heat, Wheeler is being replaced by Billy Donovan, who was acquired from Cedar Rapids. Donovan is the former Providence star who played briefly for the Knicks. And the Thrillers' general manager is Eric Musselman, the son of Bill. "Musselboy," as he's been nicknamed by one CBA coach, has not so subtly placed a Minnesota Timberwolves banner in the arena. Karl uses this for inspiration; Musselman, son and father, are getting on his nerves. He does not want to lose.

The teams split the first two quarters, with Albany out front 47–44 at the half. Most of the excitement comes from Donovan, who feeds his big men like he fed Patrick Ewing for jams at Madison Square Garden, and from the halftime show; a large fellow in a tuxedo and red tie is giving money away during a blindfolded shooting contest. Eric Musselman is telling Levy during a live interview that "we're going to be making trades tomorrow. There's no excuse for playing the way we've been playing."

"Well," says Levy, taken aback, "you didn't beat around the bush, Eric. Thank you for your candor."

Albany goes cold the rest of the way—shooting only 39 percent from the field for the game—and drops the last two quarters, and the game. Even so, Albany nearly wins it, pulling within 3 with 37 seconds left. The final is 101–94; Albany takes just one of seven standings points, but remains in first place. The team—and Karl— are looking for the leader, the man to go to. Upshaw, who played here last year, draws Karl's anger, acting aloof, not paying attention. Karl is all over him in the locker room.

"I don't think anyone is good enough to mope around. If I don't think you're playing well, or I want to play someone else, I don't need your mopin'. If I put you in the game and run a play and you don't know what the fuck's goin' on, who's fault is that? Mine?" Kelvin walks out of the locker room without showering, carrying his clothes.

"It's gonna be an expensive walk home," Karl tells him.

Upshaw goes back and showers.

Later, Karl and Oliver discuss player moves. Upshaw's name does come up.

DECEMBER 7–8

Six hours from Rapid City to Minneapolis/St. Paul to Dallas/Fort Worth. Karl and Levy stay in Dallas to hit golf balls with a friend of Karl's for the afternoon.

The rest of the team faces a two-hour bus trip to Wichita Falls.

A bottle had broken in Johnson's bag during the flight, and his things are soaked. He gets kidded for this as a matter of course, mostly from Clinton. But Clinton keeps at it, and Johnson gets annoyed.

On the way to the hotel, Johnson and Smith continue to argue. In the hotel lobby Johnson shoves Smith. Gerald rushes in to break it up. With George not here, Gerald has to maintain control. He's the boss now, more than the distributor of plane tickets and boarding passes and hotel room keys and per diem money. He is the coach. Concerned, he calls a team meeting.

It goes on for an hour. "Everybody on this team's got garbage in their heads. You all gotta start thinkin' right. Get all that garbage out of your heads. Listen to George. He'll get you to the NBA. He's a great coach. Do what he says." Gerald continues; the players are a little confused as to what this has to do with anything. "You gotta get that garbage out of your heads. If you're here to make money, you're here for the wrong reason. You're here to improve your basketball game. You all are like my team in Charleston. All they was interested in was havin' orgies. Nothin' but screwin' around an' havin' orgies . . ."

"Coach Oliver," Vince Askew asks, "what's an orgy?"

"Well, Vince, it's when one guy an' two girls, or one girl an' two guys, or a whole bunch of people are havin' sex together," Gerald explains.

"Oh. OK. I know what that is."

○　○　○

The Texans, third in the Eastern Division (for some reason, Wichita Falls, Topeka, and Tulsa are considered Eastern, while the teams in Illinois, Minnesota, and Wisconsin are in the Western), have NBA talent. Bobby Lee Hurt, the 6'10" forward, leads the league in rebounding with nearly 14 a game, and has recently been joined by Ken "The Animal" Bannister, another former Knick. Ennis Whatley, a former first-round draft pick out of Alabama, has NBA experience as well.

Even so, it looks as though Albany will win its first road game—the club takes both the first and second quarters, and leads 63–52 at the half—as Pearson hits for 15 points in the half and the team as a whole shoots over 67 percent. And the omens are strong;

Levy spots a fan in a Patroons jersey, which qualifies him to serve as color analyst on the broadcast. His name is Rob, he's from Albany, he's a soldier stationed in Oklahoma, and he wonders whatever happened to the Patroons' cheerleaders, the Patties.

But neither Rob nor the hot shooting can save this game. Bannister, in only his third game with the Texans, comes in and turns the game around. He scores 13 points over the half—9 in the third quarter—but it still takes a terrible call at the end to beat Albany. With 8 seconds left, Stroeder has a free throw to take the lead. He misses it, Whatley rebounds, Wichita Falls comes back up court. Derrick Taylor gets the pass, goes to the hoop—and plows over Keith Smith, who clearly has position. Smith takes the blow in the chest, Taylor gets the shot off, and the refs call Smith for the foul. Taylor makes his two tosses, Upshaw misses a jumper at the buzzer, and the Pats lose, 99–97.

Karl is worried; the offense has dissolved, and he hasn't found the one man he can go to yet. He's not mad. He doesn't lose his cool. The mood is edgy—a feeling that the team is trying too hard, aiming rather than shooting. Karl wants to keep the team loose. He also continues to consider changes.

Earlier this day, Dave Popson was released by the Clippers. He has 48 hours to clear waivers before the Patroons can make a move. Popson decides to spend the holidays at home, and Karl is relieved. He doesn't want to make any moves until the club returns home.

Back to the hotel, with a stop at McDonald's "Don't no brothers work here?" Clint asks the counter girl. Gerald leaves his coat inside, walks all the way to the bus in subfreezing weather, and asks if anyone has seen it. Some of the players wonder if Gerald has lost his mind.

DECEMBER 9–11

Friday morning, Braniff becomes the third airline of choice—following United and Northwest—to take the Patroons on. The bus back to DFW is followed by a flight to Kansas City; from there Crescent Charter Tours is supposed to motor the club to Topeka. But the bus doesn't show. Gerald, frantic, tries to track it down. Eventually, one shows, but the club gets in too late to practice. As the bus enters the state it passes a sign: WELCOME TO KANSAS, HOME OF THE 1988 NCAA BASKETBALL CHAMPIONS. Vince Askew chuckles. "Not anymore," he says.

These next two games against the Sizzlers are important. Topeka is not very strong—they are 2–10, in fact—and the plan is "to spend more time on ourselves than Topeka," Oliver says. "We're having a hard time finding the right chemistry for this team, and we've got two games to come up with one."

Coaching moves are also being made. In Utah, Frank Layden announces his retirement as a coach—he blames the stress of the job, noting one fan who spit on him after a game—and is replaced by his assistant, Jerry Sloan. George Karl isn't involved with that story, but his name is mentioned in the New York *Post* as an interviewee for the Indiana job. He again states his intention to stay in Albany through the season, and in fact Indiana hasn't been back in contact and he won't fly in for an interview just yet. But the question will obviously dog him just as long.

The Topeka Sizzlers provide just the right antidote for the ailing Patroons: a lousy team. Karl decides to play the entire first quarter of the first game in his passing game offense; no set plays, just pass the ball, find an opening, take the good shot. It's a more relaxed offensive strategy, and it works; the offense finds a rhythm in this quarter that it will hold for some time. They win the quarter and go on to take both games easily, winning 110–94 Saturday and 107–93 Sunday. In each game Albany takes six of seven standings points (only a missed three-point shot by Steve Shurina on the final play of Sunday's game keeps the Pats from their first seven-point sweep) to open up a 53–44 lead in the standings over second-place Tulsa. Askew, happy to be leaving Kansas—he takes a lot of abuse from the fans; "I guess I'm the villain," he says—scores 30 in the second game to lead the way.

Johnson, feeling he isn't getting enough minutes, confronts Karl. He asks to be traded.

DECEMBER 12–13

From Topeka to Rochester, Minnesota, on Monday. Shoot-around from 10:30 to 12:30 Tuesday. John Stroeder skips practice;

he's got the flu. Scott Roth is cut by the Utah Jazz today; Karl and Oliver had heard a few days earlier, through the NBA grapevine, that this would likely happen. Roth was a key part of last season's championship team, and Albany still has his rights. But Roth has said he'll play only for Eric Musselman at Rapid City. Negotiations continue.

DECEMBER 14

As of this morning the Patroons are the best team in the league. They are tied with Rockford at 9–4 for the best record, but Albany has won two more quarters, giving them 59 standings points to Rockford's 57. The Pats' lead in the Eastern Division is a solid 15 points over second place Tulsa (6–8, 44 points) and 17½ over third place Wichita Falls (7–3, 41½ points). Tonight's opponent, the Rochester Flyers, is last in the Western Division at 5–9, 39½ points. The club's five victories have been by a combined total of 15 points, and they've lost three in a row coming into tonight, and their tallest starter is only 6'9". The Pats look good to keep the road success going.

The Mayo Civic Center seats 5,200, but it's only about half full. The public address announces, "Let's play basketball!" The Patroons do most of the playing tonight. Taking advantage of the Flyers' small lineup, they get the ball inside early. Askew scores 13 points from the forward position in the first quarter; Albany takes it 31–24. In the second quarter it's Doug Lee's turn; he scores 15 points, despite the team organist, who forgets to stop playing when the action starts, and the Flight Crew, the Flyers' game cheerleading section. Leading by 12 at the half, Albany takes the first two Q points.

Halftime is another adventure for Levy. His color commentator this game has been a former meteorologist from Albany, now living in Minnesota. He is replaced for an interview with Roger Johnson, who is billed as the only team masseur—"massage therapist, as modern masseurs like to say"—in the CBA.

"So, what kind of success have you had this year, with the massage?" Levy asks.

"Sorry. I can't hear you over this band that's playing," Johnson hollers.

The second half is closer. After opening a 20-point lead, Albany falls off and loses the third quarter. And when the Flyers run off 7 straight to trail by only 4, the Patroons look tired. But they regroup, and tie the quarter with 47 seconds left. The game is in hand, but the quarter is up for grabs, and the fans remain, proving the quarter point system serves its purpose. Upshaw—who has responded to Karl's earlier bashing and is playing extremely well, becoming the man Karl looks to use down the stretch—hits a jumper with 8 seconds left to give Albany the lead by 2. But Gerald Paddio hits at the buzzer to tie it. Albany takes the game 118–107, and 5½ standings points. That makes 17½ out of 21 points over the past three games, and Albany is in first by 18.

For the first time, the team is playing solid, consistent ball. Picks are being set, the fast break is working. A cohesiveness on the court and in the locker room. Things are coming together.

DECEMBER 15

On to La Crosse, Wisconsin, with eager anticipation: La Crosse is known with little charm but genuine admiration as the Pussy Capital of the CBA. Those who have never been here are pleased when they find the hotel lobby filled with young female basketball fans. Catching a pregame rest proves difficult when the phone keeps ringing: "Hi! How ya doin'? Want some company?"

Game time is 7:30. The Catbirds, who lost to the Patroons by 18 in the Pats' third game of the season, have since added David Henderson, a late cut of the 76ers. He has been averaging over 16 a game in three games with La Crosse; even hotter is Perry Moss, on a 20 points per game streak over eight games, and center John "Moose" Campbell, rebounding nearly 11 a game, fifth in the CBA. This figures to be a tough contest.

And it is. The game is close all the way; no team ever leads by more than six. The first Q is a wash (24–24); Karl keeps it even when he gives the referees a lesson in the rules. When six Patroons somehow end up on the court during play, Albany is called for a technical. Karl leaps off the bench. "That's not a technical," he screams. "It's a delay of game. It's only a warning." The refs huddle, then agree. Karl smooths his hair and takes his seat.

The teams split the next two quarters. After three, Albany leads by 2, 80–78. That lead is only 1 with a minute left, when Upshaw scores 6 of his game-high 23 points. First, a 13-footer from in front, then four of six free throws down the stretch as the clock runs down, and the Pats win again on the road, 98–94. Add 5½ points to the standings. Much hugging in the locker room.

And much more hugging afterward. This is the only stop in La Crosse this season, so not even the brutal Wisconsin cold and a four-hour bus trip to Quad City in the morning will keep these carriers from their appointed rounds. There are some fine individual efforts, but more than that it is a tremendous team performance; even those who usually get little playing time put up some impressive numbers.

DECEMBER 16

Where is Quad City? Mostly, Quad City is the Bettendorf Holiday Inn in Moline. It isn't Boston, but for one Quad Citian, Boston is a new home. The Thunder's Kevin Gamble, the CBA's leading scorer at nearly 30 points a game, was called up two days earlier to take Larry Bird's spot on the Celtics roster. A break for the Patroons, and a chance to keep the road streak going.

DECEMBER 17

The Wharton Fieldhouse, built in 1928, has an Old World feel similar to the Armory; its court is short—only 84 feet—and the fans sit right up against the court. But it's bigger, seating 6,100, and the crowd is large tonight.

The Thunder have Coach Mauro Panaggio, who this week became the all-time winningest coach in CBA history—the Crash Davis of basketball coaches. Karl, who got his hundredth CBA win this week, hopes not to challenge the record.

A close and testy game all the way; a couple of near fights break out. Lee's two threes help take the first quarter by 4, and two Stroeder free throws with 1 second left give the Pats the second Q by 1. After building an 11 point lead, Albany fails to hold, Quad City ties. The third quarter ends 96–95, Albany losing it by 4.

They also lose Keith Smith. With 25 seconds left, he falls to the court in severe pain, and is carried off. His right knee. It appears serious. As the fourth quarter begins, the PA announcer calls for a doctor to go to the Albany dressing room. Smith, Albany's best all-around player to date, will not be easily replaced.

The last quarter stays close until Doug Lee hits two more three-pointers—his fourth and fifth of the game, a new team record—and Albany pulls away to win 126–121 (30–26 in the quarter) and take six more standings points. As the game ends the bench players leap onto the court. A 5–2 road trip, five straight wins. And tomorrow, home.

DECEMBER 18

United Airlines from Moline to O'Hare to Albany. The longest road trip of the season is completed.

○ ○ ○

In the Albany paper, Wilkin reports the CBA story of the day. Seems Topeka Sizzlers coach Art Ross traded for a player named Kannard Johnson from Cedar Rapids just before the season began. Cedar Rapids somehow forgot to tell Ross, a rookie coach, that Johnson was going to play in Europe.

"I'm not going to trust anyone. I'm not going to listen to anything anyone tells me anymore," Ross says.

DECEMBER 19

Last night, Karl reports, he took the kids to see the *Nutcracker Suite* after returning home. Gerald went to the office, trying to trade Scott Roth. Today, Karl did a little Christmas shopping. The players relaxed. Oliver worked on trading Roth. A light practice interrupts the day. It's optional; Shurina is in New York, Upshaw is still in Chicago, both with family, and Stroeder sits it out. Ozell, who did not go on the trip and has been working out all week, looks in good shape and runs well. Gerald runs the practice, Karl plays with his children and talks with reporters. "The last I heard, Keith Smith was to have an exploratory scope on his knee tomorrow morning," he says. "If it's cartilage, could be four to five weeks. If it's ligaments, could be the season."

The injury puts added spin on the Roth deal. So does the call from the Washington Bullets, inquiring about players in general and Stroeder and Askew in particular. Karl calls Stroeder the best big man in the league and recommends him highly. It looks like he may get called up soon.

Oliver and Karl have been working on dealing Roth since he was cut. They want to move him to Rapid City, but they insist on getting equal value. Eric Musselman refuses to give up Todd Mitchell, the player Karl wants, and offers cash—an ever-increasing amount—instead. Oliver calls several other clubs trying to swing a three-way deal involving a number of alternatives. At practice he discusses them with Karl, but none seems right. It looks like they will stay put, place Keith Smith on the injured list and activate Ozell, and stay with these ten—unless Stroeder gets the call. Then, they'll reevaluate.

Then the deal is further complicated—Musselman calls GM Gary Holle to tell him how much money Karl and Oliver have refused for the rights to a player who won't play for them. This infuriates Karl, and he sternly tells Gerald to let Musselman know that. "If he did that in the NBA no one would ever deal with him again," Karl snaps. "That's horseshit. I can't believe this league still works this way. Going over my personnel director's head . . . that's just horseshit."

"I know, Coach," Gerald says. "I have already talked to him about it."

That's the only dark moment in a light afternoon (not counting a screaming match between Gerald and Tony; Wilkin is laughing at the height of the fight: "I think Tony's getting canned"). Afterwards, several players head to the health club to work out. Karl takes the kids for more shopping. Gerald heads back to the office.

He calls all the parties involved—La Crosse, Cedar Rapids, Topeka, Rapid City—to make one last play. He tells them the Patroons are probably going to sit tight. He takes a call from Roth's agent to explain to him why they won't just give Roth's rights away without getting equal value. "I understand your point of view; you're saying, 'Isn't something better than nothing.' Well, from our point of view we're saying, 'This is Scott Roth. *Scott Roth!* He's more than just a player.' We wanna help Scott, we really do. But you gotta understand our situation."

"I wish Scott had never been cut," Gerald says. He means that in several ways; he truly wishes everyone was in the NBA all the time, but mainly, it's been a difficult process dealing with a complex, public situation. But now, all the major players have been contacted. All the cards are out. It's 7:30. Gerald grabs dinner from McDonald's, queues up a film of Charleston, and waits for the trade to play out.

He also thinks about things. Why does the league work this way? Why is everyone so selfish? Can't they see he's trying to help everyone, reach a common ground? Can't they get beyond self-interest and grasp the bigger picture? What is the purpose of this league, anyway? What are we trying to do here? Is the game enough? Is it enough for me? Gerald looks much older than his fifty-three years.

He also has to think about Topeka. He just found out Art Ross resigned—or was fired—as coach this afternoon.

Is the game enough? What are we trying to do?

DECEMBER 20

Nothing happens; the trade is in limbo. And further complications set in. Rick Carlisle is cut by the Knicks; Albany still has his rights. Keith Smith's surgery is postponed until tomorrow; he reports the knee is feeling better and may not be as damaged as initially thought. A trade that the coaches have been working on since training camp involving NBA veteran Wes Matthews is perhaps finally coming together; Matthews' rights are owned by Wichita Falls, and Albany has been trying to get those rights, with little success (or cooperation). Further, Derrick Rowland is back in town.

Rowland is the Patroons' all-time scoring leader, and has played more games in a Patroons uniform than anyone. He was a member of both the '83–84 and '87–88 championship teams; in all he has played in Albany for most of the past six years. He makes his home here. He's a local favorite. And after a stint in the Philippines, he is ready to play for the Patroons. He shows at practice, surveys the scene and says, "I don't recognize this. No Frankie J. No Micheal

Ray. Don't know any of these guys." He sounds like an alumnus returning to high school and realizing how quickly things change. Then he asks Laverty if the championship rings have come in yet. Karl knows him—Rowland was a final cut from Karl's Cleveland camp in 1985. But he's not sure he wants Rowland now. At 12–4, solidly in first, Karl doesn't want to break up a winning combination. If it ain't broke . . . He and Derrick talk after practice.

Gerald is feeling more chipper, though he's mad at something else. "We lost our first basketball today, Coach," he reports. He looks under all the bleachers and chairs. Basketballs, like everything else, are not easily replaced in Albany. They will have to get by with nine from now on.

Tonight's game with Charleston worries Karl. After walking through some plays, he warns everyone that the first home game after a road trip is difficult. Historically, teams come out flat; he doesn't know why. He's calm but determined outside. Inside, the game really concerns him.

He proves to be right. Although Charleston gives a lot in height, they are clearly more aggressive. The Pats are lazy on the boards, late after loose balls, and generally lackadaisical. Even so, they take the first Q by 4 and the second by 2. But late in the second Upshaw mishandles the ball on a breakaway, then throws it into the stands on a wild pass. Karl grabs his head and stares at Kelvin. And Karl is inspired to give his best halftime speech yet.

He takes a chair and, with great emotion, sits on it. He sits quietly for a moment, then starts slowly, calmly. "You are such a better basketball team than them. But you're playing in second or third gear. You might be able to beat 'em in second gear; I'm not saying you can't. But you don't get any better playing the way you played that half.

"Kelvin, that pass at the end was like an exclamation point on how we played that half. Casual. You bounce it off your knee and throw a fuckin' behind-the-back pass out of bounds. Instead of us having a 10 point lead, it's a 6 point lead. And you're not the only one. Our execution, our passes are half a second slow. Deliver the ball when the guy is open, Danny and Clinton. Not two seconds later. Vince, focus on rebounding.

"The game will come your way if you earn it."

He goes over Charleston's plays again. Then continues, his voice a little more forceful. "The refs are letting them get away with some shit, and you can't blame them. They're human beings and they see what's happening. They say, 'Shit, this team's trying.' And we're just coasting. I wish there was more I could say." And of course there is. His voice rises to fill the small room; as he gets more excited, he speaks more quickly, in short bursts of words, spitting out phrases more than sentences, trying to imprint a mood. "Stop penetration. Make smart plays. They've hurt us rebounding the ball, they're playing more aggressive. What do you have to do? Make sharper cuts. Set stronger picks. Execute with better timing. Pop to the ball rather than being lazy about it.

"It's a lazy basketball game. It's a cold gym. It's a dangerous basketball team. And it would be as embarrassing as fuckin' hell to walk out of this locker room in an hour with a defeat.

"You have the opportunity to have a fun basketball game, by just working a little bit. Have a little pride, make smart decisions, and they'll give you a game that you can score a lot of points. Run and gun and enjoy. If you rebound, play good defense, and make fundamentally sound decisions, *and everybody rebounds*, you'll get layup after layup."

Anger mixes with inspiration. "You gotta play with guts. It's an easy basketball game. You can make it easy. You can make it hard. It can be an easy win. It can be a hard loss."

The big finish. *"One time. One time! Stop the penetration! Make 'em play in a crowd! Be aggressive on the ball! Stop the penetration! Full effort!"* And then, softly, "Kick ass."

Gerald has been nodding his head silently the whole time. As the players walk out, he looks at Karl. "You couldn't say it any better."

Lee, who started in place of Keith Smith, nails two threes. Kelvin, on the bench: *"Yeah!* Let's get these motherfuckers outta here." The lead is 9 after three quarters. Lee hits a J and another three-pointer. Charleston tenses, gives up steals, and forces bad shots. Askew and Stroeder and Johnson—even Steve Shurina—grab rebounds. Ozell, who plays little, throws in an ugly hook shot off the glass, and the bench cracks up. Charleston is held to 43 points in the half. Albany wins by 24. Seven standings points.

After the game, Gerald is upstairs at the scorer's table, passing out tickets to Thirsty's, handing out rent checks, squaring accounts with various players, still solidly in the banking business. Karl walks over, beer in hand, out of his suit and in his sweater.

"I was taking this one like a playoff game." Karl smiles, more relieved than pleased after it's over.

"Great speech, Coach," Oliver says. "Best yet."

"It was good, wasn't it? How 'bout me sitting in the chair? Nice touch?"

DECEMBER 21

After last night's game, Karl sets the law: no more tardiness. Practices have been starting late, and Ken Johnson had missed one entirely this week. Karl demands it not happen again, "or it comes out of your pocket."

Tony is thirty minutes late today in delivering the players to practice.

○ ○ ○

Stroeder and Askew are excused from practice; they are sent to the Governor's Office for an anti-drug promotion with Mario Cuomo. Askew is unimpressed on the way over, so Stroeder tells him he should be more excited. "We're meeting the next president of the United States," Stroeder explains.

Askew looks puzzled. "I thought that was George Bush," he says.

DECEMBER 22

Keith Smith's scope goes smoothly. Team doctor John Kavanaugh finds a tear in the meniscus (cartilage), which he repairs, and a severe sprain, but no tear of the anterior cruciate ligament. With an ideal recovery, Smith could be back in four to six weeks. But it's a loss Karl feels deeply. Smith, perhaps the best player so far, was the glue. His toughness, more than his scoring, will be missed.

○   ○   ○

Jim Laverty, already a few egg nogs into the spirit when he walks into the Armory hours before the game, sets the tone; tonight will be filled with Christmas cheer. "I'm so happy tonight," Laverty bubbles. "George is gonna go 50–4."

"One other thing," Karl says in the pregame meeting. "Five dollars to the first guy that gets a steal when one of their guys makes a spin move."

"Every time?"

"Up to ten dollars. I'm not gonna spend more than fifty tonight."

But the Patroons are again lifeless, tied at the half with an aggressive Charleston team, up by 4 after three. Spirit comes from the lively young bodies of the Bethlehem High School cheerleaders, and the fan in the front row chanting for Grissom to get in the game.

Then Kelvin gets in the mood, leads what has become a typical Patroons fourth-quarter rush—he will finish with 31—and with 4:50 left, Albany is up by 11. The sixties hit "Shout!" booms out over the PA. Fritz Walker, the short, squat, impossibly round team photographer and one-man cheering section, dressed in green Patroons stocking cap and plaid shirt, rolls his Santa Claus–shaped body into the middle of a pile of nubile teenage cheerleaders in short skirts at center court. And things quickly degenerate from there.

2:04 left. "Ozell, you wanna get in the game?" Karl asks. Ozell hasn't played yet; he says no. "Gris, get in there."

1:34 left. Up by 17. Grissom is set up for a three-pointer. "*Shoot, Gris! Shoot it!*" Gris smiles, obliges his teammates, misses, and smiles again.. He is now 1–21 from the floor over his last several games.

0:52 left. A gentleman in a floor-length red leather fur-lined topcoat and matching red cap shuffles over to the bench. "Oze. My man." He shakes Ozell's hand. He is shooed away. A shorter, less sharply dressed man takes his place. "Later, Oze." He is shooed away.

0:02 left. Up by 13. Clinton Smith, 0–4 from the line tonight, is fouled. He tells the ref he's injured. "I can't shoot. My elbow hurts. It's bad for my percentage."

"Well, then, get somebody else up here," the referee says.

"Vince, you go in. You take it," Smith says to Askew on the bench, grabbing his arm.

"What's going on?" Karl asks the ref.

"Your shooter says he's injured. Get a shooter up there."

"Clinton, take the shot."

"Can't, Coach. Elbow hurts."

"Let's get a shooter up there. I wanna go home," says the ref.

"Who do you want to shoot?" Karl asks.

"How 'bout this guy." The ref grabs Ozell's arm. "He hasn't played yet. He can shoot. I wanna get outta here. Let's go."

Ozell doesn't move.

"Clinton, take the damn shot."

Clinton takes the damn shot, lefthanded. He misses everything. Pats win by 14.

Down in the locker room, all ten players demand five dollars. Lee wants at least two fifty for helping out on one steal. Karl says he saw nothing. Kelvin calls him a cheat, suggests he look at the film, and pads out to the shower wearing a towel and his sneakers. Mr. Red Leather Coat is gone, but his unsavory friends are in the locker room, slapping hands. Kelvin pushes past, his sneakers flopping, his towel clutched securely around his waist.

Laverty, eyes like slits, nose aglow, weaves down the stairs, a Christmas present and card under his arm. He circles the hallway unsteadily. He drops the card.

Kelvin pads back to the locker room. The doorknob, always stubborn, is now unrelenting. The door won't open. He stands patiently, in towel and sneakers, waiting to be let in.

Laverty bends down to get the card and drops the present.

DECEMBER 23

After morning shootaround, Askew approaches Karl and asks to talk. He strokes his chin, for Vince a sign of thoughtfulness. He seems concerned about something important. "Coach, what am I gonna do this summer?" he asks. Karl, expecting something more pressing, laughs. "Well, I don't know, Vince. Most guys just go home, think things over, try to get into some pro camps. I can try to help you out with that, make a few calls . . ."

Vince strokes his chin again. "Coach, I ain't got a home."

○   ○   ○

Before the game, Vince is teaching some hand jive to Luke, one of the water boys: touch opposite elbows, fake the high five, pass hands, sweep in a half circle to a low five.

At the scorer's table, pregame chatter. Stroeder and Askew have made the all-star team, and Karl, with the league's best record, will coach. Neither Stroeder nor Karl particularly wants to spend New Year's Eve in Rockford; Stroeder wants to get paid for the effort (he will get $150 for his time). Karl wants Gerald to coach in his place. Askew is happy, but wants to get into the slam dunk contest. "I'd win it. I know it," he says. He hasn't been nominated by the league, but promises to lobby hard for himself once he gets there.

More news: Wayne Engelstad, the Patroons' first draft pick last summer, is about to be cut by the Nuggets. The list of potential Patroons grows every day: Popson, Roth, Matthews, Carlisle, Rowland, now Engelstad. "They might be better than what I've got here," Karl jokes; what he's got here is, in the next three hours, about to go 15–4, 30 points ahead of second-place Wichita Falls. Some hard decisions are being made. Gerald chides Wilkin, who has been writing about possible player moves every day. "How do you know what I'm doin'?" Gerald hollers. "If you know what I'm doin' you know more than I know."

The game should be easy. Topeka has a 2–13 record, three new players, and a new coach, the franchise's fourth in twelve months. He is Ron McHenry, twenty-six, Art Ross's assistant for the past three weeks and, before that, events coordinator for the Topeka Expo Center, the Sizzlers' arena. His inexperience becomes apparent when he apologizes to the media at the press table for standing in front of them during the game. "Am I in your way? Sorry."

But it isn't an easy game. The teams split the first two quarters; it's a 2-point Albany lead at the half. Upshaw again keys a late surge with 14 points in the second half (8 in the third Q), and Danny

Pearson hits for 31 for a 117–103 win. Only 5½ standings points, but it's still nine wins in a row and a huge lead in the standings. The team is happy.

Karl isn't. He had come into the game relaxed and stayed composed throughout, but shocks everyone in the locker room with a harsh criticism. For ten minutes he lashes out at complacency— "Good teams are cocky. We're complacent. There's a difference" —indifference, inattention, complaining, selfishness, his usual litany. Again he pleads for the team to understand; they are here not just to win, but to get better, to improve. They haven't done that lately. The need to commit to him and his program. He demands it. It will work.

Gerald nods throughout. *Can't these boys see George is right? He's exactly right? Why won't they listen? Why won't they commit? What is this league for? Is the game enough?*

Karl realizes he's gone far enough. "Sorry, guys. Merry Christmas." Gerald wonders at that. Why apologize? That's what they needed.

But he heads upstairs to organize. There's a road trip coming up in two days. There are plane tickets and boarding passes and bus tickets and meal money to pass out. There's a lot he's got to do. Sure, the team Christmas party is starting at Thirsty's, sure they'll be angry 'cause he'll be late. But somebody's got to do this, and tomorrow's a day off, and Gerald's going home to see his wife, who's been ill, and he's gonna miss the game in Rockford, so he's gotta do this now. And if it takes him a while, if he's slow, it's because that's how he does things, because he wants to do it right.

And when a player pulls a fast one and cons him out of a Thirsty's meal coupon and he comes up one short, it really burns him up. It really does. What's the point, an eleven-dollar meal coupon? What are they here for? Don't they understand? Garbage in their heads.

DECEMBER 25

Merry Christmas to all . . .

6:50 A.M.: Meet at the Albany County Airport on a cold, sunny morning. "Hey yo Gris. Merry Christmas."

"Playing on Christmas," Stroeder barks. "That stinks. Don't make enough money in the CBA for that shit."

7:50–9:00 (Central Time): Fly to Chicago; try to sleep; difficult for 6'6" to 6'11" bodies in coach-size airline seats.

9:45–11:10: Bus to Rockford, Ill.; pass the Tollbooth Toyland en route.

11:15–2:00: Check into the lowbrow Sweden House Lodge; scour Rockford for an open restaurant; find only one—Grandma's; eat lunch.

2:00–4:00: Rest.

4:15–4:30: Take van, left at hotel by the Rockford Lightning, to Metro Center.

Clinton Smith arrives at the hotel from Cleveland just as van is pulling out; Kelvin Upshaw, coming from Chicago, does not.

Coach Karl drives; John Stroeder, shotgun, dials the radio. "*Si-i-lent night, ho-o-ly night . . .*" bzz-bzz-bzz . . . "*Rockin' a-round the Christ-mas tree/Have a hap-py hol-i-day . . .*"

"How much we gonna fine Kelvin?" Fifty sounds good.

"Did we forget Dan Levy?" We did.

4:30: Arrive at Metro Center. Kelvin is in locker room, boom box booming, already in uniform. "I thought I had your ass for fifty," Karl says.

4:30–6:05: Warmups. Pregame intros. As Lightning players are introduced, running through mist from a fog machine under flashing lightning bolts in a darkened arena, Ozell Jones sends a bench boy out for popcorn.

6:10: Game begins. Jones sends bench boy out for more popcorn.

6:10–8:20: Play poorly, commit 24 turnovers, lose 99–93, take only two standings points. Lose Danny Pearson, who goes down late in game with severe ankle sprain.

8:20–8:30: Karl furious in locker room. In middle of tirade, Rockford team doctor walks in to examine Pearson. It is suggested he wait till Karl is through. "Well, all right," he concedes. "But I want to go home."

8:30: Doctor examines Pearson quickly, recommends X-rays, gives directions to hospital, and goes home.

8:40–9:00: Karl drives half of team back to hotel; gets lost on the way. Pulls in to Stop-n-Go for directions. *"San-ta Claus is com-ing to town . . ."*

9:00–9:15: Back to arena for Pearson; Askew and Smith still there, come to hospital.

9:15–9:30: To hospital emergency room. Fill out forms for work-men's compensation. "Do I bill this to the team?" asks the desk attendant.

"Yes," says Karl.

"Are you the commander?"

"I am the coach."

9:30–10:45: Wait.

10:45–11:15: Pearson examined, X-rayed. Askew and Smith call a cab. Karl waits.

11:15–11:30: X-rays negative. Doctor, in stunning reversal of com-mon athletic knowledge, prescribes Pearson to place his ankle, already swollen to the size of an orange, in a hot whirlpool three times daily. Karl looks at him, incredulous. Doctor says he doesn't think Pearson should play on Tuesday, two days from now. Karl doubts he'll be able to *walk* by Tuesday, and asks for an air cast.

11:30–11:40: Wait for nurse to find an air cast; she scours the hospital, then finds one in the examining room, three feet from Pearson. She opens the box, looking puzzled. "Let me read the instructions," she says. "I think this part goes here." She slaps on cast. Pearson winces in agony. "Sorry." Karl asks for a copy of the X-ray.

11:40–12:15: Wait for copy of X-ray. Pearson sits quietly by recep-tion desk. "Merry Christmas. Damn."

12:15: Get X-rays. Get in van. "Now Danny," says Karl, "the first thing you do is forget everything that doctor told you." "All right, Coach." "If you put that ankle in a whirlpool it'll swell out to *here.*" Dr. Karl prescribes ice and elevation.

12:15–12:30: Try to find any place open on Christmas night in Rockford that sells food and beer. *"Jin-gle bell, jin-gle bell, jin-gle bell rock . . ."*

12:35: Find only another Stop-n-Go. No beer. No hot food. Buy Christmas dinner: Large bag of Doritos, one jar of salsa, one stick of beef jerky, two cans of Spam, one Dolly Madison apple pie, two cherry 7-Ups.

12:35–12:40: Back to hotel. Pass Ozell Jones in another car with someone not a Patroon.

12:45: ... And to all, a good night.

DECEMBER 26–28

The Patroons wake up to find six inches of snow on the ground.

The bus from Rockford gets to O'Hare in time, but Eastern flight 229 to Atlanta is canceled, along with dozens of others, as O'Hare becomes a shelter for the traveling homeless. Karl makes a phone call. An answering machine picks up.

"Hello, Jay Ramsdell? This is George Karl. We're stranded in O'Hare airport, there is twelve inches of snow on the ground, Eastern tells us the earliest we can get out of here is Wednesday, which is fine, I like Chicago, only our game is in Pensacola and it's on Tuesday night. Now, Gerald Oliver will be in Pensacola on time, he can probably round up ten players off the street, and I'll try to get the uniforms down there. I'm sorry you're not home, Jay. I'm kind of in a panic here. Talk to you later."

All day long, a flurry of phone calls—Ramsdell is located, the league travel agent is consulted—and it's finally determined that the team will stay in Chicago tonight and try to get on a flight tomorrow. Cabs at dusk to the Marriott O'Hare. After dinner, and over drinks, Karl plans the attack in the hotel bar. Maybe we should go in three groups. There's a 7:15 out of Eastern and an 8:05 by Delta. No, maybe it's better just to get everyone to the airport and figure it out there. Yes, that's better. Waitress, another round. Across the bar sits Orville Redenbacher, eating popcorn. Nearer is a young woman who says her name is Melanie Hatfield, of the Hatfield-and-McCoy Hatfields. George Karl switches from beer to Kahlua and cream. Celebrities banded together by adversity.

Up at 4:30 the next morning, to O'Hare by 5:30. Karl works the Eastern counter. Dan Levy, acting as assistant coach in charge of transportation in place of Gerald Oliver, works Delta. The luggage is checked through to Pensacola on Eastern, under the assumption that the team will get there sometime today. Doug Lee calls Gerald in Pensacola. "Coach Oliver, I'm doing the best I can, I'm trying to hold on here. You know, Coach Karl went home. He just said, 'Fuck the CBA,' and walked away."

"Don't tell me that," Gerald says. "That's not funny. That's mah life you're playin' with. You'll give me a heart attack."

Karl takes the phone and gives Gerald the plan. The first try is the Eastern 7:15 to Atlanta. And some success: Grissom, Shurina, and Clint Smith get on. Unfortunately, in the confusion no one gives them the continuation tickets from Atlanta to Pensacola. But not to worry. Whoever gets on the next flight will bring the tickets down.

Over to Delta. That gate is at the opposite end of O'Hare, at least a half-mile walk away. Pearson, limping heavily, takes about a half hour to get there. But no luck—the 8:05 is full, no standbys get on, not even the Eastern pilots who stand in line with Karl and Levy. Back to Eastern for the 8:45. This time, Pearson sits on a baggage cart and gets wheeled over.

Again, no one gets on. Back to Delta for the 9:53. By now, the team is starting to be recognized. The shoeshine man hits up Stroeder. "Hey! All that walkin', you can use a shine!" Ozell flirts with the woman at the security X-ray. Ken Johnson bitches. "That's it. I'm on the next flight out. L.A., San Francisco, Atlanta, don't matter. That's it." Karl wonders what Shurina, Grissom, and Smith are doing now, in Atlanta, with no luggage, no tickets, and no idea what's going on.

Shut out at Delta. Back to Eastern. 10:45. The DePaul University basketball team is booked and they get on easily; the Albany Patroons trudge back to Delta.

Kelvin pushes a luggage cart; Ozell checks the local talent.

"Hey, glamour girl. Hey, cover girl," says Ozell.

"CBA ain't worth this shit. I'm serious," says Kelvin.

"Hey miniskirt. Hey sexy. How you doin', sexy lady."

"I'm serious. League so damn cheap. Don't even pay you a professional salary. What's that, twenty thou, twenty-five? Damn. Five hundred a week, look what we gotta do, what it do to your body, walkin' around a airport all day long."

"Hey girly. Hey girl."

"This is my last year. I'm serious. I had a good job, with UPS, back in Chicago. My agent say, Kelvin, you're close, play one more year, play for George. Well that's it, I'm twenty-five."

"Sweee-eet as cherry pie."

"I'm serious."

No go at Eastern. No go at Delta. Cazzie Russell, the former Knick star and CBA coach, now an assistant at Atlanta, spots Ozell and says hello before catching the 12:35.

Karl calls the league office again. They strongly suggest the team get out tonight, but do little to help. A later flight to Charleston could be confirmed, but it's vetoed as too expensive. Down in Atlanta, Shurina et al. are told to wait it out rather than buy new tickets to Pensacola. Three more trips across O'Hare—"Them shoes lookin' beat up. I can he'p. Shine 'em up nice"—and when the Eastern 2:15 leaves without a Patroon, it's official; tonight's game will be postponed. Still, the league wants the Patroons in Florida tonight. "You mean we gotta keep doin' this all night?" Lee asks.

Karl attacks the Eastern counter and pleads with the harried counter help. "We've been here two days. If we don't get out tonight, it's gonna cost my owner fifty thousand dollars. It'll probably cost me my job. I can't believe this."

"I'll get my supervisor," she defers.

Finally, the league relents. It books a flight out of Midway at 6 P.M. It's 4:30 now. "We ain't never get to Midway in time," says Kelvin. "I need a beer," says Karl.

The league charters a bus from O'Hare to Midway; it's thirty minutes late.

While the team waits, Kelvin spots a young boy hustling unused baggage carts to return for nickels. "Hey my man. Working hard? Stayin' outta trouble?" Kelvin shakes his hand and gives him two dollars. The boy runs off. "I like to see 'em workin', not stickin' people up," Kelvin says.

Still waiting for the charter. "This shit don't happen in the NBA," says Johnson. "Up there, you just go back to your hotel, say 'Call me when you got a flight.' None of this waitin'-around shit." Finally the CBA charter comes—and boards other passengers, including, of course, a screaming baby, sitting right behind Karl's ear.

Bus to Midway. The 6:00 flight is gone, but the 7:30 is still open, maybe because the 7:30 is delayed and won't leave until 11:30. Time is passed in the airport bar, where Dan Levy meets a bleached blond girl in tight black jumpsuit who offers to show him her underwear. For Levy, it's true love, at least until her plane leaves for Philadelphia.

The 7:30-cum-11:30 flight arrives in Atlanta at 2 a.m. The league has booked rooms at a nearby motel, where Grissom, Smith, and Shurina are waiting; seven professional basketball players, their coach, and two members of the media cram into a van that comfortably seats six normal-sized people, and by three in the morning, twenty-two and a half hours after waking, the Patroons are in a dumpy Best Western in Atlanta, Georgia.

"Ozell. Here's your key," Karl says wearily.

"What? I gotta go to bed now?"

○ ○ ○

Karl wakes at 9:00 and calls Gerald in Pensacola. "Good morning, Gerald. What's happening?"

"Coach, why aren't you at the airport? Your flight leaves in an hour."

"No one told me."

Karl hurriedly calls each room to roust his players, and upon checking out finds a long distance call no one will confess to making. Detective work reveals it was made before the majority of the team arrived, leaving only Grissom, Shurina, and Clinton Smith as suspects. The evidence points to Smith, the usual suspect; he denies it and refuses to pay. Karl pays and promises to call the number and find out who called, then fine the perpetrator three times the cost of the call. Smith continues to plead innocent. "No way, not me. Not payin'." On the way to the airport, Karl rubs his eyes. "I've got such a headache. You know how they're usually localized? This one is kind of surrounding my whole head."

By 1:00 the Pats are checked into the Ramada Inn Bayview, two days late. They eat non-airport food for the first time in forty-eight hours, and collapse. The van leaves for the arena at 5:45.

Karl and Stroeder, though, still don't get much rest. Don Nelson, Karl's old boss and friend, calls from Golden State. Ralph Sampson underwent knee surgery last night. The Warriors want to sign Stroeder to a ten-day tryout to take his place. Stroeder decides to stay for the two games in Pensacola, but on Friday he'll be gone.

○   ○   ○

If ever there is a game the Patroons should lose, this is it. After the travel nightmares, the fatigue, the loss of Keith Smith and Danny Pearson and now Stroeder (who is still here, but wary of injuring himself), Albany figures to come up flat. And then the van to the game seats only eight, forcing cramped quarters in the back. And then a church league game runs long and keeps them from a proper warmup. And then the Pensacola crowd turns out small but surly, throwing epithets at Grissom and ice at Pearson. And then the refs take Albany out of the game; with the Patroons up by 5 after three, with the momentum solidly in Albany's favor, Pensacola fights back and takes the game 115–109.

Even with all that, Karl is as down as he has been all year. In the van back to the hotel, he snaps at laughter coming from the back. Maybe it's the fatigue; the NBA doesn't travel like this, and he hasn't slept much in three days. More likely it's the CBA Blues. Today, Eric Musselman came out in the Albany papers slamming Karl and the Patroons over the Roth trade. It is an unnecessary and immature thing to do, especially in print, and Gerald tries to get Karl's mind off it. "He's just a kid, Coach, just twenty-four, he's not worth your time or concern." Still, Karl is angry, frustrated, depressed, confused. In the hotel bar he looks sixty years old. He wonders, Is this team any good? They're 15–6, the best in the league, and he thinks the team stinks. His NBA system should work, but why can't they make a simple layup? Why won't Vincent Askew dunk when he has the chance? Is Steve Shurina, who has been struggling lately, any good at all? Will he ever make another jumpshot? Why aren't they capable of the NBA play? Why isn't this the NBA? This Musselman crap, this wouldn't happen in The League. It happens in this league. He feels like he needs to hit something; he may smash the blackboard tomorrow, that's how tied up he is.

He takes a piece of paper and makes out new lineups. Bring in Matthews and Engelstad and Rowland. Stroeder's gone; Keith Smith's out for a while. Put Pearson on Injured Reserve. Waive

Shurina? Waive Grissom? Waive both? What about Ozell? He looks at the new lineup and wonders. His players have worked hard, he knows that. They've won for him. It won't be easy to send them home. But are they any good? This new team is better, isn't it? Karl is still confused.

He takes a beer and pumps a quarter into a video machine and, in the empty lobby of the Ramada Inn Bayview just after midnight, he plays a game of Ms. Pac-Man.

DECEMBER 29

After the morning shootaround, the van motors back to the hotel. Negotiations ensue; Popeye's or McDonald's? Popeye's wins. The uniforms are starting to stink; will the team pay the $30 the hotel will charge to wash them? Yes, Karl promises, if they win tonight; if not, $3 comes out of everyone's meal money. It passes unanimously. "Get your uniforms to my room in ten minutes," says Grissom, "or fuck you." The van driver is asked if he'd like to come to Albany; a straight trade, him for Tony, is proposed. He declines. And then, a team mimic of Gerald's two most typical game phrases, in Gerald's inimitible drawl: "He shoots lawng! He shoots lawwwwng!" "Fo-ty-eight minutes! Fo-ty-eight minutes!"

Everyone is in a better mood today, including Karl. He takes a trip to the mall with Doug Lee, Vince Askew, and Clinton Smith. The mall crawl is a favored road diversion, good for killing several hours and making time with local women. Promising free game tickets to counter girls is the usual bribe; and everyone knows where the most likely (and prettiest) candidates work (women's cosmetics and men's cologne counters rate highly). While the players work the mall—and Clint and Askew work the girls—Karl roams, thinking.

The good mood carries over to the game. In warmups, Kelvin looks at Gerald and gets a twinkle in his eye; "Coach O, I love you so much, I'm gonna hit this." He smiles, and nails a twenty-footer. The other players are preoccupied by the Tornados hostesses, six young women wearing toothy smiles, piles of blond hair, tans, Hooters T-shirts, and orange hotpants. Even Doug Lee, profoundly married, runs to the bench for a closer look. Pearson, the Jacksonville resident, in street clothes on the bench, smiles. "Florida, man," he tells them.

The game, though close, is a quick 8-point win; six standings points put the Pats over a hundred. In the locker room, Karl is happy. He also says that there is still a lot of work to be done. "Gentlemen, we're going once hard on January first, two on the second, maybe two on the third." "Two what?" Askew asks. "Practices!" comes the chorus. And then Karl tells the team that Stroeder is going up to Golden State.

"Yeah, Stroeds, goin' to the show," Johnson yells. "Yeah Stroeder, get outta here. We don't need you," says Kelvin. For his ten days, Stroeder will make a prorated share of the minimum NBA salary of $100,000, or about $6,000—nearly as much as a full season's pay in the CBA. "Hey Stroeds, when you get there, send me a thousand bucks." "I'll take five hundred."

Out in the arena, three girls ask after Askew.

"Is there a Vince Edwards in there?" asks one.

"I think it's Askew," her friend says.

"You sure, girl?" says the third.

"I'm not sure," the first answers. "I just met him in the mall today."

DECEMBER 30–31

Up at five for the flight—or flights—back. Karl and Oliver head to Rockford for the all-star game, with Askew and Johnson, who is taking Stroeder's place. (Karl would prefer to take Upshaw, who is playing like an all-star where Johnson is not. And Karl, for all his riding of Kelvin, truly respects Upshaw's play over the last several games. But the league, which at first is reluctant to give Karl choice at all, finally relents to Johnson as a big man replacing a big man.) Karl has no desire to go himself, so he drags Gerald with him. "Tell the league if you don't go, I don't go," he says, only half joking.

Stroeder is off to Golden State. And with a few days off for the all-star break and New Year's, Upshaw goes back to Chicago, Clint Smith back to Cleveland. Pearson left the day before, leaving Ozell, Lee, Shurina, and Grissom to fly back to Albany.

Karl and Oliver will coach the all-stars to a loss in Rockford, and return to Albany New Year's Day. The original ten Patroons will be, after only two months and twenty-two games, dissipated by injuries, one call-up, and the specter of several new bodies on the way.

As 1988 ends, Albany is 16–6, with 103½ points, 31½ over second place Wichita Falls, twelve over Western Division–leading Rockford; the Patroons are the best team in the CBA.

Tomorrow, they will have to start all over.

4

JANUARY

JANUARY 1

"The Great Eight!" Gerald screams. And then he screams it again. "The Great Eight!"

On New Year's Day at 6 P.M., the Armory is frigid and messy from the New Year's Eve sock hop held last night. With Stroeder gone, and Keith Smith and Danny Pearson injured, the Patroons are indeed down to the Great Eight: Shurina and Lee, Grissom and Jones, Johnson and Askew, Upshaw and Clint Smith. "These are our eight," says Gerald, who is running practice, "until we get some more."

"We *better* get some more," Karl snipes.

Derrick Rowland is supposed to be signed tonight, and Wayne Engelstad is expected into Albany as well; unfortunately, neither can be found. Even their agents don't know where they are.

Although Karl tells Gerald to run practice, it takes only a few minutes before he is on the court, spitting orders, driving a hard, intense workout. This is really the first serious practice the Pats have been able to schedule in three weeks. With games three times a week, travel, and a schedule that leaves little free time, finding a day for real practice is a blessing. And Karl, unhappy with the team's play over the past two weeks, isn't about to let it slip by. "Don't fuck around!" he shouts. *"Work!"* Even in the cold, the Great Eight are quickly stripped down to sweat-soaked T-shirts and shorts, their warmup suits hanging limp over folding chairs. One-on-one drills turn into four-on-three's, then three-on-three half-court games. Karl works the offensive and defensive patterns back into shape. "Come *hard* off the pick"; "Pin down, Kenny"; "Wait, wait . . . now Doug Lee, *explode!*" Sets of sprints follow—sideline to sideline, seventeen in 30 seconds; base line to foul line, twenty in 30; do it again, let's go—and after two hours, they're done. And they show it, perspiration pouring off Grissom, Johnson breathing hard.

"You know, they're not in as bad shape as I thought." Karl smiles.

"A couple more practices like that, and the Great Eight might be enough," Gerald booms.

"Or they might be dead," offers Jim Laverty.

"Nice job, guys," Karl tells the huddle. They are expecting a lecture, some kind of tirade, some continuance of the speeches Karl has been giving over the last few weeks. Instead, he simply dismisses them. "Tomorrow at ten and four," he says. Then, at the sideline, "Think that surprised 'em?" He can barely contain his glee; Karl loves being unpredictable.

Before it's over, though, he confers with Ozell. For several days now, Ozell has been conspicuously unhappy over his limited playing time. At the last Pensacola game, Jones was pouting, sitting alone at the end of the bench during time-out huddles. Karl spoke with Ozell at the hotel—either do it my way or leave, the choice is yours. Now, he wants an answer.

"You want to hear it now?" Ozell asks.

"Yes."

"If you ain't gonna play me I want out," Ozell says, and walks away.

JANUARY 2

Two practices today: the first from ten to noon, the second from four to six. That makes three workouts in a twenty-four-hour period. It's a good thing Jack Moser stops by.

The Pats head trainer didn't even know the team was back in town. "George called me up and said to come by. I said, 'Where are you?' " he reports. "I thought they were still on the road."

He brings Keith Smith with him. Smith, on crutches, is progressing slowly. Moser examines him on the press table and gives him some muscle stimulation with a pocket-sized, battery-powered contraption that straps to Smith's leg. The muscle stim is his one big purchase this year; with a budget of only $1,100 for the season (and over half of that going for tape), Moser tries to save up enough for one "big" purchase a year. The muscle stim, at a cost of about $200, qualifies as this year's new toy; even that was tough to get past the front office.

In addition to his duties with the Patroons, Moser is a trainer, paramedic, and high school basketball coach. (Moser has stolen plays from all the Patroons' coaches, from Dean Meminger, the short-lived first head coach, through Phil Jackson and Bill Musselman to George Karl; he may have the most advanced offense for a losing team in all of high school basketball.) He has salt and pepper hair and mustache, bulging eyes, and an easygoing, jokey manner that works well with the players. He also seems to know what he's doing, which in this setting can be more important than actually doing it. Unlike his assistants, the whooping Rich Sill and the brooding Bob Shaffer, who seem to come and go when they please—or, to be fair, when their full-time jobs at the firehouse allow—Moser, while not always around, at least can be counted on, and counted on to do a good job. "Our training situation scares me," Karl had said earlier in the season, after a session that found him helping out with taping and icing down a sprain and bandaging a torn fingernail himself. "What if someone actually got hurt here?" he had asked. In fact, Karl had simply forgotten; that's the way it works in this league. Real injuries will be cared for, but the little things, well, sometimes you have to take care of them yourself. A full-time trainer is still a luxury. Some teams are willing to pay for one, but Albany isn't one of those teams. Moser gets $35 to show for games. Practice appearances are gratis.

While Smith is having his leg stimulated—electric pulses cause the leg muscles to contract every second or so to increase blood supply to the injury site—Moser looks Danny Pearson over. He puts Pearson through a series of exercises, balancing himself on the bad ankle, running and cutting drills and the like, and pronounces him nearly fit for the Charleston game on Wednesday, and a definite for the weekend series back home with Wichita Falls. Looking through the orange backpack/medical kit for some tape, he comes across, amid rolls of tape and pre-wrap, an unopened can of Stroh's beer. It seems somehow appropriate. "Medicinal purposes?" he asks Karl. "At least we have the kit still," Moser continues. "We usually go through two or three a year. Usually the coaches or players can't be bothered to remember it. They end up leaving it somewhere. Gerald's pretty good about those things, though."

As the Pats finish up the night session, the bodies begin to go. Grissom's leg goes into spasm during sprints, and Moser leaves his other two patients to look him over. Clint Smith leans heavily on the ball cart, complaining quietly. Johnson sits heavily on a folding chair, complaining at higher volume. "My legs, man, they gonna give out." Grissom gives some pointed, Karl-like barbs at Karl: "Yeah, I think it's real good to have three hard workouts in a day. Speaking for the players, I think we really needed that."

"Gerald," Karl shouts, "can you get us two practices in Charleston tomorrow?"

"Oh, Coach," Gerald whines. "You know it took everything I had to get one practice down there. I had to give my left testicle to get the one. You want me to give up the right one too? It's not that I'm not fired up, I am fired up about these practices, we got a lot of work done today and yesterday, a lot of work done, but I'll tell you what, I want to protect my right testicle. You don't blame me for that, do you, Coach?"

"That's all right, Gerald. One should be enough tomorrow."

"Gentlemen," Gerald shouts. "The van will be at the Quality Inn at five forty tomorrow morning. Five four oh. That means Tony, you swing by the Howard Johnson's at five thirty and then—"

"I got it, Coach. I'm on it," Tony claims.

"No excuses now, Tony. You be there at—"

"I got it, Coach."

"—Five four oh . . . I'm sorry, five three oh. Is that right now?"

Keith Smith, who hasn't been around to watch this continuing drama for a while, loses it. "Gerald and Tony, man!" He is laughing. "Gerald and Tony."

"The Great Eight, on the road." Gerald echoes through the empty Armory. "And with Mister Danny Pearson we might be the Fine Nine."

There is still no word from Rowland or Engelstad. Rowland is on Long Island for the New Year; Engelstad is in California, and his agent says he can't be reached because of snow. "Snow in California." Karl laughs. "How's that for an excuse." Then he turns to Tim Wilkin. "C'mon Timmy, buy me a beer and tell me what else Eric Musselman called me."

"You mean besides a 'fucking asshole'?"

"Aw, Coach," Gerald pleads. "Pay him no mind. Leave it alone. We got the Great Eight or the Fine Nine to worry about."

Karl just laughs.

JANUARY 3–4

Derrick Rowland signs a contract and is flown down to Charleston on Wednesday, the third of January. He will be in uniform for Thursday night's game. At twenty-nine, Rowland has seven years in the CBA already, six with Albany. He is the league's fourth leading scorer all-time; for the Patroons, he is the number one all-time leading scorer, is second in rebounding, steals, and blocked shots, and fourth in assists. He is 6' 5", 195, all arms and legs out of little known SUNY Potsdam in upstate New York, a tenth round NBA draft pick back in 1981. Rowland is the kind of player the CBA was once filled with—low- or no-round picks from unknown local colleges, midsize players who don't seem to fit at any one position—and he has managed to make a career of it. After last season with Musselman's Patroons, he looked overseas for a fatter contract and found one in the Philippines. But when the season ended there in December, he returned to Albany (where he makes his home now). Though he had said he wouldn't return to the CBA, he is back. The Patroons are happy to have him; "Dr. D.," as he's called here (a poor man's CBA version of Dr. J. perhaps), is well-known to Albany fans, obviously, and with attendance down a little this year, a familiar face might lure people back to the Armory.

○ ○ ○

The Charleston Gunners are on a hot streak, having won four in a row. Sadly, their fans don't seem to care much. The club, which drew over 4,000 for the season opener against the Patroons, has failed to top 1,000 since, despite an arena that seats about 12,000. Tonight's official attendance is 598, though it seems smaller, if that's possible.

The Fine Nine are now ten again, with the addition of Rowland; Pearson, however, is kept in street clothes to be sure his ankle is fully healed. And the Albany nine pick up the club's tenth win in the last twelve with an up-and-down 108–104 win. The bookend victory—the Pats take the first and last quarters, but get thumped in the middle two—adds five points to the standings total; it's now 108½, a full 33½ over Wichita Falls, this weekend's opponent. Vince Askew continues to improve, throwing down a career-high 32 and grabbing 12 boards, and Doug Lee, who has been averaging 24.7 points over the last four games, keeps it up with 25. Lee also hits a three for the twelfth consecutive game; with 44 three-pointers thus far, he is already only one away from the club record of 45 in a season. Rowland adds 10 points coming off the bench; only the 6 fouls he collects, which put him on the bench at the end, keep his totals from being higher. Ken Johnson, who starts at center in place of Stroeder, collects 14 rebounds as the Patroons, the league's best rebounding team, outboard Charleston by 56–30. Johnson shares time with Grissom, who gets his most minutes this season and scores his first points—he finishes with 6—in weeks. There are still too many turnovers, but all in all, the Albany contingent should be happy with the win.

Not Ozell. He's been inattentive for days now; when he plays little tonight, and takes some heat from Karl, he sulks. In the locker room after the game, Karl, who is in a foul humor today anyway, stands at the chalkboard and writes a favorite equation:

NBA Success = Talent + Knowledge × Attitude

In angry tones, he explains how important the right attitude is. It is a continuation of his season-long theme, that to get better is the reason they're all here, and that to get to the NBA involves more than just playing the game. He points fingers, he names names. He sees Ozell smirking. He throws a piece of chalk and hits him in the shoulder. Ozell challenges him verbally; Karl stands up to the challenge. No bodily contact, just an issue coming to its unavoidable climax.

That night, it is decided to get rid of Ozell.

JANUARY 5

An early flight back to Albany, and afternoon practice is quickly canceled. Karl goes home to rest; Gerald goes to the office to trade Ozell.

He also tries to track down Engelstad. For several hours Gerald is on the phone; calls are backed up like flights into La Guardia on a snowy day. Charleston needs a center; they're on line 1. Pensacola is interested; line 2. Ozell, line 3, is told to start packing. The league travel agent is looking into flights for Ozell. Engelstad's agent is on the line; Wayne should be on the flight from L.A., arriving in Albany at 10:45 tonight.

Gerald to Tim Wilkin, who is looking for the story: "You wanna go meet Wayne with me at the airport, ten forty-five? You do? That's terrific. You an' me. Yes, Ozell is gone. Not sure where yet. I'll let you know soon's I know. Now, what game we bettin' on tonight?"

To Ozell: "Pensacola looks like a no go. Charleston is pretty hot. They want you to play for them tomorrow night."

To Bill Heller, the team publicist: "Let's just announce that Ozell has been traded. We don't know where Engelstad is yet, or if he'll make it, so we'll just hold off."

To Karl: "Charleston says yes. For a player to be named later. You want to do it? You sure? Then it's done. I think it helps both clubs. And it helps Ozell."

To the Charleston GM: "Call the league, get the flight number, get a prepaid ticket waiting at the airport. Then call me back with that information. Yes, I'll be here. No, I'm not telling Ozell to get to the airport. I'm taking him there myself."

To Ozell: "Your plane leaves in exactly two hours and twenty minutes. We'll have your last check, you give us your uniform. We pay you for your days here, they pay you for your days there. You're gonna like it there, buddy. It's good for you and good for them. They're excited to have you, and I'll tell you what, you can help them. You can take them to the playoffs. Now go pack your bags. Go play."

To Engelstad's agent: "Did he get on the plane?"

To the league travel agent: "Did he get on the plane?"

To the Patroons office, now empty: "Shoot, I gotta get Ozell. We're gonna miss that plane."

He races through rush hour traffic to get Ozell, at the Quality Inn. Ozell, in his bulging hooded fur coat, is subdued. He loads his bags and a new boom box the size of a small refrigerator into Gerald's car. "Where you been, man? You said you were coming three times. We gonna miss that plane."

"Don't you worry, buddy. We'll make it. I feel good about this."

And they do make it, with three minutes to spare. Gerald helps Ozell negotiate with the boarding attendants to bring the box on board the plane. "It'll fit," Ozell insists. "It's mine, it's coming with me." He shakes Gerald's hand. "Thanks, Coach." "Thank you," Gerald answers and gives him the thumbs-up. Ozell walks down the boarding ramp, fur coat and boom box and no longer an Albany Patroon.

"Was he traded?" a woman boarding attendant asks absent-mindedly.

"Yes he was," Gerald answers. "He helped us win some ball games, and we're trying to treat him right. It just didn't work out. But we're doing the right thing, for him and for us."

The attendant, hearing more than she's interested in, nods and walks away.

Gerald drives back to the Quality Inn. He looks Ozell's room over. It's a reasonable mess; an empty cardboard carton, former home of the music box now headed for West Virginia, sits on the unmade bed, styrofoam and plastic scattered around it, warranty card and instructions unopened.

Gerald's back in the housing business; maybe Engelstad will live here. Maybe one of the boys, Askew or Pearson, still with Gerald at HoJo. Gerald's got some more decisions to make. Still in the business.

Ken Johnson walks in. "Ozell here?" He's told Ozell is gone. "Man, that's quick."

"Kenny. Do you like it better here or at the Howard Johnson's?"

"Me? The HoJo. More TV channels."

Then Kenny spots Ozell's empty clothes hangers. He grabs a dozen, with Gerald's blessing, and takes them to his room.

JANUARY 6

Out with the old ... Wayne Engelstad arrives this morning (he didn't make last night's plane) in time for the 11 A.M. shootaround. He's a big, blond, solidly built California-faced youngster, twenty-two years old, with a spiky surfer haircut. He's also 6' 8", and Karl immediately likes how he handles himself on the court.

"Wayne, how big are you? Two forty?" Karl shouts.

"Don't worry 'bout him, Coach," says Kelvin Upshaw, patting his chest. "I'm the biggest guy here."

The Patroons look, suddenly but unmistakably, different. Rowland and Engelstad are in, Stroeder and Ozell (and, still, Keith Smith) are out. Albany is now smaller, less powerful, but maybe quicker and better shooters (Rowland's shooting prowess is well documented; Engelstad, however, is also a fine shooter for a big man). Grissom, who played well in Charleston, figures to get a lot of time at center, as will Johnson. Karl realizes he has work to do.

"I don't know if it's the holidays, trades, call-ups, whatever," he tells them in the postpractice huddle, "but we've been flat. We're not getting better. We're home for a week now, so let's really concentrate on that. We take care of business the next four games, and they'll all be talking about second and third place, and we work on getting better." And then he stays on to teach the newcomers his plays.

Gerald takes down shoe sizes; it's time to order new sneakers. "Derrick?" "Fourteen." "Shurina?" "Still thirteen, Coach." "Wayne?" "What?" "Your shoe size?" "Oh. Thirteen. Low cut."

Jim Laverty wanders over. "So what did you get for Ozell?" he asks Karl with a laugh. "A bowling ball?"

○   ○   ○

Engelstad is given Stroeder's uniform (with the name plate removed but no replacement yet) before the game. He asks for a jock strap as well.

"You mean you don't have one?" Gerald asks.

"Well, no, I mean I just thought you'd have some here," Engelstad says.

Volatile head coach George Karl tried to bring NBA intensity to the CBA.

Ken Johnson, the Patroons' strong man up front, had his moments both on and off the court.

A stormy CBA season ends on a happy note as Kelvin Upshaw signs with the Boston Celtics.

Vincent Askew, who found himself at the center of a college hoops scandal, found happiness briefly in the CBA before bolting for Europe.

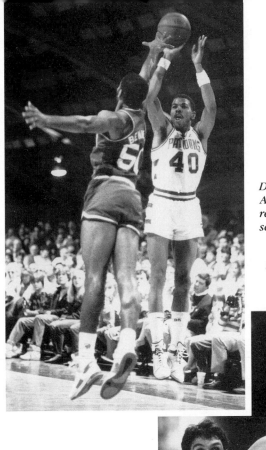

Doctor D—Derrick Rowland—Albany's most popular player, returned from overseas with his scoring touch intact.

From the CBA to the NBA and back again, John Stroeder was one of many players who lived in basketball limbo.

Fun-loving off the court but a killer on it, Greg Grissom always wanted more minutes.

Dirk Minniefield—from the NBA to rehab to starting a comeback in the CBA.

Lowes Moore kept trying to retire from the CBA, only to be called upon again and again.

A CBA record–setting three-point shooter, Doug Lee is still waiting for a call from the NBA.

Danny Pearson sprained his ankle on Christmas Day and spent the evening in the hospital recuperating.

Clinton Smith, aka "Robocop," led the Patroons in jive.

Steve Shurina, the unknown rookie from St. John's.

Coach Karl stresses defense, discipline, and teamsmanship—three elements of the game rarely seen in the CBA.

Greg Grissom

Keith Smith

Kelvin Upshaw

Ken Johnson

Danny Pearson

Ozell Jones

Steve Shurina

John Stroeder

Lowes Moore

Clinton Smith

Dirk Minniefield

Doug Lee

Derrick Rowland

Vincent Askew

Coach George Karl

*Assistant Coach
Gerald Oliver*

"Welcome to the CBA, son." Gerald laughs at him. "And by the way, last guy here who didn't have a jock scored 38 points."

The Patroons face further troubles. A stomach virus has invaded; Doug Lee is home in bed, Clint Smith is here but weak, and Ken Johnson can barely hold his head up. Jack Moser runs to the pharmacy. While Karl further explains his codes in the pregame—"Red means double-team the ball, Wayne and Derrick. White means push the ball toward the center of the floor"—Moser pours Ken a capful of Imodium A-D. Then he hands out vitamins to everyone.

Karl is deeper into his pregame funk than usual. Always nervous and edgy before a game—he talks a little faster, paces a little more, and his stomach flares up on him during pregame talks—he seems particularly anxious tonight. It's going to take a concentrated effort on his part to win under these conditions, and he is feeling more of the burden than usual.

The fans know none of this, of course; they've packed the Armory—nearly 4,000—mainly to see Dr. D. Until now, the crowds have been polite but reserved, slow to warm to the new faces even though the team is so successful. The fact bothers Karl—he feels they haven't given his club a fair chance—but he may have forgotten that Albany is perhaps the most stable franchise in a transient league. Albany's fans aren't used to wholesale personnel changes; Rowland has been on the team every season, which makes him more of a Patroon than anyone else (except, to a lesser degree, Grissom). Now that the fans have a real Patroon back, they are back. Tonight's crowd is easily the liveliest, most enthused of the season.

They are treated to an immensely entertaining game. With two new faces in the lineup, Karl calls for a fast, loose offense; few plays, lots of running. Wichita Falls is hurting; Bobby Lee Hurt and Derrick Taylor are out, and Ennis Whatley is playing for the first time in several days. The first two quarters are split, but the Patroons are having offensive trouble. Askew is missing easy layups. Grissom and Rowland are playing well (Engelstad isn't playing at all, instead sitting close to Gerald for instruction), but what should be a big lead is only 3 at the half.

Karl implores his team to pull together; start playing fundamental defense, he says, and the offense will come. But the Texans shoot out quickly in the third quarter, and after a 16–4 run puts them up by 9, Karl calls a time-out.

Rather than the usual huddle at the bench, he calls everyone out onto the court. In controlled, quiet tones, he is emphatic. We should be kicking this team's ass, he says, not losing. It's time for a gut-check; the next six minutes will say a lot about this team. Relax, play your game. And they break.

The ploy works. Askew comes alive with 6 straight points, including a slam; Grissom rejects two shots, rebounds well, and starts the fast break. Kelvin runs and runs, dishing to Pearson—not at all hobbled, despite the air cast he still wears on his ankle—and Rowland and Askew. Although they just fail to take the third Q— losing by 2—the fourth is a rout. Grissom takes down 11 rebounds for the game, Kelvin finishes with 14 assists; Askew takes scoring honors with 21 and Rowland adds 20, and the crowd can hardly contain itself, spilling out of the seats and surrounding the Pats bench. "Great game," says one fan, intoxicated by victory and beer, as he slaps Askew on the shoulder. Vince nods politely and offers thanks.

Karl is drained, but pleased, in the locker room, still amazed at the CBA. How could the other team play only six guys the second half? He could see they were dead, couldn't their coach? And how can these teams continue to throw up threes all the time? Every team in this league attempts twenty against us. Can't they see it doesn't work? Michael Tait, seven for fucking *sixteen* for threes? Jesus.

Rich Sill brings in the tray of soda and beer. Karl grabs two of the latter. "See, Derrick? Things are different than when Musselman was here. We get beers when we win."

Rowland smiles. "Only when we win?" he asks, before three reporters surround his chair.

JANUARY 7

The toughest two minutes for a coach might be those quiet, internal moments that it takes to walk from the court, after the first half ends, to the locker room. In those moments a coach must quickly summarize the strengths and weaknesses of his club, describe the flow of the game, come to understand the moods of his players, his opponents, and the officials. He has to distill all the technical and emotional information of the past 24 minutes into a ten-minute . . . what? A lecture? A shouting match? A fit? How should he react? How best will he fix what's broken, change the course of his team and this game? Loud or quiet? Stern or relaxed? What will it be?

Tonight, at the half, Albany trails by 10—at one point they are down 17—after perhaps the least effective 24 minutes of the season. Wichita Falls, still without Hurt and Taylor and now also without Ennis Whatley, who has reinjured his leg, nevertheless blows Albany out for two quarters.

Before each halftime talk, Karl stands outside the locker room for a few moments, conferring with Gerald or composing himself, while fans push past to get to the rest room. There's no coaches' room here, and Karl has no place to hide. Tonight he seems fit to burst; his face is blazing red, his brow creased. When angry, Karl tends to put his hands to the sides of his head, as if he is trying somehow to keep his skull from exploding. It looks like it might not work this time. His fury even keeps away the drunken fans, who usually try to shake his hand or give a high five.

He finally steps into the locker room. For a minute, then another, he says nothing. He paces about the tiny room, still gaining his thoughts. Everyone in the locker room feels the pressure rising and prepares for the storm. And then . . . it doesn't come.

"You know, guys, the only thing I can say is, fuck, let's forget about it," Karl says quietly, looking at the floor. "We were so fucking bad it's . . . it's . . . I . . ." He almost loses it here, struggling to maintain control. He doesn't really know why, and he hasn't planned this, but somehow he feels it's right. He's not going to go crazy. Two years ago, he might have thrown a chair or tipped a table over. And he might have been justified. But Karl is learning a lot about coaching here; that's part of the reason he took the job, to improve his own talents. Sometimes, quiet works better than loud, and he's giving it a try now.

It isn't easy. When talking about keeping composure (Kelvin has gotten into early foul trouble from unnecessary aggressiveness when provoked by the rough-playing Texans, and Askew is simply not in the game, missing layups and foul shots and ignoring the defensive end of the court), he nearly loses his. Talking about what he calls brain-locking—running plays incorrectly, finding themselves out of position—his brain, it is clear to everyone, is seizing up within his head. But still, he is still. "When the game is tough, make it easy. Hustle. Get a layup. Rebound. Cover people. Earn it. Earn the game." Shifting to the bigger picture, he again almost shakes with internal combustion, but keeps from igniting. "I know it's a long year and maybe I should just sit back and say, hey, it's gonna happen once in a while. But for your careers, you can't let it happen. There's two NBA guys here. There's one European scout here. And they're watching, gentlemen. They don't want to see bullshit professionalism. They don't want to see CBA basketball. They want to see someone who can play NBA basketball."

As always, Karl ends on a positive note. His locker-room technique, like his on-court tactics, is systematic and fundamental. Tonight, he has added a touch of subtlety. As everyone files upstairs, and Karl pushes quickly out to find some solitude in the rest room, Moser and Rich Sill and Gerald are left behind.

"He's really a master of knowing this team's mood," says Moser, a fellow coach, with admiration. "I just learned so much from that one talk."

"A lot different than last year, eh, Jack?" says Rich. "Musselman woulda been through the roof."

"I would have been hiding in the corner," Jack says.

"Remember that one time, I walked out in the middle, and thought he was coming after me," Rich remembers. "He threw a bottle at the door, sounded like he was coming through."

" 'Course, the only guy who ever really did damage here was Dave Cowens, when he was coaching in the league," says Jack.

"What'd he do?" Gerald asks.

"Ripped the door out. Bolts, hardware, wood frame, everything. Just ripped it out."

"Yessir, Cowens could do that." Gerald nods. "One time, during a game, he lifted Bill Musselman right off the floor. Right off the floor he lifted him. Yessir, Cowens could do that."

"That was some speech just now, though," Jack Moser says, and walks upstairs.

○   ○   ○

Grissom scores, blocks a shot, rebounds, even dives for a loose ball; his large white body sliding across the floor brings the season's largest crowd—4,327—to its feet. Askew starts making layups off fast breaks. Doug Lee, a mass of energy after missing last night's game, gets his shots to fall (he will finish with 30). Upshaw runs the break. Engelstad hits two free throws with 28 seconds left in the third Q, and Albany has the lead for the first time, 77–76. Wichita comes apart; their coach, Tom Schneeman, gets his second technical and is ejected—escorted out as the accordionist serenades him with "Deep in the Heart of Texas"—and, moments later, Ken Bannister is also ejected. He walks off more slowly. "Shit stinks," he mutters, as the crowd, sensing victory for the first time after a long, quiet, ugly night, boos riotously. From there on, Albany is in possession of its game. With a minute and a half left, and the lead a comfortable 15 points, Karl takes off his tie, his symbol of victory. It ends 115–97. With six standings points added to yesterday's five, Albany now leads the division by 41½ points. It is time to start talking about second and third.

With sickness rampant—Ken Johnson stayed home tonight—Karl gives the team tomorrow off and most of the next day as well. Next practice is Monday night at 6 P.M. Then he sucks down a postgame beer quickly.

Even he is surprised at his halftime performance. "Two years ago, this table would've been in trouble." He smiles. Moser, still impressed, hangs on his words. As coaches, they know just how impressive it has been. Even if the rest of the rowdy room doesn't.

In a battle of southern accents, Gerald is challenging Grissom, who played a stellar game (11 points, 12 rebounds) to keep working, to lift weights, to get in better physical condition. Gerald suggests Grissom cut his beer intake down; Grissom promises to reduce consumption from a case to a six-pack per sitting. Gerald is aghast; Grissom is firm. "Coach, ah'll cut down but ah won't give it up. A six don't hardly give me a buzz."

Then Gary Holle walks in; the championship rings have arrived. They had been presented to Grissom and Rowland in a pregame ceremony. Now the rings, handsome gold with a jade-colored setting holding two diamonds, are being handed out permanently. Keith Smith, leaning on his crutches, grabs Rowland's ring for a look at the diamonds. "That's some real ice 'n' shit," he says, impressed.

Rowland calls over to Grissom: "Has everyone got one?"

"Naw. Bobby Davis, he wasn't here but a couple weeks, he wanted the seven hundred bucks instead."

JANUARY 8–9

Sunday the eighth is, as promised, a day off, and the ninth might as well be. Practice is from 6 to 8 P.M.; unfortunately, so are two high school track meets. Karl tries to run the offense through, to bring Rowland and Engelstad up to speed, but with several hundred fans watching and cheering as their kids run around the Armory floor, it's not easy to stay on top of the mood. In the end, Karl gives up and sends everyone home.

The days off aren't wasted by Gerald, though. He's still organizing the housing and financial situations of various Patroons. He's also catching up on player moves. The Scott Roth deal is on hold; Roth was signed by San Antonio a few days earlier. (In fact it's been a busy week for call-ups; Andre Turner, Mark Davis, and Todd Mitchell are all signed to ten-day contracts.) And the Wes Matthews trade is also snagged, but for some other reasons. While working out the specifics—which has become difficult, in that Wichita Falls, which owns Matthews' rights, is asking for some unusual compensation agreements, like collecting any money the Patroons might get should they sell Matthews later (in addition to the money they would get in selling Matthews to Albany)—Gerald learns that Dirk Minniefield is available. Having coached the University of Kentucky alum at Cleveland and Golden State, Karl likes Minniefield as a guard more than Matthews (despite the fact that Dirk is in a rehab center for substance abuse). So Karl tells Gerald to hold off on Matthews and get Minniefield, which Gerald does today, in a three-way trade with La Crosse and Rapid City. When Minniefield might come in is an unanswered question. But the way players are moving lately, Minniefield gives Karl another card.

JANUARY 10

Greg Grissom begins his day by stuffing his large body into a small seat at the Eagle Restaurant, a greasy spoon across the street from the Armory. He stops here nearly every morning before shootaround. Today he orders a light prepractice breakfast: a stack of pancakes, a couple of fried eggs, a double order of sausage, a pile of home fries, toast, and coffee, and reads about himself in the morning paper. Tim Wilkin is telling of how Gris asked to be traded earlier in the season, when he wasn't playing, until he wrecked his beloved Mercedes in a car accident. Rather than leave his pride and joy behind, he decided to wait it out. And now with Stroeder and Ozell gone, Gris is playing a lot, and playing well. A naturally easygoing, good ol' Texas boy with a goofy smile (he looks eerily like the actor Randy Quaid), his contentment shows, if in nothing more than his robust appetite.

The shootaround is typical. Karl runs a few plays, goes over the opposition, wins $10 (this time from Danny Pearson) by sinking a half-court, back-to-the-basket shot (Karl's favorite trick shot) and following it up with a half-court, one-bounce toss that's all net (his second favorite). Gerald passes out the money, being that it's payday, and Karl gives him a hard time over it, being that it's Gerald. "When you gonna stop baby-sitting these guys, Gerald?" Karl laughs. "I gotta go cash some checks," Gerald answers, and, pulling his wool cap down low over his head, he ambles out, a couple of Patroons in tow.

Back at the office at around 1:30, Gerald has a call. Stu Inman is phoning from Miami. The Heat need a point guard. If you're not taking Kelvin, Gerald tells the Miami GM, you're not taking the best point guard in the CBA. The Heat take Kelvin. Karl has been talking up Upshaw—as well as Johnson and Askew—around The League, and people are listening. Upshaw is to be on the 5:55 flight to Miami.

Karl goes to the hotel to tell him. Their relationship, which was decidedly testy at first, has come to be closer. Kelvin has learned to take Karl's rough-edged methods and live with them. "He just sees me as this bad, street-kid type," Kelvin had said a few weeks earlier. "He don't see the rest of it. That ain't me at all." Karl, for his part, has come to respect Kelvin's play. When he tells people Upshaw is the best down here, he means it. And he has lightened up on Kelvin in return. At the hotel he gives Upshaw some advice. Play defense, be professional, don't lose composure, and no one will say anything bad about you. And he suggests looking at the stat sheets once he gets to Miami. "Find out who's scoring," Karl says, "and get him the ball. A lot."

Kelvin gives Karl a hug.

Now, Albany is without its starting center—an all-star—and its point guard, the quarterback of Karl's offense. And Clint Smith has been diagnosed as having walking pneumonia. Somebody needs to be found, and fast. Bill Heller, the Patroons' public relations director, suggests Lowes Moore.

Moore, perhaps the most popular Patroon ever, retired after last season to coach at a local community college. His last competition was in those exhibition games in early November. But there isn't much time, and there isn't anyone else. And, fortunately, his school is on break. Karl gets him on the phone:

"Lowes, it's George. Wanna go for a run tonight?" Lowes thinks it's a joke. When he realizes it's not, he does what any professional would do. He says he needs a pair of shoes.

○   ○   ○

Before the game, Karl and Oliver sort things out at the press table. George can't really believe it; what was the most disciplined, most NBA-like team in the CBA is quickly turned into a new, unknown club. Three guys are new, they don't know any of the plays. His point guard is a thirty-one-year-old coach who has un-retired for the games tonight and tomorrow, and will then re-retire. He's playing a team—the Topeka Sizzlers—that has lost its last fourteen games and is now on its third coach (Mike Riley, an assistant at Rockford, has replaced Ron McHenry, who replaced Art Ross), but that has a seemingly tough lineup and that scares Karl immensely. "I wish Doug Moe were here," Karl says. "He'd love this."

Gerald calls Moore over during warmups. "Lowes," he bubbles, "are you as happy as I am? If so, sign this here contract, so the league don't fine us fifty bucks."

"They can't fine him fifty bucks," Karl says. "He's not making fifty bucks."

"He's making a hundred a game," says Gerald. "That all right with you, Lowes?"

"Whatever," says Lowes, holding the pen with his left hand, holding a basketball with his right.

"A hundred a game?" Karl says. "That's seven hundred a week. Congratulations, Lowes. You're now our highest-paid player by two hundred dollars a week. That's why you won't be here long."

"Whatever," Lowes says again, and walks off to take some shots.

"What the hell am I gonna do tonight?" Karl shakes his head.

"I gotta get outta this damn financial bidness," Gerald says and flips through his notebook.

○ ○ ○

Karl runs an offense with limited structure; since no one knows the plays, he doesn't call many. His eyes are focused tonight on Steve Shurina. Steve has been playing poorly, thinking too much, turning the ball over, missing shots he must hit. In Karl's mind, this should be Shurina's chance; Kelvin's gone, Lowes won't be able to run the offense, so Shurina's the only point guard left. The job is his for the taking.

He doesn't take it. In 27 minutes of playing time he scores 6 points; Moore, in 18 minutes, scores 8. Shurina simply looks outmatched, perhaps over his head. After the game Karl seems almost hurt; he wants Shurina to succeed. He even whispers to himself when Shurina takes a shot from the corner: "Hit one." And he winces when the shot bounces away. He's given Shurina every chance. Steve was his first surprise, he really thought he could make something out of him. Now it's slipping away, and Karl may have to make a move. Minniefield, Matthews, Upshaw if he comes back . . . Shurina just doesn't seem to have it, and it's a shame.

The game turns out to be as scary as Karl felt it would be. With no structure, none of the things that made Albany so much stronger than the rest of the CBA, the team never gets its rhythm. Kelvin is missed; the Patroons are not quick without him, and the fast break never develops. The game is slow, pedestrian, sloppy, and only a tap-in by Grissom as the clock hits zero (*after* the clock hits zero, according to the Sizzlers, who protest) salvages the game, 107–105.

"It's a win, guys. Thanks," Karl says afterwards. "Shootaround at eleven tomorrow. Lowes, it'd be nice if you can make it."

"Yeah, if you're not teaching or anything," yells Grissom.

"If ah owe any o' you any damn money, come up an' see me after you dress," Gerald yells. "I'm gettin' out of the damn financial bidness."

Gerald sets up shop at the table upstairs. He flips through his notebook, cash and checks bulging out, notes to himself that only he can understand spread in front. He flips to each player's personal sleeve and adds up the accounts. He crosses off Ozell Jones's name and adds Engelstad's. He leaves Upshaw's name for the time being. He proudly shows Karl how everything is working, how his system is under control. He flips to a page marked JOHNSON. "See? Here's Ken Johnson. We're even." He flips to LEE. "See? Here's Doug Lee. We're even." Flip to GRISSOM. "See? Here's Greg Grissom. I owe him forty dollars, which is right here in this note." He flips to a blank page. "See? Here's a player, I don't even know who it is."

JANUARY 11

After the pregame talk, Karl says to Oliver, "Gerald, we're not a very good team," chuckling. "Lowes is one of our best players, and he's only been here a day. And he's leaving."

"I know it, Coach," says Gerald. "I'm gonna get us a point guard tonight. I have a feeling I'm gonna be on that phone a long time tonight. I got you four options, unless you say to forget it."

"I don't say forget it. I just say fuck you."

The four options are Matthews (if the deal works out, which Gerald doubts), Minniefield (if he can be found), plus two new possibilities, Ken Patterson (a free agent) and Dominic Pressley (a recent cut by the Bullets, whose rights Albany owns). Without Clinton Smith and with Moore about to be re-retired, Albany will be down to only eight players. Tonight's game is almost a sidelight. And for some reason it's easy. A lifeless Topeka team takes the floor in a lifeless gym with a lifeless crowd. Albany zips to a 66–40 halftime lead, then coasts home to win 135–114. The only laugh comes when, after losing the third Q, and in danger of losing the fourth (it is tied at 36 with 44 seconds left) a fan yells, "Hey George, we don't give up points here."

"Yes we do," Karl says on the bench.

JANUARY 12

Gerald has been up all night. It's 7 A.M., he's tired, but he's gotta get things done and get the boys on the plane. He doesn't want to hear the bitching. Tony messed up again—he had a spot in line at the ticket counter and then he gave it up—and if he even sees him he'll holler he's so mad. And Ken Johnson is bitching, he don't even know we were on the phone at 11:30 last night trying to get him an NBA job, getting people to look him over. And now he's complaining again, got all that garbage in his head. Gerald doesn't want to hear about it, but he has to, it's his job, and he's gotta be positive. Gotta be positive.

Talking with a player on the plane, he falls asleep in mid-sentence.

○　○　○

"Dad gemit, we're here." Gerald beams happily as the van pulls into the Sheraton Kensington in Tulsa, Oklahoma. "We got us a gymnasium, a 7-Eleven, and cable TV. What more do we need?"

The players need some rest, but Karl calls for practice immediately. The van leaves in forty-five minutes. More complaining ensues.

"Don't worry," Karl says. "it won't be a hard one. It'll just be a cerebral practice."

"What's that, Coach?" Vince Askew asks.

"Cerebral. For your mind."

"Oh, OK. Cereal. OK."

Arriving at the gym, they find no lights, no balls, and no one to get either. To keep the mood light while help can be found, Karl tells stories about gym gamesmanship in the NBA. "Boston never lets visiting teams practice in the Garden. They always have some excuse—the floor isn't down, the ice is still down. One day I went walking past the place when we were supposed to practice and snuck in. The floor was all ready to go. I asked somebody about it and he said, 'Well, it's a tradition that no one practices in the Garden.' Boston's terrible. And another thing, it's amazing, but whenever Boston's in a seventh game situation, somehow the fire alarm always goes off in the visiting team's hotel. At three or four in the morning. For about half an hour."

Still no lights. "Hey guys, who talks the most shit in the CBA?" Nominations are offered: Ken Bannister. Shouse. Andre Patterson, no contest. Steppe.

Lights, but no basketballs. "Everyone get a coin. We'll have a little contest. First guy to pitch his coin from the sideline into the X in the center circle wins a buck from everyone." It takes three rounds, but Doug Lee connects. Then the balls are found. Karl now runs practice.

He does it with a mind full of distractions. He learned at the airport, upon calling in to the office, that the Italian scout wants Vince Askew. On Sunday. He also learns that the L.A. Clippers might be interested in him to take over as an interim coach. What does he tell Vince? It's $40,000, much more if they make the playoffs, plus a sports car and an apartment. But is he ready for Italy?

What does he do himself?

○   ○   ○

After practice, Karl and Oliver call Vince into Karl's hotel room. Gerald is sprawled on the bed, listening. While George explains the situation, his phone rings. He goes to answer it. Gerald is fast asleep, snoring.

Vince shakes him. "Coach Oliver. Coach Oliver . . ."

○   ○   ○

"Levy, find us a satellite dish. I want to watch Upshaw tonight." Dan Levy runs off to make inquiries while Karl nurses a gin and tonic in the hotel bar. Vince wants to go to Europe. Karl doesn't know if it's right for him, but for some reason the NBA isn't taken with Vince. Karl isn't sure why; Vince is playing too well to be ignored, but his name isn't exciting NBA people. Still, Karl refuses to tell Vince what to do. Part of his relationship with Vince has been to help him grow up, make him responsible for his own life. Vince would rather be told what to do; decisions like this come hard to him.

"I can't find a place," Levy says on return.

"Try again," Karl orders. Levy trots off.

Karl doesn't like the idea of interim coach. He's been told that if he does a good job in L.A., they could give him a long-term contract. Of course, if he does a good job, there's no reason he can't get a job elsewhere. But the Clipper job is hardly ideal, a lousy team (that just got lousier, losing star Danny Manning for at least the season with a knee injury) in a tough market with an owner with a difficult reputation. What should Vince do? What should he do?

"OK, I found a place with a satellite, but they say the Miami game isn't on," Levy says.

"Man, Levy, I'm disappointed in you. Here's what you do. Call Ricky's in San Leandro, California. Ask for Ricky. Tell him I sent you. He'll know what the coordinates are. Here's the number." Levy leaves, replaced by Gerald. "Ollie!" Karl screeches, using Gerald's newest nickname.

"Ollie, we're going to watch Uppy. You're coming."

"Coach, I can't, I got—"

"*Ollie!*"

"You know what? I'll tell you what. I will come and watch Uppy play. I'll even have a drink."

Levy runs in. "OK. I got Ricky. Spacenet two, Transponder sixteen."

"Ricky's the greatest!" Karl laughs. "Let's go."

They pass Derrick Rowland in the lobby. "Derrick," Karl says, "didn't I trade you once? I did. I traded your ass from Montana to Rochester in, what, '81? I remember that call."

And then, to the bar, only to find the game is scrambled and unwatchable. Eating and drinking ensue.

JANUARY 13

Dominic Pressley, three suitcases at his side, is waiting at the gym before practice. When the other three options fail to gel, Pressley is called into service. He enters talking. "Here I am reporting for duty. Not here to shake hands and say hello, I'm here to go to work. I'm gonna be the second Albany point guard called up to the NBA. First one got eight points last night. I was at the game. Kelvin played good. I'm next. Where do I change at?"

Pressley, the former Boston College star, was cut by the Bullets last week. He flew in this morning and came right to the gym. A fast talker, assured and confident, he makes an immediate presence.

Gerald is distressed; the Tulsa trainer has been told not to tape the Albany players. This is just the kind of thing Gerald hates about the CBA. People not treating people right, not helping each other. The rule is, if a visiting team doesn't travel with a trainer, the home team has to make one available. The visitors pay for it, that's not the problem. It's trying to get an advantage on a team, and it's not right in Gerald's mind. It's not the right thing to do. Gerald makes a note to talk to the Tulsa general manager.

The shootaround over, the team loads up to return to the hotel. Grissom leads the charge. "Let's go. My soap's on in fifteen minutes."

But it's not to be. Pressley, flipping through his luggage in the van, cries out. "Shit! I left my $350 watch on the table back there. I know right where it is. We gotta go back. Hillbilly Joe gonna be wearin' my shit tonight. I'm sorry, Coach, I'm messin' up already, I know it. We gotta go back."

"There goes 'All My Children.'" Grissom sighs.

"What's the fine, gentlemen?" Karl asks. "Buy us all diet Cokes at the next airport?"

Pressley says, "I can handle that. All right. What's the per diem here anyway? Twenty-two dollars? Man, it's fifty in the NBA. That was nice. Eat well on fifty a day."

○   ○   ○

According to the league grapevine, the Tulsa cheerleaders, the Heartbreakers, are among the best equipped in the CBA ("The Bra-Breakers," as they are called by Tulsa's van driver). As the Patroons file into the Expo Square Pavilion before the game, the Heart-breakers are practicing a routine to "Sweet Georgia Brown." A quick look reveals the scouting report to be accurate. Even tonight's officials are impressed, taking extra time to check the floor markings.

"How do they look?" asks ref one.

"So far, they look all right," says ref two.

"Got your socks and jock?" Gerald asks Dominic. "I'm ready to play," he answers. But Danny Pearson, suffering from a severe charleyhorse, isn't. That means only eight players are in uniform, three of whom weren't here three weeks ago. As a result, the game is over almost immediately. After Albany wins the first quarter by 2, Tulsa dashes off to a 12–0 start in the second. Tulsa's press gives Albany fits—they commit twenty-four turnovers, including three from Pressley in his first 30 seconds of action. ("Nice start," Karl says to Oliver after the third one.) There is little togetherness, no adherence to any system, bad communication, no productivity from the point guards (Shurina nets 18, but adds only 2 assists and five turnovers). It's no surprise that Albany loses by 13, taking only one of seven points.

Karl doesn't know what to do. Coaching, he often says, is giving players the best opportunity for them to win the game. That's how he coaches, giving players the plays that will let their talents shine, creating systems that will work with given individuals. But how can you do that when half your team is brand-new? How do you coach like this?

To add to the confusion, two NBA scouts are in for the game. Gar Heard is in from Dallas, and it seems the Mavs are interested in Askew. That's not news. But Elvin Gentry is in from San Antonio, and Karl gets the impression they are interested in Engelstad. That's news.

After the game, Karl goes to eat with three friends who drove up from Texas, golfing buddies all. They drink beers and talk of the NBA, golf, and old friends. Karl's mind is elsewhere. Back in his hotel room, he takes a vote.

"Should I take the Clippers job?"

One friend votes yes. The second votes no. The third says, "Are you crazy? Benoit Benjamin? You thought Joe Barry Carroll was bad . . ."

Karl rolls over on his bed, covers his head with a pillow, and orders everyone out.

JANUARY 14

It's becoming apparent that winning games is taking on less importance than getting a team together. With Stroeder (who has signed on for another ten days with Golden State), Upshaw, and Keith Smith gone, and Clinton Smith out sick, not only are four starters missing, the others, forced into different roles, aren't performing as well. Doug Lee is an excellent player when his job is just to shoot; now, as one of the better players on the court, he is struggling, running plays wrong, messing up on defense. Karl is all over him lately, and Lee can't seem to un-brain-lock. Shurina is fine off the bench, a smart player, but he hasn't the talents of the lead point guard (he'd rather play shooting guard, anyway). Pressley has the speed Karl likes at the point, but he doesn't know the plays and may be too out of control for Karl's system. Ken Johnson has become a distraction, complaining about nearly everything, challenging the coaches, blaming other players in games. Vince is playing well, but now his mind is filled; he simply can't decide what to do. With no family to talk to, he relies on Karl and Johnson (his mentor on the team) for advice. He is leaning toward Europe, and the money, though he doesn't really know where Europe is. (He tells another *Times Union* reporter, Keith Marder, he wants to go to Italy and "see other parts of the country.")

Karl is still confused. Not enough players for a decent practice (Dan Levy runs drills and occasionally helps in a scrimmage); the NBA job a possibility; the CBA Blues setting in.

In Albany, Bill Heller is angry too. He was never told that Dominic Pressley had joined the team. In fact, no one in the front office was told, but only Heller got mad about it. He heard it on the radio.

○ ○ ○

Picture this: A statewide cheerleading contest is winding down as the Patroons enter the arena. Several hundred girls, as young as five or six and as old as the Heartbreakers (mid-twenties), in all manner of hormonal distress, all packaged in spandex and glitter and pom-pons, are spread about the pavilion seats and on the basketball floor.

There is much shrieking as winners are announced, the kind of shrieking only teenage girls can effect. There is much enthusiasm, much perkiness, much teased blond hair, much leaping and bouncing about, much ... cheerleader-ness. Into this mass walks Greg Grissom, 6' 11", in uniform, striding through a mass of young girls like Gulliver among the Lilliputians, his head and chest well above the level of the highest ponytail, checking it all out, eating a candy bar. It is, perhaps, the CBA at its finest.

The game itself is the same as the last one. The only difference is that tiny Eric Newsome, who was not a factor last night, is a big one tonight. "The Little Shit" (as in, "someone cover the Little Shit, fer chrissakes") knocks down five of ten three-pointers. Pressley and Shurina continue to turn it over, and plays continue to be run incorrectly. Albany manages to pull within 3 points at the end of three quarters, but the fourth is no contest. It ends 116–106 against, with only one standings point to show for the effort.

The game was there for the taking, in Karl's mind. He just can't get them to take it. He still can't figure out why. Worse, the bitching is getting worse. In the locker room he gives a typical win-as-a-team, lose-as-a-team speech. "Stay above the CBA bullshit. Have some character. Believe in one another. Don't point fingers at one another."

After, Gerald and Karl confer. "The question is," Gerald says, "can we improve these players? If not, we got to get more players."

JANUARY 15

The van sits outside the hotel door at 9:44. Karl, in his usual position in the front seat next to the driver, looks at his watch. "They have thirty seconds." "I'll go get them," Gerald says. "No," Karl answers. Thirty seconds pass. "Let's go," Karl tells the driver. The van leaves at 9:45, just as everyone knew it would. Ken Johnson and Vince Askew aren't in it. Karl isn't waiting.

With only seven players at practice, Karl runs a few plays, then settles on three-on-three and one-on-one games. Karl is good at mixing up practices, making them fun and relieving the monotony. (Yesterday he offered five dollars for any half-court basket), and today he has each player coach an offensive series to see if they know the patterns. With everyone tired, the workout is more mental than physical, which seems fine to those in attendance.

Gerald is upbeat. He says he is happier now than he has been in a long time, that he loves coaching here, loves working with and learning from George, even if he's got to take care of all the businesses he's in. He's also concerned. He doesn't know what George will do about Johnson. (Vince is a different problem.) Gerald is thinking philosophically again, as he has been doing a lot this trip. Do leopards change their spots? How can he communicate with Ken that Ken is blowing his chances? How does he relate this to Ken? The season, he says, has entered a critical point. "There's no growth without crisis," he says. Then he smiles. "I am so happy here. So happy to be here with George. I've learned so much of what I wanted to learn."

Across the gym, a side door is open to the outside. Tulsa is covered in fog today, and looking across the brightly lit basketball floor, with sharp, crisp images of colored practice jerseys and basketballs and young men in motion, through that door and out to the misty, gray, enshrouded, unclear fairgrounds is like looking through a window into another, more mysterious world. Gerald looks through that window and says, "Don't think I'm crazy for askin' this, but have you ever thought about how you're going to die?"

○   ○   ○

After practice Gerald visits George in George's room. George tells Gerald to trade Ken Johnson.

JANUARY 16

Vince Askew says some quick good-byes, gets and gives some phone numbers, hears a few "Good luck in Italy"s, and boards the private car to the airport. The team thinks he's going to Bologna. He thinks he's going to Dallas. Karl had talked to Vince at breakfast, telling him that Dallas might take him for a ten-day tryout. Vince says he'll stay if it's for the year. "I won't stay for no ten-day," he says in the car to the airport. "I need the dough. If something happens over the summer, I don't want to regret not going." Right now he's headed to Albany, to await Dallas's decision, and make a final one of his own.

The rest of the team vans to the airport for the morning flight to Kansas City, and then the bus to Topeka. Karl is in a foul humor. He and Gerald are talking over the Matthews deal; the two clubs are now haggling over the schedule of payments, which Karl had thought was a closed matter.

"You don't change a deal in the middle," Karl snaps angrily.

"You do in the CBA, Coach," Gerald tells him.

"Well, you don't in the NBA—you don't with me," Karl says, and walks away.

Karl is in no mood for CBA bullshit. Gerald had told him earlier that if Vince went to Italy, he couldn't be replaced on the roster for ten days. When a player is called up to the NBA, he is placed on the league's NBA Suspended list and replaced immediately. However, the same is not true for European contracts. Vince must either be waived (in which case his rights are gone forever) or suspended for ten days (so that his rights are still held). "It's a great league that punishes teams for helping its players become successful and make money," Karl said sarcastically when he learned of the rule. "More Druckerisms, I'm sure." Further, the deadline for placing Vince on the correct list comes before Dallas will make its final decision; if Vince goes to Dallas and isn't on the NBA Suspended list, Albany will have to forfeit the $1,000 a CBA team gets whenever a player is called up.

One forty-five-minute flight, fifty minutes of video games, and a one-hour bus ride later, the Patroons are in Topeka, Kansas. Doug Lee tapes his own ankle in the hotel, and it's off to practice. With Vince gone, the team is back to eight players. Dan Levy, the only 5′ 6″ Jewish radio announcer/point guard in professional basketball, runs hard in practice. The energy level is surprisingly high, but Karl is not his usual self. His sarcasm is more biting, his joking less funny.

On the bus back to the hotel, Gerald and Danny Pearson get into a screaming argument. Pearson is owed money for a plane ticket he bought. He wants reimbursement. Gerald, who is overtired, in poor health, and looks like he needs a vacation (despite his professed happiness), is talking in tongues. He shouts Danny down. Pearson, normally quiet, shouts back for a few minutes, then, realizing it's not getting anywhere, tries to end it.

"Let's leave it, Coach," Pearson shouts. "Let's leave it."

Other players chirp in. "Game over, Coach O." "That's all, Coach."

Gerald goes on, his voice booming through the bus. The tension is high; Gerald's theatrics are often funny, usually amusing in their eccentricity, but today they are just annoying.

And when the bus pulls over at a video store for Gerald to rent a VCR, Karl, who has been sitting silently in the front, staring at the floor, asks the driver to open the door. He gets off the bus and walks down the street to the hotel, two miles away, alone.

The bus pulls out and passes him on the way. Engelstad spots him and starts to sing: "He's got the CBA Blues . . ."

○ ○ ○

Back in Albany, Vince Askew has changed his mind. He phones Karl and tells him, "I been poor before. I can be poor a little longer." Even though Dallas has decided not to sign him, he chooses to play in the CBA a little longer. His confusion is obvious, and painful to watch. It seems that whoever has Vince's ear last, wins. He tells Tim Wilkin, "I talked to some guy in Italy, and I couldn't understand a word he said. I ain't going."

For Karl it's a small piece of good news. Vince's growth as a person has been a personal challenge of Karl's. It's one of the reasons he coaches and likes coaching. In the same way Karl feels he made a difference in Kelvin's life, Vince's progress over the past two months has been tremendously satisfying. To see Vince make this decision, however belatedly, is pleasing, and Karl is ready for a beer or two.

His mood is enhanced in the hotel lobby when a cab pulls up from the airport, carrying Dirk Minniefield. Karl steps through the door and gives Minniefield a hug around the neck.

JANUARY 17

Before practice. Karl calls Shurina aside. "Shurina's an Italian name, right?"

"No. It's Slavic," Shurina answers.

"I think you're wrong," Karl says. "It's Italian."

"What are you talking about? It's not Italian."

"It is now." The Italian league is looking for a guard, and Karl says they are interested in Shurina.

After practice. "I need a cut, man."

"Tough to get a good haircut. Brother got B.G."

"Got the B.G. real bad, man, that's the truth."

"What the hell is B.G.?" Karl asks, overhearing the conversation among various Patroons and Sizzlers as morning shootaround ends.

"B.G., man. The Bad Grain. Brothers all got the Bad Grain, can't get a good cut. Big Daddy Ken got V.B.G. Very Bad Grain. Ain't that right, Big Daddy."

"Bad as a mo-fo, tramp."

"B.G." Karl laughs. "That's a new one."

Karl is in a better mood. He has a real affection for Minniefield, whom he coached in Cleveland and Golden State. Minny is the type of point guard Karl likes. Not only does he have NBA talent (he last played with the Celtics in the 1988 playoffs) he also has the energy and life the team needs right now. Minniefield is short (about 6' 2"), slim, with a high forehead, a missing front tooth, and a spark in his eye. Yet he looks much older than his twenty-eight years. His face shows troubles, his eyes reveal pain. After seventy days at the ASAP rehab center in California, Minniefield is both profoundly happy to be playing ball again and continually aware of how he came to be here.

He and Karl seem like old friends reacquainted. In the shootaround and before the game, Karl goes over the plays, which are similar to the ones he ran in the NBA. "That was Joe Barry's play, right?" Minniefield asks. "I got it." "You do it right, though," Karl says. "Joe Barry always hit the decoy instead of the shooter." Minniefield laughs.

At the press table before the game, Gerald calls Dirk over. "Got your jocks and socks, Dirk? Great. Now sign this contract and we're in bidness."

"What if I'm an illegal alien?" he says, and signs.

"Coach," Gerald says, "I'll tell you what, I am organized. I am more organized than I ever been. Me and Danny are square, aren't we, Danny?" He flashes Pearson a thumbs-up; Pearson, on the court, flashes one back and giggles. "I am gettin' out of all these bidnesses I am in. I am fired up. This game is gonna be a war." He takes a bottle out of a plastic bag and shines his shoes.

"Hey Minny," Karl yells, "you know the white line in this league is the three-point line."

"Don't know nothin' 'bout lines, George. Just know if I'm behind the furthest one, it counts as three." To prove it, he cans a jumper from about twenty-five feet.

"Ollie, what are you doing with your shoes?"

○   ○   ○

Three NBA scouts—from Denver, San Antonio, and Indiana—push the crowd into the low three figures. Though Topeka is playing better under its new coach and new players, it is still by far the worst in the league. With an empty gym and a lifeless team, Albany is in a good position to end the losing streak. Even though Askew can't make the necessary connections to play tonight, the Patroons should have enough to win.

They are blown out in the first Q 33–17. But when Minniefield enters the game early in the second, he sparks a comeback. "Pressure don't mean nothing to him," Gerald says on the bench. "He's the leadership we need." Minniefield pushes the break, makes the passes (mostly to Doug Lee, who has the hot hand tonight), and at the half Albany has tied the game at 59.

Earlier in the season, this is the kind of game Albany would have run away with. Not now. The same problems—turnovers, poor execution, lax defense, cold shooting (except for Lee, who finishes with 37)—continue, despite Minniefield's efforts. Topeka takes the third Q by 3, and then builds the lead to 12. The Patroons do fight back—lack of effort has not been a problem—and cut the lead back down to 3, but they can get no closer. The final is 121–114, and for the third straight game Albany notches only one standings point. Their lead is still a healthy forty points—the Eastern Division is clearly the weaker of the two—but Karl is interested in championships, not division titles. While the lead gives him the luxury of a few losses, he knows he hasn't got a championship team right now.

The locker room is silent. Karl's postgame talk is calm but concerned, his brow heavily creased, his eyes tired. He can't be angry with the team's effort—they are trying, he knows that. What he doesn't know is why the brains are locking, why the things that worked a month ago aren't working now. Why his players just aren't that good. After the talk, he and Gerald disappear into an empty room to confer. The players dress quietly, congregate in the lobby amid the jubilant Topeka players and staff, and plan a night out.

Several Patroons players, short-tempered and foul-humored, are off to a local club. There one learns about dreams in the CBA.

A Topeka cheerleader named Becky, a rail-thin blonde bursting with squeals of energy and lust in her eyes, dreams of furthering her career as a Los Angeles Laker cheerleader in the future. For now, loving a Sizzler will suffice.

A waitress named Wendy, nineteen, unwed, mother of one, anorexic, with stringy blond hair and crooked teeth, dreams of joining the Air Force, which she will do in two weeks.

A Sizzler front office worker named Jill, pretty, heavyset, lively smile, dreams only of a fun time in a near-empty bar on a Tuesday night in Topeka.

A Sizzler player named Mike Davis, little used by Topeka despite his abundant defensive ability, dreams of playing in Albany for George Karl, and getting a European contract and some real money to support his wife and two kids back home in Alabama.

The Patroons players dream of ending this losing streak, of surviving the CBA Blues, of temporarily curing a lousy mood with the pleasures of the flesh.

JANUARY 18

Up at 5 A.M. for the bus to Kansas City, and the flight to Pensacola. Change flights in Atlanta, where Vince Askew rejoins the team.

"So, Vince, what you been doing with yourself the last, oh, forty-eight hours?" Steve Shurina jokes.

"Eating," Vince answers.

"So, this plane stops in Pensacola and then goes straight to Italy, or what?" Shurina says. Vince laughs.

Karl again calls for practice immediately on arrival in Pensacola. "I won't kill 'em today," he tells Gerald. "I feel a little sorry for them." Nevertheless, he still gets a good run going.

In the back of the van, Minniefield tells Vince about rehab. He talks calmly but directly at Vince, making eye contact, speaking with no remorse and little emotion in a deep, husky voice. "We had to meet every day, just for an hour."

"Just one hour? For real?"

"That's all. Just talk like we're talkin' now, about being responsible for yourself, about knowing why you get high an' why you don't need to get high. You know what I'm sayin'? Some guys don't know that they don't need to get high, you seen it, right? You seen it in the ghetto, guys be thinkin' they don't get a right deal, see other guys in The League they know they're better than, but they can't get up, so they get high all the time. You seen it in the ghetto, right? We'd talk 'bout gettin' through each day, not gettin' high, just bein' responsible for you own self. Basketball's just one thing in life. It's not life."

"For real? One hour is all?"

A quiet night at the hotel. Some laundry is done, a lot of Ms. Pac-Man is played. Dominic Pressley destroys Dan Levy to take over the team crown; "I've never lost," he says as he is setting a new record. Levy, ever competitive, promises to get him next time and pumps some games out by himself. Everyone orders dinner and falls out.

Gerald orders the hotel special Dinner for 2, $14.95, all for himself. "I can't decide between soup and salad, so I'll get both." Two slabs of prime rib, soup and salad, rice and potato, two vegetables, and two ice creams later, he is satisfied. "Now, I'm gonna go do some work. Got to get organized."

JANUARY 19

The talk in the van turns to last night's dirty movie on cable. "Nekkid movies," Vince calls them. Dominic Pressley shakes his head.

"Man, some of these guys scare me. One week on the road, they all be losin' their cool. So horny they balls swell up like *this.*

Can't handle it. Stiff wind comes up they gotta pour cold water all over themselves. I don't even want to shake hands with these guys. Man."

Engelstad has a sprained foot; X-rays are negative, but the doctor tells him to sit out today's practice. With little to do, Engelstad, who possesses a dry, sardonic, laid-back California humor, gets on Gerald. Gerald is full of fire today. He's cashing checks for players, setting up practice time, renting a VCR, "solving problems."

"Coach O, why don't you get out of the business already," Engelstad says. "You been sayin' you're getting out of the business for three weeks, now."

"I am getting out of the bidness very soon."

"Without the business, though, what would you be here for?"

"You keep giving me a hard time, you'll see what I kin do," Gerald shouts. "You'll see. I don't mind bein' the 'ee' some of the time, but I don't have to be the 'ee' all of the time."

Engelstad and Karl pass puzzled looks. "What the hell is the 'ee,' Ollie?"

"The fuck-ee. I am the fuck-ee, but I don't always have to be the fuck-ee. I can be the fuck-er. You all keep on ol' Coach O, you'll see how he can be the fuck-er, and not the fuck-ee."

"Dan Levy, you're playing," Karl yells. "Anyone lets Levy score, we run five suicides."

Karl runs a tough practice. When brain-lock sets in, he gets them running suicides anyway. They line up on the base line and sprint to the near foul line, back to the base line, to center court and back, to the far foul line and back, and to the far base line and back. A few of those "to wake you fuckers up," and then some serious scrimmaging. Levy holds his own and even scares everyone by getting open for a couple of J's—he misses both—though he does take a hard fall on a fast break. ("Jewish guy slips in practice. There's gonna be lawsuits," he says, and races upcourt.)

After two hours, Karl ends it. "Hey Minny, I don't know who was better, you or Levy."

"Oh, George, that's cold-blooded. I'm gonna remember that. Very cold-blooded."

"Gentlemen," Gerald yells, "I need to talk to y'all. Two minutes. I am gettin' out of the bidness."

"Aw Coach, you been sayin' that for two months," Grissom moans. "Let's go. 'One Life to Live' is waiting. And it's Friday. Shit happens on Friday."

"Gentlemen, you want your uniforms washed, get them to Doug Lee in room 284 in ten minutes after we get back to the hotel. Ten minutes. Not half an hour. Not an hour. Ten minutes. Those that got bidness with me come see me right after, in room 290. Right after. That's 284 for uniforms washed, 290 to see me. I am out of the bidness."

"We got it, Coach. Let's go."

○   ○   ○

"Time to strap on the beer goggles," Engelstad announces. That night, in serious pursuit of happiness, the taverns of Pensacola are toured. As usual, the team splits into two groups. There is no racial disharmony here—nearly everyone gets along just fine with everyone else—but there are cultural differences. The blacks and the whites enjoy different music, different atmosphere, different style. So tonight, as with almost every night, the blacks go in search of one kind of fun, the whites another. Except Doug Lee; his parents are here for the week to watch him play yet again, and he spends the night with his family, which is his most comfortable version of fun anyway.

JANUARY 20

A call to the hotel front desk, around 9 A.M. "Hello, this is Sandy, can I help you?"

"Yes, can you tell me if the basketball team left for practice yet?"

"One left, by himself."

"One? Which one?"

"Askew. He checked out. Around eight thirty. He said he was going to Baloney, Italy. I guess he meant Bologna."

"No one else was with him, Sandy?"

"His roommate, Mr. Johnson."

"Not the coaches?"

"No. Just Mr. Askew and Mr. Johnson."

"Thanks, Sandy."
"Is he in trouble?"

○ ○ ○

Gerald sits on the couch in the lobby at 11:00, waiting for the van to shootaround, when he is told.
"So, you lost another one?"
"What do you mean?" Gerald asks.
"Vince checked out this morning. Didn't you know?"
Gerald smiles a weak smile. "I hope he left his uniform." He lets it sink in a moment. "If that's true, then I better tell George. I hope that's not true." He gets up to call Karl.
Vince has changed his mind once more, and gone to Italy. He hasn't told anyone on the team, other than Johnson.
He has simply left.

○ ○ ○

It is cold and raining in Pensacola, and no one is in a good mood now. Karl is terribly disappointed in Vince's move. He had heard last night, in talking to various NBA friends, that the word was already out that Vince was going to go to Italy. According to Johnson, the Italians upped the offer. "It was strictly a financial decision," Kenny tells Wilkin by phone, "he really did want to play in Albany, but this offer, I guess he really couldn't pass up." But Karl never expected Vince to leave like this, without talking to him. Vince had made such progress....
At practice Karl turns everything over to Gerald and climbs the empty arena to the top row, where he sits alone in the dark. The players wonder what happened, and whether Vince has just blown his last chance at the NBA. First the Kansas thing, and now this; his talent now may never overcome his reputation.
The calls have been coming in from the Albany media, but Gerald and George don't want to talk about it. "He's gone, and I'm thinking about the game tonight," Gerald says with a forced smile. That may be true, but it's also hard to believe. On a cool, rainy day at the end of a long, draining road trip, the CBA Blues are raging.

○ ○ ○

"Just relax, play fast, have fun, let's win the fucking ball game," Karl says before the game. By the half, they are down 11.

"What do I tell them now?" Karl asks Oliver in the hallway outside the locker room.

"Same things you been tellin' 'em."

They walk in. "Gentlemen," Karl begins slowly. "Right now, the pieces of the puzzle just aren't fitting. We get some rebounding, some offense, some passing, but it's not together. We're not making things easy for ourselves, not finding the open man, not making each other better. We get too many easy basketball opportunities that become turnovers and a layup at our end.

"The effort is there, I know that. I don't know how to give you confidence, to relax you. You have to make the easy play. Maybe your shot is good, but the better shot is over there. Find that shot. Then you're better. Then the team is better. Something about chemistry. Something about character. You start to win games. There's not much heart here right now, not much brains, not much team. Whether it's CBA Blues, call-ups, I don't know, but you're all hanging your heads. Get your heads up. Play with pride. You were really good two weeks ago. Remember?

"Now go out and kick some ass."

"You said it all, Coach," Gerald says after they leave. "You said what needed to be said."

"I'm so confused. I have no idea how to coach these guys. They were really good two weeks ago."

Gerald generates the energy. "Forty-eight minutes! We need forty-eight minutes!" "He shoots long! Get the rebound, he shoots long!" Karl runs some new plays. Slowly, the Pensacola lead, which reaches 15, is chipped away. After three, Albany is down by 5.

"We got 'em by 6 that quarter!" Gerald yells. "We get 'em by 6 this quarter, we win! Right, Coach?" They get 'em by 10. Rowland keys the fourth quarter drive, with steals, rebounds, and key buckets (he nets 31, including back-to-back layup and slam dunk) to give the Pats their first lead in days. The fight continues to the end. With the lead at 4, and 10 seconds left, the irrepressible Brook Steppe throws up his eighth three-pointer of the night. He's already made five, but this one comes up short; Pearson grabs the rebound and is fouled, and the victory is won. Karl removes his tie and shakes hands with every player on the bench. Then he turns his back to Gerald.

"Hey, Coach, fuck you!" Gerald laughs. "What about me? Fuck me? Fuck you!" George smiles and grabs Gerald's meaty paw. Both break into wide grins. "I got him good, didn't I," Gerald yelps. "I surely did get him good."

It is amazing what a win can do for morale. The previous week has been forgotten, at least temporarily. The Domino's pizzas supplied by the Tornados are devoured. "Hey guys, one slice," Gerald yells. "One slice, not two. Somebody takes two, somebody else don't get one. One slice."

Karl looks over the happy scene and shrugs. "When we win I have no idea why we win. When we lose I have no idea why we lose. I'm totally confused." He smiles and drains a beer.

JANUARY 21

Life on the road, CBA-style, in four acts.

ACT I   "I think it's Coach Karl's sheer will and determination that makes them a good team," goes the quote in the morning paper from Brook Steppe. And as the Tornados hand the court over for morning shooting, he hears about it.

"Hey Brook," Minniefield starts, "why you breezin' George like that?"

"Hey Brook," says Engelstad, "Coach has five dollars for you."

"Hey Brook," says Grissom, "you wanna get out of Pensacola? I guess we know where you wanna play."

"Man," says Steppe, "I shoulda known better. Next time I don't say nothing."

○   ○   ○

ACT II   Doc Nunnally, the Pensacola Tornados' young trainer, says he's quitting today. Doc is known throughout the CBA. This is his second year here—he's just out of school, and last year he worked in Savannah when they had a franchise—and he's one of the friendliest, most helpful, most pleasant fixtures on the circuit. A diminutive young man, just a few inches over five feet tall, with fair hair and the rumor of a mustache, Doc speaks from experience when he calls the CBA the Crazy Basketball Association. And for his lousy $150 a week, he doesn't need the abuse anymore. He's been having problems with the front office here, and he's had enough. "I'm only two years out of school, so it's not the money," he says in a soft southern voice. "I'm livin' at home anyway, so the money don't matter. I'm doin' it for experience. But it ain't experience if you're not happy. I already talked to Gerald, I'd love to come work in Albany. I'm gonna talk to George later, he said he'd talk to people up there. Though I know they don't want to pay for a trainer. If not, I may go work at Georgia Tech for Bobby Cremins. I hear the Atlanta Braves are looking for someone too. It don't really matter. I'm quittin' today, at one o'clock. I'm goin' home."

At gametime, Doc is still working, taping ankles, bagging ice, fetching sodas. He says he's leaving tonight instead.

○   ○   ○

ACT III   "Hey Dan Levy, where'd you go to lunch?"

"Place called Maguire's. Great place. Ever hear of it, Dominic?"

"What, is it some kind of famous place or what?"

"Somewhat famous. They have Irish folk music at night."

"Oh, yeah, Irish folk music, well, I guess that explains why it ain't too well known to the Brothers."

○   ○   ○

ACT IV   A certain member of the Patroons entourage has had no luck with women. Not on any road trip, and not on this trip. He has taken a good deal of abuse; his plight is public knowledge, and mercy is not a sportsman's most useful quality. Today, though, is his day. Or so he claims. Having met the girl of his dreams the night before, he has set up a rendezvous this after. There is no doubt in his mind but that love will find a way.

His roommate, Steve Shurina, has doubts. Shurina, a criminal justice major at St. John's, graciously leaves the accused (he shall remain nameless, to protect the embarrassed) the room key, then puts his considerable sleuthing skills to work. Upon returning from practice, he finds the room empty; the alleged lover is not back from his lunch date. Shurina grabs a bite of his own at the hotel restaurant, then returns.

Peering under the door, he counts four feet—two in men's shoes, two in women's. Perhaps he is wrong, Det. Shurina thinks, perhaps the accused will succeed, and he wanders off to play Ms. Pac-Man.

An appropriate amount of time passes. Shurina calls the room. He notes the time: 4:37. The accused, in sleepy voice, says he will be right down, as soon as he says farewell to his paramour. Shurina hangs up and plants himself on the couch by the front door. Again he notes the time: 4:38. The stakeout begins.

At 4:42 Shurina walks over to the Ms. Pac-Man game, and finds the suspect hard at play. Shurina notes the score: 30,000 points.

Shurina interrogates the accused. "So, did you say good-bye?"

"Yes, I just walked her out the front door."

"*That* front door?" Shurina asks, pointing to the stakeout site.

"Yes, that door."

"You walked her out *that front door*?" Shurina asks again.

"Yes. That door."

"I've been sitting by that door for five minutes and I never saw you."

"Oh, uh. . . . I meant the side door over there. That door."

The interrogation ends. Shurina visits the scene of the alleged crime. He checks the bed. Messy. But dry. He sniffs the pillow. No perfumy residue. He sniffs the air. No musky afterscent. He checks for the leftovers of love. No empty boxes. No torn foil. Toilet unflushed, but no sheathlike evidence in favor of the accused.

Later that night, at the game, Det. Shurina, now disguised in the uniform of Steve Shurina, Albany Patroon, sits at the press table. Putting pen to press notes, he writes his final report:

FACTS

4:37 Called accused

4:38 In lobby

4:42 Accused at 30,000 pts. in Ms. Pac-Man

　　　Perjured himself during interrogation (see interrogator)

IN ROOM

　　　Bed messy

　　　No signs of rubber use

　　　**No wet spot!*

CONCLUSION

It would take much longer than 5 min. for accused and his friend to dress, go to her car and get 30,000 pts. in Pac-Man. That, along with the perjury, the lack of a wet spot points to the logical conclusion that the accused did not get *laid!*

Det./Patroon Shurina presents the report to Judge Karl. He reads it and renders his verdict toward the accused, standing nearby.

"There is no fuckin' *way* you got laid! No way!" Karl howls, since it is he who has given the accused the most grief over his failures. Shurina, satisfied in a job well done, goes off to get his ankle taped. The accused, protesting mightily, cries out for justice. Karl dismisses the case. "No fucking *way!*"

○ ○ ○

Shurina continues his fine work on the court. Playing his best game this year in place of Minniefield (who has an injured ankle and plays only a few minutes), Shurina exhibits his best qualities: heady play, crisp passes, fearless drives to the rim. He has 11 points in the first half, and Albany takes both quarters and leads 62–54. Things seem to have turned, both for Shurina (who only a few days ago was in danger of being released) and the rest of the team. Gerald asks, "Is this the same team that played Tulsa?"

Steppe comes over to Karl as the teams warm up to begin the second half and says, "You teach your guys to play dirty. You're a dirty coach. That's what I'm gonna put in the paper tomorrow."

But then, within moments, it is the team that played Tulsa once again. Pensacola scores the first 16 points of the third quarter, and Albany loses 112–105. And all the good cheer has washed away. Karl is angry in the locker room. "That third quarter was a character test, gentlemen, like we talked about at the half. Well, we flunked that test. We flunked it big time."

Sitting outside the locker room a few minutes later, sipping a beer, he suddenly hears screams from within. Gerald and Ken Johnson are having at it. It's about Vince's phone bill, which he left without paying. Ken Johnson, Askew's roommate, used his credit card to charge their room's phone charges (the team pays only the player's room rate; all incidentals, like phone calls, meals, and mov ies, are paid by the player). Johnson thinks the team should pay Vince's part of the bill. Once again, Gerald isn't making himself clear, shouting at Ken to be a man, and Johnson isn't helping. "I can't pay *my* bills, Gerald! Support my family on this CBA shit? You're fuckin' crazy, Gerald!" It quickly gets ugly. Karl lets it play itself out, then steps in. He calms Gerald down, explains how they can take care of the problem, and tells Gerald this might not have been the best time to bring it up.

On the other hand, it might be the perfect capper to twelve long, sad, frustrating days of CBA Blues.

JANUARY 22

Back to Albany. It's Super Bowl Sunday. Karl, Oliver, Shurina, and Grissom watch the game together at a Knights of Columbus hall. That is, three of them watch.

Gerald lies down under a table and falls asleep.

JANUARY 23

Bill Heller, the typically high-strung part-time publicity direc-tor, is more tightly wound than usual. "Closed practice!" he says to Tim Wilkin. "Unless Gerald says you can go in, closed practice!"

The cause of Heller's concern: The nine Albany Patroons are now twelve. Clint Smith, fifteen pounds lighter but fully recovered, is in the Armory for practice. So is John Stroeder. His twenty days at Golden State are over, and he stands ready, in jeans and work shirt, along the sidelines. The twelfth, and the biggest problem from Heller's standpoint, is Greg Ballard. No one can know that Ballard, the long-time NBA veteran just returned from Italy to work with Karl, his friend and former coach, is here. Tim Wilkin asks Karl what Ballard will do here.

"Ballard's not here. You don't see him," Karl answers.

"Where isn't he staying?" asks Keith Marder, another reporter.

"If he were here, then, what would I say about him? Player? Coach?" Wilkin asks.

"Wait till tomorrow, when I know the technicalities of the league, whether I can have a voluntary assistant coach," Karl says.

Roster decisions are being made once again. With Vince unreplaceable for ten days, the Patroons will be allowed only nine players tomorrow night against Rapid City. Stroeder can be kept inactive for five days without losing his rights; he may be picked up again anyway, by someone else in the NBA. Clint Smith could come off the injured list. Engelstad and/or Minniefield could go on it. Ballard . . . well, he's not here yet, so there's no decision.

One move is made, though. Charley Rosen, desperate for a point guard, calls from Rockford asking about Dominic Pressley. With Minniefield in and Shurina playing better, Pressley is excess. It is done quickly; Pressley is off to Rockford, for a draft choice and $2,000. After joining the club in Tulsa, he spends one night in Albany and is gone, never to bounce a ball in the Armory as a Patroon.

JANUARY 24

And now Minniefield is out. He had twisted his knee in practice a few days earlier and what was thought to be a sore left knee is, on doctor's examination, torn cartilage. For the coach who needs his point guard most, Karl is down to the one he now likes least. "What the hell am I gonna do tonight?" he asks out loud with a laugh, looking at his lineup before the game. "Do you realize how many times the look of this team has changed in the last two weeks? How the hell do I coach this?"

Minniefield is placed on the injured list, Clint Smith is taken off it, and John Stroeder is activated. "I might play all big guys tonight," Karl says.

The game tonight features the two best teams in the league. Albany is now at 22–10 (and still forty points up on the rest of the division). Rapid City, at 21–8, is only 1½ points ahead of Rockford. But the game itself is almost a subplot; Rapid City means the Musselmans, man and boy, are in town. The feud between Karl and Eric Musselman has cooled, but Karl is tired of the never-ending comparisons to Bill's team of the previous year. And Bill is flying in to watch the game tonight.

The Rapid City club, like the Musselmans themselves, are a cocky bunch; they sport RAPID CITY VICTORY TOUR T-shirts, with a map of the country pinpointing all their stops on the circuit. The elder Musselman walks into the arena and receives a hero's welcome. Minniefield, in street clothes, looks him over and shakes his head. "Look at him. Thinks he's a god or something. I heard some weird shit 'bout him, man. They won't put up with that shit in the pros. Be real interesting next year."

The talk around the league is that Musselman, not Musselboy, is calling the shots. Tim Wilkin quotes one CBA coach as saying, "They tell the players if they play for Rapid City, they'll get a chance to play for Bill in Minnesota next year." And when the elder Musselman takes a seat by the Rapid City bench and begins telling coach Flip Saunders what to do, the connection becomes clear.

As if the Patroons needed any extra incentive tonight, more comes. Some of the Thrillers players tell some of the Patroons that they have been offered a $50 bonus if they win tonight. That practice is wholly against the rules, but everyone knows that it's happened before, so no one doubts its truth.

It's a game Albany wants badly. And things look good in the first half. Shurina, playing the entire 24 minutes, runs with renewed confidence, performing as well as he has all year. Minniefield, sitting right behind him, offers endless encouragement, patting him repeatedly during time-outs, giving advice, playing cheerleader: "You're doin' it, man. You're doin' all right." And Stroeder, barking like a drill sergeant, seems at home even though he doesn't play much in the half. The game plan is sound, the defense is all hustle, and the half-time lead is 10, 60–50.

But the quick pace takes its toll. Shurina, unused to this amount of playing time, tires and cramps up, making him less effective. The defense breaks down as it did on the road, turnovers return to haunt, and Rapid City's Milt Wagner eats up Doug Lee (Wagner scores 12 in the fourth to finish with 37). The fourth period is as hot, angry, and closely contested as any period this season. Bucket for bucket the teams trade the lead, the benches and the building energized, the air electric. Stroeder and Shurina score big baskets, to be answered by Wagner and Clint Wheeler. For 6 minutes the score is essentially tied; it's 98–98 with 5:35 left. Then Shurina drives to the basket, but his shot won't fall; Lee suffers the same fate, Wagner hits two baskets, and it's 102–98. Lee and Wagner trade jumpers as the action swings from end to end, then Lee hits again. Another thriller bucket, and it's 108–102. Shurina nails a three-pointer from the corner; the lead is 3. Only a minute left. A Wagner free throw, and it's 4 again. Karl calls time-out and draws the play, which Albany executes to perfection—Engelstad takes the ball on the right side and drives to the basket for the layup. It's 109–107. Free throws make it 111–108, then 112–108. Eighteen seconds left. Karl draws another play and Lee works himself inside for a short jumper—112–110. Wagner makes another free throw. A 3-point lead for Rapid City. Karl draws the play. Pearson launches the three-pointer . . .

And misses. The final is 113–110. Rapid City reacts like it's won the league championship. Karl knows it's just one game. Fifty-dollar incentives, true or not, don't win championships. He tells Clint Wheeler, "We're gonna be in the finals. I don't think you will."

Still, the loss is painful. Five of six have now gotten away. A 21–5 record was a lot more fun than 22–11. Shurina sits exhausted in the locker room, too tired to undress. Karl, still confused as to how to coach this group of players—it almost can't be called a team—and how to make them smarter, keep them from brain-locking, stop them from beating themselves, loses his cool and throws a cup of ice at the wall. Like the rest of the team's luck recently, this move backfires: the cup hits Doug Lee in the eye, opening a small cut.

Later, calmer, Karl and Greg Ballard go over the final stats. Ballard, not yet officially a player or a coach, sat behind the bench and watched. Now, noting Shurina's numbers—15 points, 6 assists, 6 rebounds—Ballard comments on how the point guard tired out at the end.

"He's not used to that many minutes," Karl tells him.

"What's he used to?" Ballard asks.

"Try seven."

"*Seven?*" Ballard looks amazed.

"Hell, last week I almost cut him. He was gone."

The two look at each other and they laugh and laugh.

○   ○   ○

At Thirsty's, a few beers into his recovery, Karl walks up to Shurina. He offers his hand, they shake, then he pats him behind his head. "You played great," Karl tells him.

At a nearby table, Greg Grissom sits with a pitcher of his own. With Stroeder back, Grissom played only 2 minutes. It seems like nothing has changed, like all his patience and, when he got the chance to play, good work, was for nothing. He is far from happy.

JANUARY 25

Practice is delayed one half hour. The players have to clean the court. Six mops are recruited from the Armory basement, and six professional basketball players swab the deck. Karl looks on in amazement. "There's Greg Ballard, a ten-year NBA veteran, championship ring on his finger, it's his third day in town, and he's mopping the floor."

"You do it all in the CBA, I guess," Ballard says good naturedly, wringing out his mop.

"That's right," offers Clint Smith, pushing across the floor. "Like being on welfare, work relief or something."

"OK Doug Lee, get this team stretched," Karl yells.

"Gotta get these puddles up first, Coach."

Today is a day to tie up some loose ends, from last night and the last several days. Ballard will be signed today as a player and work as an assistant coach. ("We get you cheap, too, Ballard," Karl says. "We got a salary cap problem and you just solved it." Ballard doesn't mind. His contract in Italy, where he was most recently playing, was bought out at an attractive sum, and, at the age of thirty-four, he's here more to start a coaching career than continue as a player.)

The Musselmans are discussed. When asked, Karl says he never met with or said hello to either Muss, even though he made himself available for Bill Musselman several times. "Is he always that way?" he asks Rowland and Grissom. Both shake their heads and smile. "You have no idea," Rowland says. "He's so unbelievable it's ... unbelievable. You don't think he wanted to win that game last night? I saw him. Could see it in his eyes."

Minniefield says he'll be 'scoped on Friday the twenty-seventh;

he'll be out two weeks, he figures. Then he tells Tim Wilkin the frightening details of his drug problems: of sleeping alone in hotel rooms away from his wife and three children, of the hypocrisy of telling kids not to use drugs and then going to get high, of not wanting to live, of turning down a contract from the Boston Celtics three days before training camp to check himself in, voluntarily, to rehab. The memories are still so recent that the pain leaks from his entire body. Only when he talks of getting himself together, of his happiness at being in Albany, of his chances to work with kids and "talk to people like you about my problem" do his eyes look like the eyes of an athlete—confident, secure, strong, and wise.

Jim Laverty comes up to tell Minniefield he can get him a job at a local counseling center. Minniefield says he has decided to stay in Albany, to set down some roots, to work with kids.

Karl goes up to Grissom after practice and says, "Somebody fucked you last night."

"Who?" Grissom asks.

"Me," Karl says quietly. "I'm sorry. I don't know what I'm doing."

And, finally, thirty-three games into the season, the team sweat suits have arrived. Gerald lays each pair—green hooded top with the Patroons wooden-shoe-and-basketball logo, green bottom with the logo and PATROONS spelled out down one leg—on individual chairs, all in a row, for everyone to see.

"I think they will get a real charge out of seeing them." He beams as he and Jack Moser, the man responsible for getting the sweats donated, look at the ten suits in a row. "I get a charge out of seeing them myself. I am fired up just looking at 'em."

JANUARY 26

The good news is that the Rochester Flyers, tonight's opponent, are in disarray. They are in last place in the Western Division; they average less than 100 points per game; rumors are out that their coach is to be fired, perhaps tonight; they have just traded Michael Graham, the contentious former Georgetown player; and they seem to be generally in a lousy mood. They should be easy pickings, just the kind of team a struggling club like the Patroons needs after tough losses to Pensacola and Rapid City.

The bad news is that San Antonio called looking for a shooter, and Karl thinks he's sold them on Doug Lee. After Rochester, Pensacola comes in for two games. "They'll be fun without Lee," Karl says sarcastically.

○   ○   ○

Doug Dickinson, the statistician, stands by Karl. "You know, last night I think you set a CBA record. Four white guys on the court at one time. I went home and checked through all the old rosters; I don't think many teams even *had* four white guys." Karl laughs, then tells Dickinson tonight's starters: Lee, Shurina, Engelstad, Stroeder, and Rowland.

"You're *starting* four whites?" Dickinson smiles. "That *is* a record."

"I am starting four whites, aren't I?" Karl laughs.

The game itself is easy; Albany is up 73–52 at the half. A typically awful third quarter follows—for some unknown reason, the Patroons always seem to lose the third Q—and the lead is down to 14. But the fourth is another rout, and the game is quickly over. The fun begins. Ballard, the old man, takes some ribbing when he scores his first points. Ken Johnson starts calling him Pops, and Engelstad reminds him he could have dunked on that play in his younger days.

Grissom, who still didn't play much in the first half, gets a lot of time in the second (Stroeder is not playing well at all, perhaps rusty from two weeks of benchwarming in Golden State—or perhaps unhappy at finding himself back in the CBA) and plays with fury. In 15 minutes of playing time Gris scores 11 points, hauls in 6 rebounds, and blocks two shots, in an obvious effort to prove his worth all over again.

Only Karl seems to be unhappy. The refs, eager to keep the game close, have called everything Rochester's way, and Karl, despite the huge lead, is afire with anger. He paces, yells, pulls players on and off the court angrily. To Minniefield it's the Karl of old. "He's going too crazy, too hard," Ballard whispers to Minniefield. Dirk whispers back: "That's how he was in the NBA. Takes everything too personal, like every loss is his fault, you know. He expects too much. Like Dean Smith, you know.

"Course he's much better now, much calmer. He's calmed down a lot."

In the locker room after the win, Karl seems decidedly uncalm, but the raucous good humor that fills the room after the win—the final is 141–120, and six more standings points boost the lead back to thirty-five—seems to overtake his bad mood. Three quick post-game beers also help, as do a few more at Thirsty's.

Tonight, Cathy Karl joins the team at the bar. When asked how she and George are enjoying Albany, she is quick to answer. "George is so happy, the happiest he's been in years," she reports. "Maybe the happiest since he was a player. He's having fun again. The NBA was almost never fun."

George is over at another table, telling Doug and Becky Lee that Doug may be leaving soon.

JANUARY 27

No one wants to practice. Gerald has a proposition.

"Gentlemen, here's the deal. We go hard today, and we kick Pensacola's ass twice on Saturday and Sunday, and then we have Monday and Tuesday off."

"And if not . . ." comes the response.

"If not, then we have two-a-days. Are you for it or against it? Hard today, then two wins, then two days off, or then two-a-days. Right?"

The vote passes, over John Stroeder's protests. "Two-a-days?" he barks. "That's bullshit! We don't make enough money in the CBA for two-a-days!"

"Gerald, straighten Stroeder's attitude out," Karl chirps from the sidelines.

"Do we have a deal, gentlemen?" Gerald asks.

○ ○ ○

San Antonio has decided not to take Lee. Like Shurina, who wasn't chosen by the Italians, Lee just misses the CBA's brass ring. Still, without Karl's prodding, Lee and Shurina, both of whom have struggled in this league, might not have been considered at all.

JANUARY 28

A 128–81, seven-points-to-zero thrashing of Pensacola, for two main reasons.

In the morning paper, Tim Wilkin calls Wayne Engelstad a bust so far as a Patroon (Engelstad, Cal-Irvine's second all-time leading scorer, is averaging only 9.9 a game here), and Engelstad responds with a vengeance, scoring 27, grabbing 13 boards, dishing 4 assists, and making two steals. "That article was just what I needed," he admits afterwards.

And Doug Lee shuts down Brook Steppe, the league's leading scorer, holding the 25 ppg ace to just 7 (including just 2 points—on free throws—in the first half).

The only casualty: Ken Johnson is pulled in the third quarter when he stops playing hard (even in a rout, Karl demands effort), and he sulks. When Karl tries to put him back in in the fourth, he refuses to go, then visibly pouts the rest of the way.

But after the game, much celebrating. Bob Ryan, the Boston *Globe* writer, is in town for the two games; he and Karl reacquaint (it was Ryan who called Karl the Billy Martin of basketball) over a few cold ones.

"Can you believe the refs called that traveling on Ballard?" Karl laughs.

"I know it. I've watched him make that same move for ten years in the NBA, and this jerk calls him on it," Ryan answers.

"Hey, Clinton Smith," Karl yells. "Where's that girl?"

"What girl is that, George?"

"The one that bought you a thirty-inch color TV."

"Oh, George, don't be on that, now. Don't be gettin' me in trouble."

"I hear she bought you some furniture for the apartment, too."

"George, she likes me, what can I say."

"Why is she buying him a TV set?" Ryan asks.

"Why do you think," Karl answers.

JANUARY 29

Ken Johnson knows he did wrong, and he apologizes to the team, personally and in print. Karl benches him anyway for the Sunday afternoon rematch with Pensacola; he doesn't play a minute. And the Patroons lose.

Johnson might have helped—lost rebounds are a major factor—although the team's cold shooting (14 percent in the first Q) and uninspired play have more to do with it. Engelstad has a one-for-nine night of shooting and 4 points, Shurina has six turn-overs, and Delray Brooks (in for Steppe, who is ejected in the second quarter after his second technical; he fights with Rowland, then tosses a ball at a ref) lights up Lee for 28 points. The final: 100–95, against.

Afterwards, Karl says little. A pre–road trip team dinner sched-uled for tomorrow at Thirsty's is vetoed when only four players say they will attend. Karl decides to give a day off—despite the deal of a few days earlier—and hold one practice on Tuesday. Then, tired, he goes home.

Ballard, stepping out of the shower, is approached by a young fan for an autograph. "Are you new?" the boy asks.

"Yes." He smiles. "Very new."

JANUARY 31

Greg Grissom, at breakfast, scanning the newspaper. "So, any trades?" Not yet; Ken Johnson is still a Patroon.

George Karl, after practice: "So, do you want to stay in Dallas instead of Wichita Falls? It's a two-hour drive each way, which means we'll leave around three o'clock before the game, and won't get back till after midnight, but I got a hotel lined up, and Dallas is a lot more fun than Wichita Falls. And I want to play a lot of golf." The motion carries: Six days in Dallas, and not in Wichita Falls. "And Clinton, the hotel is near three malls." "My boy, George Karl."

"Another thing. Do we want to leave right after the Cedar Rapids game and bus to Rockford? It's about three and a half hours—we won't get in till late, two or two thirty in the morning." This, too, carries.

Karl, to Wilkin. "Miami is supposed to decide on Kelvin today, but they want to wait till Friday. They have another guy on a ten-day, and his doesn't end till then. So they're gonna keep Kelvin around for a few more days. Which pisses me off."

Gerald: "I guess I am back in the transportation bidness. I'll get you all to the airport on Thursday." Tony, in a fit of insubordination, tried to tell off Gary Holle, his nominal boss, after the Sunday game. With some prodding from the coaching staff—Gerald directing up front, George the producer behind the scenes—Holle has summarily dismissed Tony from his position. "You'll see, you won't be able to do nothing without me," Tony says. "You need me."

Karl offers to improve Gerald's wardrobe, at a cash value of $1,000, for Gerald's good work in effecting this key transaction. "Ollie! First you rob Rockford for Pressley, and now this," Karl says. "That might get you CBA executive of the year."

"Are my clothes that bad, Coach?" Gerald wants to know.

"Yes, they are, Ollie," says Karl.

5

FEBRUARY 1–2

"Are these the ten who will go on the trip?" Karl is asked.

"Yeah, plus a couple of extra uniforms. Just in case . . ." he says, smiling slyly. Another road trip, the last long trip of the season, begins Thursday the second. If history is any indication, the ten who leave—Shurina, Clint Smith, Pearson, Lee, Rowland, Grissom, Ballard, Johnson, Stroeder, and Engelstad (Minniefield, on IR, stays home)—won't be the ten who return a week from Saturday.

○   ○   ○

On the second of February, a frigid Thursday afternoon, Gerald, wearing his usual travel uniform—a retina-burning sweater featuring four horizontal blocks of solid colors, colors not found in nature—steps into the Albany airport, coatless. Once inside, he then pulls his blue wool cap on (first removing a wad of money from within) and organizes the trip. Karl, sitting out the two-hour weather delay, slips on a pair of headphones for his portable CD. He then starts shouting over the music to Dan Levy, which causes heads to turn and his players to giggle uncontrollably. "What? Am I shouting?" he asks sheepishly when he figures out the problem. "I guess I'm not used to these like Danny Pearson over there." Danny Pearson over there is, as usual, slouched in an airport chair fast asleep, headphones in place.

On the flight to O'Hare, Karl assigns homework: Each player lists his five favorite plays, and the team's five most effective plays. Grissom leans over the seat in front of him and taps Tim Wilkin, who is making this trip (his first of the year; CBA newspapers, like CBA teams, don't have—or don't want to spend—the money for coverage on the road, and Wilkin normally writes road-game stories by listening to the game on the radio) to write a diary for the newspaper. "I hate these little tests," Gris tells Wilkin. "You can quote me on this. I don't like these head games. They make me an emotional wreck." John Stroeder, sitting next to Greg, writes down two plays and asks Grissom for some more. When Gris fails to answer, Stroeder copies off his paper. Then he hands his food tray to Doug Lee, who is returning empties to the galley in hopes of scoring another dish of lasagna.

The weather delay back in Albany forces the team to miss its first connection to Cedar Rapids, and Gerald is furious. Sweat pours off his brow as he argues with the counter help at O'Hare, until Lee figures out that the team is indeed booked on the next flight. He mops Gerald's head with his scarf. All is secure. All to the airport bar.

Beers, Cokes, hot dogs, chitchat ... when suddenly a large, unnaturally tanned gentleman in sunglasses, bandanna, stretch pants, boots, and bulging biceps walks past, pushing a baggage cart. "Isn't that the Hulkster?" Engelstad makes the I.D. It is indeed Hulk Hogan, quickly followed by living cartoon characters such as the Macho Man, Jake the Snake, The Gorgeous Elizabeth ("She really is gorgeous," Shurina reports), and an unidentified fellow with a long, pointy goatee. The World Wrestling Federation, its members bedecked in traditional wrestling mufti—leopardskin tights and banana-yellow boots and dark sunglasses and loud jewelry—all weave in varying stages of unsteadiness down the airport aisle on their way to a flight to Milwaukee. Engelstad isn't impressed. "Hulk's not so big. I'm gonna go kick his ass, won't take long," he says and heads after them. Lee and Ballard, more deferential than Wayne, go for autographs.

Wilkin, intrepid reporter, approaches the group. "Mr. Hogan, have you ever heard of the Albany Patroons?"

"No," he rasps, looking elsewhere behind his shades.

"Ever hear of the CBA?"

"No."

"Do you like basketball?"

"No."

"Thanks for your time."

At the gate, Stroeder, hearing the wrestlers are nearby, is miffed he missed them. "Clinton," Karl orders, "Stroeds is pissed. Take him to see Hulk. And bring me a diet Coke."

Karl giggles helplessly. "What has happened to my life?"

His life has much further to turn. On arrival at Cedar Rapids, where it is a comfortable five below zero, there is no van waiting, Gerald is sweating, the players are tired and cranky. Karl plots his escape. "Timmy, you got an expense account, right? Get a cab."

Karl, Wilkin, and Levy abandon ship and motor to the Best Western. The cab's driver, a very short, very round, late-model woman with silvery hair piled on her head in a bun, learns that Wilkin is a newspaperman.

"You a writer? I'm a writer too," she says. She looks not at all like a writer. "Mind if I ask you a question?"

Wilkin considers the request carefully. "No, I don't mind."

She says, "I have a virgin. I have a good guy and a bad guy. Who should get her first?"

The cab pulls up to the hotel. "The bad guy," Wilkin says and quickly pays the fare. "Did you say 'virgin'?" Karl asks. "Did she say 'virgin'?"

"I thought she was looking to fix us up," Wilkin says. "Then I figured out it was characters in her book."

"I have no idea what she was talking about," Karl says, giggling crazily. He orders three beers from the now-closed hotel bar. The desk clerk has a six-pack brought up. It is well after midnight, and feels like it.

"Have you ever seen a Fellini movie?" Karl asks, cracking open two beers. "My life is like a Fellini movie."

FEBRUARY 3

A very busy day.

The good news is that Kelvin Upshaw has been released by

Miami. The Heat sign Craig Neal, their other CBA call-up, instead. Upshaw plans on meeting the Patroons in Dallas later in the week. The bad news is that Wayne Engelstad is going to Italy. "Hey Ollie," Karl yelps at Gerald before leaving for shootaround. "You know that stuff you said would probably happen? It's happening."

"Well that's fine, George. That's great. I am happy for Wayne. I will hug and kiss him good-bye. Just get someone else to pay his dad gem way and get his ass over there."

In the second of two vans driving to the practice, Engelstad says he has to go. He's been talking to Rome for a few days—almost a week—and it comes down to money. Sixty thousand dollars, plus incentives, tax free, for three months. "Can't make that kind of money in the NBA this year, even if I played the rest of the year. I can still go to an NBA camp next year, or play in the CBA again if they pass that rule." (A new rule allowing players to move back and forth between Europe and the CBA more easily is expected to pass in the spring.) "I can't lose," Engelstad concludes.

"Too bad they don't have a European league for writers," Wilkin says with envy.

Just then Karl, in the front seat, lets out a whoop. He spots the other van—being pushed into a gas station. "There's Ollie! Pushing! Look!" Ollie is indeed pushing the gasless van into the station. It is three below zero.

As long as they're there, the players pick up breakfast: donuts, fruit pies, juices. "Hey Clinton, buy me a diet Coke," Karl orders. "Oh, George . . ." Clinton says, and complies.

"Where's Ken Johnson?" Karl asks.

"Couldn't find him at the hotel, George," Clint says. "Here's your Coke."

○   ○   ○

"You wanna play tonight?" Karl asks Engelstad in the lobby, just before the van leaves.

"It's your call. I'll play if you want."

"No, it's your call."

"I guess I'll leave then, get back to California for a day or two."

"Leave me your uniform and warmups," Gerald says.

With that, Engelstad says good-bye to the team. His palm is

sweaty, he appears nervous, it was a tough decision to make (sixty thousand reasons notwithstanding), but he has decided to play in Rome. Shurina, his roommate on this trip, shakes his hand and does some totaling. "So far I roomed with Kelvin, he's gone. Keith Smith, knee surgery. Ozell, got the boot. Now Wayne. I guess I'm the kiss of death. Gonna room by myself, maybe *I'll* get to Europe."

And the Albany nine get ready for the game (Johnson included; he apologizes for missing the practice, and Karl accepts his return). Gerald loads those players who need taping in the first van to get them to the arena early, and the rest file into the second. The first van, which is the Best Western's own vehicle—the one that ran out of gas—loads up with Karl and Gerald, Rowland and Pearson and Lee and Stroeder, Levy and Wilkin, and most of the luggage. (The team is bussing right to Rockford after the game.) Loading goes quickly—it's still below zero, and a stiff breeze has the wind chill around thirty below. But all proceeds well.

Until, a mile from the arena, a tire blows on the interstate. The van pulls over onto the shoulder. "I don't believe this is happening to me," Karl moans. The van's driver, a wild-haired, wild-eyed youth, says there isn't any spare. He doesn't know what to do.

"Rim it to the arena," Lee suggests. That doesn't work. Sit for a few minutes. "I can't believe this," Karl says. "We can't just sit here. We'll freeze to death." The driver looks at Gerald and says he'll go get help. He dashes out, down the embankment, waves down a car—with a pretty blonde at the wheel—and speeds off.

"I bet we never see him again," Lee says. "I have a feeling he just quit his job."

"You know, Gerald," Karl agrees, "there's a chance that guy just said, 'Fuck this.' "

Gerald nods. "I don't think he's coming back. That boy looked strange. He had some eyes. Them eyes had seen some things."

"Gerald, let's rim it. Start driving."

"I cain't, Coach. He took the keys."

"Ollie, the van is still running! How could he take the keys?"

Ollie thinks about that one. "I don't know, Coach." He smiles. "I guess I was just kidding."

"Think we can walk it?"

"It's twenty below out! Walk it? With the luggage?"

"I can't believe this is happening to me!" Karl says. "Hey Pearson. Can't you smile? Can't you laugh at this?"

"This ain't funny, man," Pearson grumbles, then leans his head against the window and falls asleep.

"This is like the old CBA, ain't it, Gerald," Rowland says. "Drive eight hours, get out, get dressed, play a game, get back in the van. Drive all night to the next game."

The group sits for several minutes, traffic humming past on the interstate. Gerald starts writing on the frosted windows. Three capital As and an O with a line under it—secret hieroglyphs from Gerald's undecipherable past. He explains: "Back in Tennessee, in '71. Or '69. Or '71. We had the A, the A, the A, the zero with the bar. Can't remember what it means. It was our slogan. Had it on our T-shirts."

"Gerald, you're talking in tongues again." Karl laughs. "I can't believe this."

"I remember now. 'Any time, Any place, Anywhere, bar none.' Three A's and the zero. That meant, 'Get it done.' An' we're gonna get it done. Ah'm fired up. This is a motivatin' experience."

"Gerald," Levy asks, "Can you turn on the light? I have to write my show."

"Don't do it, Ollie. He isn't worth it," Karl says. "This isn't happening to me."

Thirty-five minutes pass this way. Then, miraculously, wild eyes returns with the other van. This vehicle seats perhaps six normal-sized people comfortably. Now it seats four basketball players, two coaches, three media members, and one extra driver, plus luggage. Gerald is fahr'd up. Squeezed onto Lee's lap, elbows and knees in his face, bouncing dangerously down the freeway, he chatters away, volume set at 10.

"This *motivates* me! I ain't kiddin'! We're gonna use this. A-A-A bar *none*. Kick Cedar Rapid's *asses*. This is adversity. I *love* adversity! Bar nothin'! I am glad o' this.

"That young fella, the driver, he got it done! Stopped that car, pretty girl an' all, coulda run off with her to Florida or somewheres, but he had the courage. He got it *done!* Any time, any body, any how, any where, any which way, bar zero—bar nothin'! I love it.

"Timmy Wilkin! I am glad you are here with us, buddy! You're seein' some things. You're learnin' some things. Maybe now you'll understand what our life is, what we motherfuckers go through! Won't write all that bad stuff about us now in your newspaper. Yessir, maybe now you understand some. What it's like to have no water, walk ten miles, haven't slept in 'bout three weeks, your clothes stink. Now you know what it's like, why your legs get tired, why maybe you don't play so well. You have lived it. You have paid the price. Yessir.

"I'll tell you what! Ah am *fired up!* This motivates me! A-A-A. Bar none! Let's go kick Cedar Rapid's ass!"

And with that, the van pulls up to the players' entrance. Hysterical with laughter, the passengers untangle, collect their bags, and beat the cold into the arena.

"I can't believe this is my life!" Karl cries for the last time.

The team files into the tiny locker room, luggage piled high in front of the chalkboard. Karl leans over it all, sitting precariously on the edge of a valise, and tries to write his pregame notes on the board. This is his life.

○   ○   ○

Oh, yes, the game. Albany wins the second and third quarters, and is down 1—73–72—after three. Throughout the fourth, the lead changes hands; each team takes, then loses it. Only at the end, with just 38 seconds left, when Shurina misses a layup and the Silver Bullets' Lewis Lloyd (in his first game since being reinstated for drug use) scores, does Cedar Rapids build a 3-point lead. Rowland's last attempt is blocked, and the final is 100–96.

The bus—a big, comfortable coach—leaves from in front of the arena at 10:15. The temperature is now about five below, the wind has picked up, and a steady snow is falling. Gerald steps on last. "Let's see, we got nine players an' Dan an' Tim an' me an' George. An' the driver. Let's hit it."

"What do you guys want, Kentucky Fried Chicken or Mc-Donald's?" Karl asks. The winner is Burger King, since that is what's found first. Everyone de-busses and gets in line.

Greg Ballard asks if he has to pay for the food himself. "Yeah, you gotta pay," Ken Johnson tells him. "CBA rookie."

And three and a half hours later, at 2:30 A.M., the Patroons pull into the Alpine House Motel. Trudging with their bags through a persistent snow in subzero temperatures across the slippery parking lot to their rooms—this is a real motel; the doors face the cold—they are too tired to complain.

FEBRUARY 4

The day is spent in and around the scruffy Alpine House. Morning practice is canceled, everyone sleeps late, then grabs lunch across the street (although it's almost too cold to walk even that far). The phone company is busy, though. Gerald is trying to get Kelvin, who is just fifty miles away in Chicago, for tonight's game, but no one is answering at his home.

And coming in, from Seattle, is a call from the SuperSonics' coach, Bernie Bickerstaff, for George Karl. Sedale Threatt broke a finger, and Seattle is interested in calling on Greg Ballard.

This is a shocker. Karl can't believe it; even Ballard is surprised he'd be called this quickly. His name still carries weight, obviously, and Seattle needs a veteran who is both good for character and can still play some. It's not official, but he might be called up later this week. "This one hurts a little," Karl admits. Ballard has been, in his short time, a valuable addition, not so much as a player but as a mature, steadying influence on the moody, bitchy Patroons of late. If he should go, he will be missed.

So it's appropriate that the old man win one before he goes. This is a game Albany figures to lose. They have never played well here; Rockford matches up nicely against them, and the Lightning have the added boost of the return of Pace Mannion, back from a ten-day trip to the Pistons. Dominic Pressley, momentarily a Patroon, now starts for Rockford. Karl starts a new five: Stroeder, Grissom, Shurina, Lee, and Rowland.

Lee hits an early three-pointer, and the 40 or so members of his family and friends in attendance make conspicuous noise from the Albany rooting section. But then the Patroons start playing dumb again. Stroeder misses a couple of layups and has two shots blocked—his play has been dismal since returning from the NBA —and Rockford takes the first Q by 9. That lead bulges to as many as 17, and at the half it's 10. (It should be 6, but Lee tries to dribble through two defenders at the end, is stripped of the ball, and Rockford scores at the buzzer.) At halftime, all Karl can tell them is, play smarter.

And somehow they do. The defense swarms all over Rockford—Mannion, standing by the Patroon bench during a delay, tells Karl, "You must of really got on 'em at halftime," though Karl didn't—and cut the lead to 1 after three quarters. It slips away a bit in the fourth, though—missed layups continue to hound the Patroons—and with 3 minutes left Albany is losing by 5. Then Ballard takes control.

He hits two straight jumpers—the same ugly, line-drive J's he made famous in the NBA—to cut it to 1 with just over a minute left. Then, on defense, he makes a baseline steal, starts a fast break, and watches Stroeder lay one in for a 98–97 lead. And when Shurina feeds Stroeder underneath for another hoop—and the foul—the bench erupts, and Karl jumps three feet in the air and dances onto the court, breaking into a wide grin. It ends 102–97, a stirring, emotionally uplifting win.

"Maybe this'll put a smile on my boy George's face," says Clint Smith in the locker room. "I hate him when he loses. He's no fun at all."

"Yeah, Pops!" Johnson yells at Ballard. "CBA rookie comes through. Yeah, CBA rookie!"

"Isn't Ballard's shot the ugliest thing you ever seen?" Karl laughs as he heads out to meet a friend, who tells him, "You said you were starting four white guys, but you didn't say it would be four *slow* white guys."

"And I told them I wanted to play fast tempo tonight," Karl says. "Let's go eat."

Life is good after a win on the road.

FEBRUARY 5–6

To Dallas, for six days of fun and sun and lots of golf—except that it's below freezing, and the roads are glass-slick from a recent ice storm (Dallas has no salt or sand trucks, so the ice stays on the roads all week). Still, it's better than Wichita Falls.

On the trip down, Wilkin talks with Greg Grissom, looking for an angle for today's diary. The flight leaves at 10 A.M. and Gris, looking forward to meeting his college buddies from TCU—he's staying in Fort Worth to be near the action—gets right to work with five quick beers on the plane. He rates this year's team in terms of partying, womanizing, and general good-timing prowess, and comes to the conclusion that he, Grissom, is one of the few live wires. "We really do have a boring team. I had more fun on my high school team, and I didn't even drink then." Gris tells some favorite drinking stories—thirty-six Lite beers on a fishing trip, twenty-four on a hot day of golf ("I was asked never to come back to that club"), etc. He gives some high marks to Shurina, Rowland, Clint Smith, and now-departed Patroons Keith Smith and Wayne Engelstad, flunks Lee and Stroeder ("them married guys are worthless"), then orders another beer from the stewardess. "I mean, there's nothin' wrong with a good time, y'know? You don't have to be a drunk or anything."

"How many beers for you to feel it?" Wilkin asks. Gris thinks hard for a minute. "Ten, maybe." "So these five . . ." "Just warmin' up, gettin' a base." At DFW, Gris meets his boys, and is off. "Practice tomorrow at ten? See ya then."

Karl takes a few travelers one way to get his rental car, Oliver takes the rest to get the van. Karl brings Clinton along. "Clint, get me a diet Coke."

"Oh, man, George, I spent thirty-five dollars gettin' you Cokes."

"How many minutes you want to play? I think I see Danny Pearson getting some more."

"I'll get it, George," Shurina jumps in. "Whatever you want. I need those minutes."

"Hey, Clint," Karl says, "you know the hotel is near two malls."

"My boy, G.K. Two thumbs up. Siskel and Ebert. I'm ready. Look at the chickadoos."

"Who does Clint Smith look like?" Karl asks.

"Louis Farrakhan," says Levy.

"No, man, don't be sayin' that. Even the fellas don't like that guy."

"Stan Laurel. A black Stan Laurel," says Wilkin.

"He looks like one of the California Raisins," Shurina whispers. "We call him Cal."

"No Cal. None o' that Farrakhan. Call me Robocop."

○ ○ ○

Practice on the sixth is at the Royal Haven Baptist Church/Bateson Rec Center, where the Dallas Mavericks sometimes practice. With some help from his friends in the Mavs' organization, Karl has secured gym time and a duffel bag full of basketballs.

Practice starts light; Shurina and Lee are banged up—the former has a sprained knee, the latter's shoulder hurts. Kelvin isn't in yet. And Gris is late. Gerald is worried. "He called at eight thirty this mornin', said he'd be here. I thought the big guy was a winner, thought he had the courage."

"Maybe the ice on the roads slowed him down," Wilkin says.

Gerald's face falls. "Here I am cussin' out the big man. And he's out there fightin' the ice and the roads and the thing, and the big man could be dead."

Soon, though, Gris walks in, with two pals who can't quite hide their physical state as well as the big man. Gris, bleary-eyed and flushed in the face but in full control, takes his position in practice, shouting and cursing and having a good ol' time. His friends pass out on the sideline.

"It looks like my boy Grissom got into the buttermilk last night," Clint says.

Danny Pearson sits practice out. He is the latest problem child, and Karl jumps on his attitude. Pearson looks to be twenty pounds heavier than earlier in the season, is complaining on the bench and not playing well. Karl tells him, in no uncertain terms, that if things don't change, he is gone. Pearson watches practice for an hour silently, then walks to center court and tells Karl he understands. He'll try to do better.

Pearson has taken Johnson's place in the doghouse as the Johnson situation has nearly reached its conclusion. Johnson has decided to head home for a while to take care of some personal problems. Both sides will then evaluate whether he comes back. Johnson will finish the road trip, play one game at home on return, then fly to California. As this has resolved itself, Johnson's mood has improved, his attitude has gotten better (even if his minutes haven't increased) and, with Ballard leaving, he might come back yet. Then again, he might not.

Practice ends. Gris tells of his nighttime activities—"I lost my damn wallet, all my money, my license, everything. Had a great time"—rousts his buddies, and heads back to Fort Worth. Back at the hotel, Clint Smith puts on his finest clothes, dabs some cologne on, and heads to a nearby mall. "Just a warmup before me an' the fellas go to the Galleria, the big mall downtown. Gonna meet the community.

"Hey Timmy Wilkin. You call me Robocop in that story of yours? You did? All right. My boy Timmy Wilkin. Don't call me no Farrakhan in that paper. I'm Robocop."

Karl, Oliver, Levy, Wilkin, and Karl's golfing friends find a cheap, unknown barbecue joint called Moore's. It's excellent—all agree it might be as good as any they've had—and many enormous piles of beef, sausage, ribs, fried okra, fried corn, beans, raw onions, sweet peppers, cole slaw, and potato salad later, it's time to leave. But first, Gerald is talked into trying one of the onions.

"*Whewwwweeee!* Mah *lord* that's hot. Mah goodness. Those onions, they go straight through your brain and out your head. They'll straighten your life out. Make you think right.

"Maybe Ken Johnson oughta try some."

FEBRUARY 7

No shootaround. Instead, a team meeting. Karl says the next six games—against probable playoff competition—are important in terms of making the right statement, that these teams have no chance of beating Albany in the postseason. He also reiterates the need for proper attitude. The season is nearly over—only sixteen games are left, and the division title is all but assured—and the championship drive is officially on.

Ballard and Clint Smith get Karl's rental car to pick up Kelvin at the airport. Before going, Karl asks Smith if he wants to room with Upshaw. "Shoot, no, George. No way. I don't need that. He'll be comin' down here with that big NBA head. Head so big it won't fit through the door."

"Clinton, are you the jivest guy in the CBA?" Karl laughs.

"No sir, George. Not anymore. Used to be, but no more. It's still in me, though. It's in my roots. Can come out at any time."

"How 'bout a diet Coke?"

"My boy, G.K. All right. Diet Coke. I got it."

He's then off to the airport. The others get their rest. The coaches and media head back to Moore's, Gerald only a bit reluctantly. "Tim, do me a favor. Stop off and get me some Rolaids. Those onions straightened me out some."

○ ○ ○

"Hey, Kelvin Upshaw! Your head too big to shake my hand?" Karl smiles, spotting Upshaw on the van before leaving, and offers a typical Karl greeting. Upshaw smiles, shakes his hand, and the van—just the players, Doug Lee at the helm—begins the two-hour-plus drive to Wichita Falls.

Karl and Oliver take Karl's rental car—a Cadillac, of course. (Wilkin and Levy, in Wilkin's more economical rental, follow along in the media caravan.) The two coaches talk trades, throwing around names. "Ah can get you Perry Moss," Gerald says. "You want him? Eric Newsome? I don't think I can get Rob Rose. Ah know ah cain't get Jimmy Miller."

"Get me Winston Bennett," Karl says. "I kind of like his athletic ability. We have no athletes on this team since Vince left. How can I win a championship without one athlete?"

"I will try, Coach."

Karl makes some mental notes. "We get Bennett. Johnson is out. Bring Dave Popson in. Coach Smith is on my case about Popson." Karl laughs. The Carolina fraternity is strong, and when Dean Smith tells Karl to bring in Popson (who has been sitting at home doing nothing since being released by the Pistons) Karl knows he better listen.

They drive on, through the flat, dry plains of Texas, talking about life, basketball, players, friends. Gerald, loving Karl's company, is at one point laughing so hard his massive belly heaves and perspiration drips down his forehead as he struggles to catch his breath.

"Ollie, are you having the big one?" Karl asks.

"You know somethin', Coach. If I'd have the big one now, I'd die a happy man. I'd have lived a good life. How 'bout you?"

"Ollie, please! I'll be happy when you get me Winston Bennett."

Gerald promises to call about Bennett. Then he asks, quietly,

"You think Coach Smith can help me get the Loyola, Maryland job next year?"

○   ○   ○

The three vehicles pull into Midwestern State University and park by the Coliseum. In the pregame meeting, Karl goes over the Texans' team, his game plan, and the matchups. "Anybody know who this guy Ervin Dillon is? Any idea? How about this Henry James? Anybody?" No one knows either of them.

"Coach, should I wear the Colonel Mustard coat tonight?" Gerald asks as they dress for the game. He pulls a loud yellow polyester sports coat out. "Is it too ugly?"

"Ollie, I gotta take you shopping. With that $1,000 for getting rid of Tony I owe you." Ollie, in Colonel Mustard, and Karl, in gray suit and silk tie, then take the floor.

Kelvin starts the game hard by Gerald. "I gotta refresh my memory," he says. Once he's in, though, it is clear: With Kelvin playing well at the point this team can win a championship. Shurina moves over to the 2-guard and plays perhaps his best game of the year—19 points, 7 assists, 6 boards—but it is mostly Upshaw. In 27 minutes of playing time he pops for 26 (19 in the second half), plus 5 assists.

The Texans are a tough team, though, with Ennis Whatley, Derrick Taylor, Rob Rose, and 7' 3" Martin Nessley (and the unknown Dillon and James), and the game is close to the end. Down 5 at the half, Albany builds a 9-point lead of its own, then sees it slip to 4.

"Gerald, how many time-outs do we have left," barks Karl, his concentration deep into the game as he plans his strategy over the final minutes. Gerald lumbers to the scorer, then lumbers back.

With all due seriousness, Gerald reports, "Coach, we have two. But they're not too smart here; I don't think they know the rules. I think we can get three."

With 58 seconds left, Rob Rose scores to cut it to 2, 106–104, and on the next posession Lee loses the ball. Derrick Taylor scoops it up, drives over Shurina, and scores—but is called for the offensive foul. Like the first game here back in November, the Albany defender gets good position. Unlike the first game, though, when the call went against Keith Smith, this time Shurina takes the charge, and the ref calls it that way. It's Taylor's seventh foul, too; Lee hits the technical and it's all but over. Gerald tells Wilkin at courtside, "Tim, let's win this thing an' get the hell outta here." Upshaw's two free throws ice it, 110–105, six standings points. And a second consecutive road win.

"Stupid fresh game, 'Shaw." "Yeah, 'Shaw dog." " 'Shaw ain't won since he left here for Miami."

"Naw, I won one," he corrects.

"Yo Gris, puttin' the block on big Nessley, gettin' Big Daddy's shit outta there. Yeah."

"Hey, I can take the white guys." Grissom laughs. "Don't know about the brothers, but I can take a white guy!"

"Great job, gentlemen." Karl smiles before taking on dinner with Gerald and friends. "Just hide the cans on the drive back."

For those scoring at home, Grissom finishes fifteen beers on the ride. Shurina adds thirteen. Clinton Smith has two wine coolers. Gerald Oliver eats one ice cream bar, then finishes a pint of Haagen-Dasz Praline Swirl, then a vanilla milk shake. Then the waitress brings over the hamburger he ordered. He looks at it, puzzled.

"Miss, I gotta ask you a question. What is this?"

FEBRUARY 8

"The Nets signed Corey Gaines," Stroeder, reading *USA Today*, tells Ken Johnson in the lobby before practice. "And the Bucks got Tony Brown." More CBA call-ups, but not the ones they were hoping for.

The mood is good, the spirits high. Winning helps; so does staying in Dallas. The players are enjoying a big city and the use of wheels. Vanning together has brought them a little closer, and with a forty-two-point standings lead and two days off in Dallas, life is pretty good.

At least that's what Grissom announces before practice. "Day two in Dallas. Still hung over." Wilkin tells him it's day four. Gris doesn't seem to care. Upshaw finds a beat-up football in the rec center storeroom, and after running a few plays, Karl announces that if anyone can make a half-court shot with the pigskin, there will be no practice. Pearson, the fifth up, hits a swish. He is surrounded and high-fived amid whoops of good cheer. Karl, all smiles, shrugs his shoulders, heads to the bleachers with Gerald, and puts Greg Ballard in charge of a fun-filled, if not too strenuous, hour and a half of drills.

Pearson is happy; he played his best game in quite a while, despite limited time, last night. He talks to Wilkin about his junk food diet for Wilkin's diary. "First, I start with a Snickers, man. They're the best. I'd rather have a double cheeseburger than a steak any day." Clint Smith is happy; he is the early star of Wilkin's diary back in Albany. "My boy Timmy Wilkin, what you writing about me? The ladies are calling already. You call me Robo?" Gris is still happy, too, for obvious reasons.

○   ○   ○

Back at the hotel. "Miss," Greg Ballard tells the desk clerk, "I just lost seventy-five cents in the soda machine. Can I get a refund?" She complies.

Clint Smith, watching intently. "Hey, I lost six bucks in the soda machine, too." Nice try.

"Hey Clint, you wanna go with Shurina and me to Dealey Plaza later?" Wilkin asks.

"What's that?"

"It's where John Kennedy was shot."

"I don't think so. You gonna drive through it? I wouldn't see anything. Too scared. I'd be duckin' in the backseat. They might be someone takin' shots at me."

The fellas go off to the mall, the coaches to Moore's for more barbecue. Then Wilkin takes Shurina, the criminal justice major, to Dealey Plaza. Shurina is deeply interested; despite a sore knee that has him hobbling and a steady cold wind that bites through his sweats, he stares at the Book Depository Building, wanders the grassy knoll, watches cars speed by on Commerce, discusses the various theories—the second gunman, the Mafia connections, Castro's role, the CIA—checks out the parking lot from where the second assassin might have escaped, tries to figure where the Zapruder film was taken. For Shurina, it's fascinating ancient history. Kennedy was shot three years before he was born.

○   ○   ○

No game tomorrow, so it's Married Guys' Night Out. With Shurina and Wilkin as chaperones, Doug Lee and John Stroeder are looking to strap the beer goggles on. When Karl walks in on them at the bar next door to the hotel, they are already several pitchers into the evening.

"Hey Coach!" Lee shouts/slurs, offering a shaky hand. "I'm drinkin' tonight!" Karl shakes his hand and laughs at him, then joins for a few cold ones of his own and the Lakers game on the big screen. But soon, new pastures need be roamed, so Wilkin and his car are recruited. Off to do Big D.

First, being full of life, the boys must destroy everything in the car. They tear up newspapers, empty ashtrays, play with the radio, readjust the mirrors. Of course, at the toll plaza, Shurina is challenged to toss the exact change in from the shotgun seat, hook shot–style, over the top of the car. (He makes the first of two— the quarter—but tosses a brick with the nickel.) All the while, also of course, there is much cursing, ragging, ribbing, and verbal mayhem. The overall feeling is of sophomore year, high school, cruising for action that is never found. These guys, it is obvious, don't get out much. The fellas, were they here, would be embarrassed.

To an area called the West End, and four separate bars to indulge. The first, a jazzy/urban/funk club, has the most stylish and attractive clientele; it is deemed inappropriate. Lee and Wilkin find an arcade downstairs and engage in a basketball shooting contest at one of the booths. Lee's touch has gone the way of his sobriety, and Wilkin dismisses him. Upstairs, Stroeder and Shurina have stumbled on a piano bar. Two pianos, back to back, on a small stage facing a small crowd in a smoky, Western-style saloon.

"Who has a request?"

Stroeder doesn't hesitate; in his barking baritone—if a seal could talk it would sound something like big John—he calls out for "New York, New York." Three bars into the tune, and Stroeder glowing with glee, a Texan stands and shouts out:

"Fuck New York!"

"For twenty bucks I'll play something else," the piano man tells the audience. The intruder steps up, plunks down a twenty, and whispers his choice. And the musician complies.

"Flintstones/Meet the Flint-stones/They're a modern stone-age fam-i-lee . . ."

Stroeder is stricken. His eyes bulge, his voice jabs out in disbelief. "Steve, can you believe this? Twenty dollars for the Flintstones. Shiiiiit. I don't believe it. Can you believe it? Twenty dollars. Shi-i-i-i-i-it. Moron."

Lee, downstairs, continues to play in the arcade. After a while he tallies his success: thirty-eight redeemable coupons. "I'll get something for my wife," he announces, but, when the booty is seen to be unacceptable, he gives the coupons back to the gamekeeper. "Give 'em to some kid," he tells her magnanimously, then wanders upstairs for another beer and a good view of the dance floor.

Stroeder bulls in to the dance club, red-head-and-broad-shoulders taller than the crowd, and stands by the bar in his long black overcoat. He draws a few double takes from the barflies, but is not in the mood. "Twenty dollars, Steve. Can you believe it? I hate that song. Shi-i-i-it. Loser."

It's getting late, the crowd is thinning, danger lurks in the hearts of the remaining patrons, so it's time to leave. Wilkin leads the boys back to the car. Stroeder sees two young ladies nearby, walking to their own car.

"Twenty dollars!" he howls at the ladies. "For the Flintstones! Can you believe that? I can't believe that!" The ladies hurry on. "Shi-i-i-it, Steve. The Flintstones."

To the car. To the highway. More paper tearing. More exactchange tossing. "Shi-i-i-it. Twenty dollars, Steve. The Flintstones. Moron."

And so, to bed.

FEBRUARY 9

"Look at Doug!" Grissom yelps at practice. "Trying to hide it. Not doing a very good job. He don't have the experience, like me." Lee, carrying with him a headful of last night, tries gamely to contribute at practice, but bleary eyes and heavy limbs give him away.

By 2 P.M. this afternoon, he will be in bed, and not heard from again until tomorrow.

Other developments: Greg Ballard will be signed to two ten-days; he leaves as soon as the team returns to Albany on Saturday, the eleventh. "This hurts a little more than Engelstad," Karl admits. "We needed his glue. Now we need another glue guy." His replacement will most likely be Dave Popson. Dean Smith has been trying to get Karl to bring Popson in for a while, and Coach Smith still has power over his former charges. "El Deano is mad at George for not getting Popson in before," Gerald says.

With the trading deadline on Sunday, the twelfth, Karl has Gerald pursue some leads. Pensacola will trade Bennett for Danny Pearson; "That's gonna make George squirm, put his nuts in a bind," Gerald predicts. He says he wouldn't make that trade. Karl says it's a steal, and tells Gerald to make it tomorrow.

Ken Johnson, it is decided, will reinjure his back on Monday and fly to California.

○ ○ ○

Laundry day after practice; Johnson and Smith meet with dirty uniforms at the hotel washer/dryer. Wilkin wanders by.

"My boy, Timmy Wilkin. Writin' about ol' C. Smith. The girls are callin' already, sayin', 'I gotta meet this Clint Smith.' "

Wilkin and Johnson talk some, and Kenny impresses Clint with his vocabulary.

"Timmy Wilkin oughta do a book on my boy Ken Johnson. He's so phil-o-sophical. So smart."

"Do a book on me, huh?" Johnson shakes his head. "Well, then, someone should do a comic book on you."

FEBRUARY 10

Winston Bennett scored 22 points last night; Pensacola retracts its offer. Gerald ups the ante—Pearson, plus cash and a draft pick —but Pensacola says no. Karl is distraught, in part because the deal has fallen to what he believes is CBA bullshit—"They won't trade a 10-minute player because he has one good game"—and in part because he desperately wants an athlete, and Bennett filled his needs.

Grissom, his Fort Worth play nearing a close, needs to get a new driver's license before returning home, but is told he'll need some identification to procure it. Since all his ID was in his lost wallet, he faces a problem, until he spots a CBA media guide. With the guide in tow, he walks into the motor vehicle bureau, opens to his entry, and points out his birth date, birthplace, and photograph. And with that, he is licensed again. Fame has its perks.

○ ○ ○

At three, the Patroons saddle up and drive to Wichita Falls for the last game of the road trip. The players pile into the van—Doug Lee again the skipper—the coaches take the Caddy, Wilkin and Levy comprise the media bus.

Karl, still mad about Bennett, vents some spleen, then sleeps in the backseat. Before losing consciousness, he tells Gerald he'll be fined for driving less than seventy. Gerald sets the cruise control at a firm seventy, and happily complies. Happily, that is, until the state trooper spots him. Officer Slaton pulls Gerald over, and walks him back to the police car.

"I am sorry, officer," Gerald begins, "but we all are with a basketball team, an' we're tryin' to get to a game in Wichita Falls, an' the team left earlier, an' I'm tryin' to catch 'em."

"That's gonna be hard to do, since they were goin' eighty an' you're only goin' seventy." The officer smiles. "Your boys came through here about fifteen minutes ago."

Gerald laughs. "Well, officer, it was mighty nice of you to let my boys go through an' not give 'em a ticket or anything."

"Who said I didn't give 'em a ticket? Let's see ... a Mr. Lee. Yessir. Eighty miles an hour."

The officer and the coach talk a while longer; the policeman suggests Gerald call the local justice of the peace and explain the situation. He thinks there's a good chance they'll get off.

Says Gerald, climbing back behind the wheel and setting the cruise control for a gentlemanly sixty-four, "I'll say, 'Judge, don't fine me an' my players. That's just the way travelin' is in the CBA.' "

○ ○ ○

"How you feelin'?" Gerald asks George just before the game begins.
"I've got a headache and a stomachache."

"You got 'em both? Then you are ready to go."

Everyone, in fact, is ready to go. Doug Lee hits his team record
seventy-fourth three-pointer, Grissom blocks four shots in the first
half and the Pats are up 55–44 after two. From there it gets pro-
gressively worse for the Texans; the Patroons lead steadily increases,
to 14, to 19, to 22. The Wichita Falls crowd is growing incensed
with the officiating, which is giving many of the calls to Albany
(justifiably, perhaps, since Albany is playing the more aggressive
ball, and as Karl often says, refs reward hustle as much as fans do).
The crowd is getting nasty, occasionally tossing paper and cups on
the court, howling at the officials, cursing the Patroons. It seems
fortunate that beer is not served here, or things could get ugly. But
beer or no, things get ugly anyway.

With 2:28 left in the third Q and Albany up by 25, 83–58, a
spark ignites an inferno. The lead official, Mike Bobiak, finds a cheerleader's pompon on the floor and tosses it to the sidelines, but a
fan tosses it back on the court at him. Bobiak orders the fan thrown
out. The fan has a few things to say first, and while he does, more
debris comes down. Included in the projectiles are two or three
small plastic basketballs—about the size of a softball—that each
fan received as a promotional give-away before the game. Before
things get too out of hand, Texans coach Tom Schneeman is asked
to get on the PA and calm the crowd. He has other ideas. Taking
the mike, he announces:

"We understand your justifiable upsettedness at the *terrible*
officiating, but—"

He doesn't get the chance to finish. Bobiak races toward him,
slaps a T in his face, and tosses him from the game. And immediately,
a deluge. Red and blue plastic balls, hundreds and hundreds of them,
rain down from the seats. Most are directed at Bobiak and his
partner, Doug Rogan. A few head toward the Patroons. The balls
are soft, so no real danger exists; still, it's a scary sight, and for a
moment everyone is frozen, watching the storm like a cloudburst
that is awesome in its sudden, unexpected power.

Until Shurina, in his New York wisdom, sizes things up: "Hey George, let's get the fuck outta here!" he yells over the booing.

"Yeah, yeah, right," Karl agrees, snapped out of his momentary trance. "Everybody in the locker room. Let's get the fuck outta here!"

The Patroons race off the court, as do the Texans—and, of course, the refs. Schneeman stops to pick up a ball and toss it at Bobiak—missing the referee, but not by much. A fan, in imitation, races up behind Rowland and plugs him in the back of the head. Rowland spins, takes off one of his sneakers, and starts after the criminal, who wisely spins on his heels and runs away. More balls continue to fall onto the court. Gerald grabs Rowland and pushes him toward the locker room; Rowland, seething, relents, one shoe in his hand.

Once inside, stock is taken.

"I was gonna hit the motherfucker in the head with my shoe," Rowland, now laughing, admits.

"Hey, is 'upsettedness' a real word?" Shurina asks.

"I don't know; if it were Scrabble I'd have to challenge," Grissom answers.

"Hey, Kelvin, you ever seen anything like this?"

"Hell, in my high school people be gang fightin' in the stands, bring pistols, start shootin'. This ain't nothing."

Karl confers with the officials and the Texans' GM, and calls the league office. He is willing to forfeit the fourth quarter, take the win and six standings points, and go home. The refs want to finish the game, as does the league, and Karl relents. But a suitable amount of time must pass to calm the crowd. While waiting, the two teams meet in the runway that leads from the locker rooms to the floor. Watching the maintenance people clean up, they shake heads and smile.

"Hey Nessley," Ballard asks, "think it's safe?" Nessley, the big center, walks out on the court to talk to the crowd—more rationally than his coach.

Gerald spots Rob Rose. "When you all come to our place we're givin' out cue balls," Gerald tells him. Rose laughs.

Ennis Whatley announces he isn't worried. "Them balls got your names on 'em, not ours," he tells the Patroons.

A security guard stops over. "We are ready to play," Gerald says. "Nothin' is gonna happen now." The guard raises his eyebrows. "I don't know. They gave out three thousand of them balls, and only fifteen hundred came down." Gerald wonders if this is true.

After thirty-five minutes, the teams take the floor—warily. The Patroons warm up, shooting with one eye on the rim and one toward the stands. Gerald is fired up. "We were speedin' on the way in, and we're speedin' on the way out," he tells his team—three times. Kelvin has a better idea: "I'm gonna pull out a pistol and kill all these motherfuckers."

Fortunately, such drastic measures aren't needed. The game concludes without incident, except that the refs refuse to call anything against the Texans, who win the fourth quarter. It all ends calmly—with Kelvin, who has played another fine game, signing some of the little plastic balls for appreciative fans while he's on the bench and tossing them back playfully.

Everyone is amused by it all when it's over. Everyone except Karl. Schneeman's childish move depresses him, embarrasses him as a coach and as a member of this league, and reminds him, once again, that this isn't the NBA. Even when things like this happen every day, when the CBA bullshit seems more than he can be expected to understand, something worse happens. With several friends here watching the game, Karl almost wants to hide. He doesn't care to be a part of it.

But dinner and a few beers will cheer him up.

Gerald drives back to Dallas alone, to organize for the trip back home tomorrow. When he gets to the hotel, though, he first checks in on Wilkin, to make sure Tim got back safely. Gerald knocks on the door, and when Wilkin opens it Gerald asks, "Tim, are you here?"

The players take the van. Clint Smith drives, and gets lost. The team is in Fort Worth before it realizes the mistake.

Heading back to Dallas and arguing about what is played on the radio—"The Brothers all wanna listen to that Luther Vandross shit," Shurina tells Wilkin later—they pass a car alongside the road. A man is seated by the car, alone. He could be injured—or dead. Lee tells Clint to stop and help.

"Oh, no," Clint says, speeding past. "Police'll come, think C. Smith did it. Haul me away. I ain't stopping."

FEBRUARY 11

Because of silly scheduling, the Patroons have a game at home tonight, and a day off tomorrow. So it's up at 5:30, leave the hotel at 6:15, at the airport at 6:30.

"Hey, Clint Smith, how 'bout a diet Coke."

"Oh, George, here we go . . ."

"I got it," says Shurina. "I don't wanna get waived." Shurina isn't joking this time. His knee is still sore, and he sprained his wrist last night and won't play tonight. "If I go on George Karl's IR, I may never come back," he says with a smile. He knows roster moves are being made, and he knows that, with Minniefield and Upshaw back, he is a likely candidate—despite his excellent play of late. He is worried. "I'd have to fight for a job all over, new guys are coming in . . . and I don't want to miss the ESPN game." The Patroons-Texans game at the Armory next Monday is the ESPN CBA telecast. "Don't think I'm not psyched for that," Shurina says.

Ballard, though, has no worries. He leaves Albany for Washington, D.C.—his home—and then Seattle. "The CBA has been . . . different," he says. Now it's back to the NBA. Karl can only hope Ballard will return for the playoffs.

Gerald, of course, has worries enough for several men. He's on the pay phone at the Detroit airport while waiting for the connecting flight to Albany. Hanging up, he tells Karl, "George, I got Tulsa a ride from the Albany airport to the hotel. They are all set."

"Who's picking *us* up?" Karl asks.

Gerald thinks a minute. "I don't know, Coach."

"What about Minniefield? Isn't he supposed to?"

"Yes, he is, George. Maybe I should call him again and be sure."

"Maybe you should. Hey Clint, how about gettin' me . . ."

○   ○   ○

Minniefield is indeed waiting at the airport with the van. All go home, only to reconvene in three hours for another game.

And already, there are changes. Ballard is out—he is placed on the NBA/suspended list—and Dave Popson is in his place. El Deano is happy, as is Popson. Minniefield announces he is ready to play, but Karl keeps him out until he sees Minny practice. Shurina doesn't play, but is not put on IR either. The Patroons go with nine players tonight.

The Tulsa Fast Breakers have a new face of their own: Eric Newsome, the Little Shit, has been waived, replaced by Otis Bird-song, the NBA veteran. He shakes Karl's hand before the game.

"Why didn't you call me?" Birdsong asks. "I only live an hour and a half from here."

"How much did Tulsa get you for?" Karl asks.

"Fifty dollars."

"The way you've been playing that's about right."

Birdsong laughs. "So how's World B. Free? Talk to him lately?"

The game is an ugly, poorly officiated, why-are-we-here contest. Both teams traveled into Albany today after games last night, arriving just before the game, and both are tired and sloppy. The Patroons win, 102–92, and take six more points. But Karl blasts the officials in the paper, perhaps the combined outrage of last night and tonight boiling over.

He had considered giving the team tomorrow—Sunday—off, before Monday's rematch with Tulsa. Now he's not sure. In the locker room, looking as tired as his players, he says, "I was thinking about a day off, but I might want a couple of you—"

"Don't do it, Coach," Gerald jumps in. "Follow your instincts. Off tomorrow, bust 'em on Monday. Go with your gut. Go with your feel. You made a feel call earlier, in the game, and it worked, right?"

Karl laughs. "I did? When the fuck was that?"

Gerald thinks again. "I don't know. I just know you should go with your gut."

"All right, Ollie. Day off tomorrow."

FEBRUARY 13

Gerald, to Wilkin: "When George talks about the refs, don't write it, OK?"

"But Gerald, that's my job."

"I know. Just don't do it."

Wilkin, to Clint Smith: "You're back with your girlfriend?"

"Yeah, that's right. We tryin' to work things out."

"I thought you said she was on your case, always saying 'Clinton do this, Clinton do that.' "

"Now don't go around sayin' that, we gonna work things out."

"What about the girl who bought you that TV set?"

"C. Smith gonna have to go in-cog-ni-to for a while. Like Fletch."

Gerald, to Jim Laverty: "Lav, will you take these here keys an' go pick up Tulsa at the hotel an' bring 'em here so's they can play a game tonight?"

"Ollie, for you, anything."

Minniefield, in street clothes, to Luke, the bench boy, as the game starts: "Get me two hot dogs."

"They're on sale today. Fifty cents each."

"Fifty cents? Then get me four."

George Karl, to referee Ed Clarke, with 6:53 left in the game and the score tied at 83: "Get that guy off his fucking back!"

"That's it, George. Technical foul on George Karl."

"Go get fucked!"

"Yer outta here!"

With that, Karl has made his best coaching move of the game. The Patroons, lethargic all night, have lost a 14-point lead. Nothing Karl tried worked, the crowd was dead, the team flat. Upshaw's play, in particular, has incensed Karl; his first two games back had moments of inspiration, but since returning from the NBA, Kelvin has reverted to some of his wilder habits, forcing bad shots and not running the offense like Karl wants it run from the point. All Karl's screaming is having no effect, however. Sometimes, a coach has to sacrifice himself. He had been considering the move the entire fourth quarter; now he acts. Walking off the court, slowly, for maximum effect, he brings the crowd to life. Gerald escorts him off, says a few words, lumbers back to the bench, pulls up his pants, tucks in his shirttail, and gets to work. So does the team.

Lee pulls his favorite ploy, sticking his leg out to initiate contact with the defender and then hitting the deck on a three-point attempt, and tricks the ref into calling a foul. He makes all three free throws. Clint Smith, off the bench, dunks, rebounds, and drives in sequence, scoring all 11 of his points in the last quarter to key the charge. Stroeder hits an important jumper from the corner, later nails two free throws, then feeds Clint for another jam. Grissom feeds Upshaw underneath for a layup. All in all, the Pats run off an 18–4 burst, go up 101–90 in short order, and get the Armory rocking.

Gerald is fired up, coaching as intently as he knows how, his face beet red, sweat running off his tight brow, eyes squinting at the action. He makes a wise substitution right off, getting Clint into the game. He tries to call plays with his fingers, like a third-base coach giving signs, but in his excitement his gnarled fingers won't cooperate. Shurina, on the bench, tries desperately not to laugh as Gerald attempts to call the play 4-C, only to look like his hand is slipping into uncontrollable spasms. But Gerald is too involved to notice. He just wants to win a ball game.

Which he does, 107–94.

"George, the best thing you did all night was leave," Minniefield says on entering the locker room.

"I was thinking about it a lot earlier," Karl admits.

Meanwhile, the room fills with Clint's new nickname: Chuckie Brown. "Attaboy, Chuckie! Chuckie Brown off the bench." No one knows why he is Chuckie Brown. No one seems to care.

Kelvin, towel wrapped around his waist, heads for the shower. "You stunk, Kelvin Upshaw," Karl hollers after him with a hint of real anger. "Awful. No leadership at all."

"Hey, we won. Without you."

"Ooh, Kelvin!" Jack Moser calls out. "From downtown—it's good!"

Karl laughs—just a little.

FEBRUARY 14–17

Four days without a game, the longest time off since the New Year's break. On Tuesday, the fourteenth, Ken Johnson flies home to California. Officially, his back has acted up, and he is placed on the injured list. Unofficially, it is something of a trial separation between Johnson and the Patroons. Neither side is sure if reconciliation is possible.

Johnson takes Minniefield's place on IR (teams are allowed only two players on the injured list at a time; Kenny joins Keith Smith, still recovering from knee surgery). At practice on the fifteenth—the fourteenth is a day off—Dirk joins Kelvin Upshaw in the backcourt, and the challenge is met. Karl is concerned with Kelvin's attitude all over again. His stint in the NBA, while good for him in that it instilled confidence in his game ("I know I can play up there," Upshaw says now) has also given Kelvin a little cockiness, that big head that Clint Smith was worried about. Little confrontations, like the one after the last game, threaten to become bigger ones. And with Dirk back, presenting an added challenge, Karl is watching Kelvin closely.

On the sixteenth, Karl introduces two new plays, including a new alley-oop play for Dave Popson. Popson, with his sweat jacket zipped tightly to his throat, is learning about Armory practices: "Man, it's cold in here."

"You haven't *seen* cold yet," Karl tells him, this being a comparatively mild day. "Some days you see your breath in here." The new plays are Karl's way of keeping up with his ever-changing personnel; he designs his plays, and his overall offense, around his players. When the players keep changing, so do the plays. A playbook in the CBA would quickly become obsolete.

But this team will presumably stick for a while. The trading deadline for active players has passed; from here on in, trades can be made only for the rights to players not in the league. So the Patroons won't get Wes Matthews (whom Wichita Falls trades to Tulsa instead) or Rob Rose or Winston Bennett or any of the others. One name, though, does begin to pop up, the name of a player whose rights Albany acquired earlier in the year, an NBA veteran whom Karl had in Golden State and calls a scoring machine. His name is Steve Harris. Karl has been mentioning him on and off all year. Now, it is more on than ever.

But some other business needs to be done first. Gerald sits at the scorer's table on the sixteenth and announces, "Ah got some big things accomplished today. I got the van exchanged, I've taken care of some of the players' phone bills, I've taken care of some workmen's comp problems.... They might don't sound big, but they are." And then he watches Karl coach some zone defense, some things Gerald has drawn up. "That's one thing I know about, is zones," Gerald says with pride. "I learned from Ray Mears."

"Was he good with zones?" Gerald is asked.

"He was as good as there was," Gerald says quietly. "Maybe better than there was."

Practice ends, but not without Karl hounding Kelvin relentlessly. Even in practice, Kelvin has been a bit too cool for Karl's liking. "Upshaw, your game stinks," Karl spits at Kelvin. "*Stinks!* Everything about it sucks." Kelvin, his own anger rising, tosses a ball toward the ceiling, and it never comes down. The ball lands on one of the crossbeams, and sticks there. Kelvin just shrugs. Gerald's eyes pop. Then he sighs. "Dad gem it. Now we're down to seven balls." Karl calls Kelvin over for a stiff lecture.

FEBRUARY 18

First, the team picture isn't taken before the game; the photographer is there, the front office is there, but no one told the players. "I think I screwed up," Gerald says, "and I'm tryin' to figure out *how* I screwed up." Team owner Ben Fernandez, who flew in just for this occasion, doesn't care who screwed up; he only knows he's angry, and leaves before the game starts.

Then, Shurina learns that the Patroons won't hold three tickets for his girlfriend and her parents, who have driven up from New York to watch him play. They'll be stuck in general admission— the cheap seats—so the front office can sell a few more choice tickets. "Is this a fuckin' cheap organization, or what?" Shurina asks. Every day, things prove, it is. But, heck, good seats cost eight dollars, and eight dollars is eight dollars....

And then, Steve Harris walks in, in street clothes, to watch his first Albany Patroons game. Press pundits look over the Albany roster, wondering who is about to get injured in tonight's game to make room for the new entry.

"Will Steve Harris play Monday?" Wilkin asks Karl.

"On the record?" Karl asks.

"Yes."

"Fuck you."

"All right, off the record."

"Probably." Karl laughs.

Karl also admits that he knew Portland Trail Blazers coach Mike Shuler would be fired, which he was today.

"Have you talked to them yet?" Wilkin asks.

"I heard they were gonna fire him on the road, next week. I guess they decided not to wait."

"Are you interested in the job?"

"On the record?"

"Of course."

"Fuck you."

"Off the record . . ."

"I think it's a pretty good fit."

Karl tells Wilkin he thinks he has a good chance at the job. Portland has named an interim coach for the rest of the season, so it appears Karl will have to wait for the off-season. On the other hand, things can change quickly. But Karl isn't talking. Add Portland to Indiana and the Clippers—all intriguing rumors, all to be played out later. Stay tuned.

There is a game tonight, against the Wichita Falls Texans once again. Tom Schneeman is not coaching; he was suspended for two games as a result of his incendiary behavior in the now-famous riot last week, and this is the second game of that suspension. And that might be to the Texans' advantage; Schneeman is not a very good coach, and his team appears more relaxed under the laissez-faire leadership of interim coach John Treloar, the team's basketball operations veep. The Texans, in fact, take a 14-point lead early, and win the first quarter by 7. But Treloar follows what seems to be typical CBA coaching behavior, and plays his starters to death. Ennis Whatley, Derrick Taylor, Rob Rose, and Cedric Jenkins all log 40 minutes or more, and Albany's deeper bench—all ten Patroons play between 15 and 32 minutes—eventually wears the Texans down. Up by 1 after three quarters, Albany scores 47 in the fourth—a season high—and wins going away, taking six more standings points. The Patroons file off the court, mixed in with the fans as they stride toward the staircase down to the locker room. "Nice game, Keith," a fan offers to Lee as he fights through the crowd.

"It's Doug. Thanks." Lee shakes his hand, and bounds down the stairs, laughing. "He must've thought I was Keith Lee. Believe that?"

Karl evaluates. Popson, in his first full game, plays well: 23 points, 9 rebounds. He can't rebound like Ken Johnson, but his overall game is better. Perhaps Stroeder, Grissom, and Popson are enough. Stroeder, too, is coming around a bit; John scores 27, and 9 boards. Minniefield and Upshaw form a fine backcourt, combining for 25 points and 13 assists between them. The only real problems are with Upshaw's and Stroeder's shot selections—Stroeder still plays like he thinks he's a shooting guard, putting up too many twenty-footers when he serves better in the paint, and Kelvin continues his impatient play, shooting more than he should and finding others less. But the more subtle problem is this: who goes when Steve Harris comes on. Both Shurina and Clint Smith, the likely candidates, are playing well off the bench (both contributed key baskets in the fourth quarter run tonight).

The decision will wait until just before Monday's game—the ESPN game. Tomorrow—Sunday—will be a closed practice, Karl tells Wilkin. "You can come, but you can't write anything."

"Why? Will Harris practice?"

"On the record? Fuck you," Karl booms with a laugh, and takes off for Thirsty's.

FEBRUARY 19

Practice is closed, so, as far as the world knows, Steve Harris isn't here. Karl doesn't tell him he'll be making $10 a game, and doesn't add, "Hell, you're making $390,000 from the NBA, you don't need our money." And Harris doesn't laugh.

If Harris had been here—which he wasn't, honest—he would have heard Gerald's prepractice lecture. Gerald gathers the team and talks about renewing commitment to George. It's directed mainly at Kelvin, but it also is intended to sharpen everyone for the playoffs. Unfortunately, it's also in tongues.

"He said something about the Japanese," Grissom says later,

trying to recapture the moment. "They have better memories or something. He kept saying, 'Give me a piece of paper, I'll memorize it.' There was some more about the garbage in our heads—nothing about orgies, though."

"There was a couple of 'fuck me–fuck you's in there, too," Shurina adds.

"Yeah, but he messed one up, didn't he? He said fuck you–fuck me instead," Grissom says.

"The scary thing is, Stroeder is starting to understand him," Shurina says.

"Yeah, well, they're kind of on the same wavelength," Grissom answers.

Shurina changes his shoes and leaves. He has been quieter than normal today. Usually an extraverted, story-telling, easygoing kid, he seems preoccupied. And for good reason, perhaps. Someone is about to be hurt, and he's afraid it will be he.

Clint Smith is afraid, too, but he's more vocal about it. "If it's me," he tells Wilkin, "it's dy-no-mite time. I'll blow this place up."

FEBRUARY 20

In the middle of the frenzy that comes with a television broadcast, among the newly arrived trucks parked outside the Armory that feed in the extra cables and wires and monitors, among the harried Albany execs and frenzied league officials and ESPN technicians, with the heightened excitement that fills the Armory air and elevates the moods of Patroons staffers and Armory volunteers and ticket takers and popcorn vendors, in the midst of all this, Steve Shurina sits, alone, dark-eyed and sullen, on an empty staircase. His face hangs to his chest, his eyes flame with the toxic mix of anger, frustration, embarrassment, confusion, resentment, disbelief . . . fury. "Sometimes," Karl has just told him, "the good guys get fucked. And you've been great." But something has to give to make room for Steve Harris, and that something is Shurina. He's placed on the injured list, two hours before his chance to shine on national television. And he is taking it hard.

He and Clint Smith have both been talked to; Karl says that Shurina is the guy now, and Clint is next—in all likelihood, they will alternate places in the lineup until (and if) someone is called up to the NBA or goes to Europe. Clint, while sorry for his apartment-mate's demotion, is nevertheless relieved. "If it had been me," he tells Wilkin, "no game today. Dy-no-mite." Five games from now, though, Clint might be in Shurina's sad shoes.

And sad is hardly the word. Shurina's girlfriend spots him sitting alone, stands by him a minute, then leads him out the door. They don't stay to watch. Instead, with a road trip coming up—the team leaves tomorrow morning—a trip on which he won't be invited, Shurina is going home to New York, to worry about his basketball future. Karl assures him he will play again this year. Shurina has heard things like that before.

And up in the wives/girlfriends section, the women sit and sympathize. They also wonder: Couldn't Karl have waited one more day? Who is this Steve Harris, anyway?

Steve Harris is, just now, signing a contract in the locker room. When all is over in about three hours, he will have played just 6 minutes. Couldn't Karl have waited one more day?

○ ○ ○

Bill Heller is frantic, trying to keep up with the added responsibility of putting on an ESPN show; he spots Wilkin and tells him—voice down low, as if he's revealing insider information—that Keith Smith has been waived to make room for Shurina on the injured list. Wilkin nods, then laughs when Heller bustles away. Once again, the reporter knows more than the team publicist. Wilkin knew Smith was going to be waived three days ago; he also knows Karl has somehow swung a deal with the league to let the Patroons keep Smith's rights—waiving him would make Keith a free agent—for the promise that he won't play again this year.

Karl is in fact now talking with the CBA's commissioner, Jay Ramsdell, who is in town for the ESPN game. Karl is trying to swing another, and much more intriguing deal. He wants to get Larry Bird, recuperating from foot surgery, to play a rehab game in the CBA, and he wants Bird to play in Albany (even though Rockford has the rights to Celtics players, Karl argues that Albany is much closer). It's nearly impossible that Bird would want to or be allowed to play in the CBA, but you never know. . . .

What you do know is that general manager Gary Holle would milk it for every penny. There is precedent: When Ron Guidry was recovering from arm trouble a few years back, he rehabbed one game for the Albany Yankees, New York's Double A affiliate. Holle, who also works for that team, rarely lets things like safety, common sense, or professional appearances stand in the way of an honest buck; he sold tickets for folding chairs set up along the warning track—in fair territory—to accommodate the overflow crowd. Signing waivers of liability in case they should be bonked in the head by a fly ball, the fans were allowed to sit in the outfield while Guidry pitched. Today, the speculation is how many chairs Holle could sell at half court, should Larry Bird play a game here.

In the meantime, and serving to further Albany's reputation for fiscal responsibility, the Patroons have placed the ESPN crew at the seedy Howard Johnson's Motel. One can only imagine Brent Musburger being treated this way.

The ESPN crew takes over; this is not so much a game as a TV show. Everything is scripted, from the advance whoop-de-do that PA announcer Jay Silverman is instructed to whip the crowd into (you can't have a quiet crowd when the red light comes on) to the shortened halftime to the wireless mikes that Karl and Schneeman must wear. (Karl, however, reports his isn't working and hands it back. It's not working because he doesn't want it to work.)

But Karl has done a good job of downplaying the significance of a televised game. "When I was at Golden State," he says at courtside before the game, "I can distinctly remember being on the stationary bike in our training room one afternoon, and I had the option of watching a CBA game or 'General Hospital.' I watched 'General Hospital.' No one in the NBA watches this. They've had their scouts here, and by now they have their lists of who they like. Being on TV doesn't mean anything."

Once all the hoopla is over, the game takes command, and like many Patroons games lately, it's tougher than it should be. Albany and Wichita Falls split the first two quarters, and then, after the shortened halftime, Albany goes into its usual third quarter funk. A 16–8 run puts the Texans up by 5, 71–66, with 4:25 left. Karl then pulls Clint Smith off the bench—he hasn't played yet—and Clint once again provides the spark. First he grabs a defensive rebound and feeds Minniefield for the layup. Then his persistent defense forces a turnover. But most important, he follows this with a one-man slam dunk contest. Over the next minute and a half, Clint slams three dunks in a row, all to finish fast breaks, the last one giving Albany a 3-point lead and real—not scripted—enthusiasm to the crowd. The quarter ends with Albany up by 2. A few minutes into the fourth, Clint checks out of the game. The crowd stands and cheers; the bench rises, too, calling him "Sparky" for obvious reasons. Clint, keeping his game face on, calmly slaps hands and coolly takes a seat. Then he turns to a reporter at the press table. "I shoulda been in in the first half," he says.

But, as usual, it's not quite over. Derrick Taylor finds his rhythm—he will finish with 28—and brings the Texans back to the lead, only to have fatigue strike once again. Pearson's baseline J puts Albany back on top. Doug Lee follows with a three-point play, to be followed by Pearson's three-point bomb from the wing and another three-point play by Lee (Lee and Pearson finish with 22 and 21 points, respectively). And then it is over, 115–105. Minniefield wraps a towel around his shoulders and walks off court. Only a few notice his towel—and others like it—sport the Hilton logo.

"Yeah, Sparky!" Grissom hollers in the dressing room. "A win on national TV!"

"Word," Sparky says.

"Gentlemen," Gerald breaks the celebration, "we leave the Quality Inn at six forty-fahve tomorrow morning. Make it six forty. Six four oh. Be down in the lobby at six thirty-fahve loading your bags on the van. Six three fahve."

"Yeah, Sparky!"

Out in the hallway, Karl talks with some reporters. A fan walks up, as fans often do down here in the Armory basement. But this fan has a look about him. He has glazed eyes, ringlets of jheri-curled hair falling around his face, and is dressed in tattered sweat clothes. It appears he is here to offer more than congratulations.

"Nice game, Coach," he begins, and Karl shakes his hand. Then comes the rest. "Can I talk wichyoo?" he whispers to Karl. George considers the request, and against his better judgment accepts. The two step aside. Karl listens a moment, then looks around for help. He spots Gerald stepping out of the locker room. "This is the man you need to talk to," Karl says hurriedly, pushing the gentleman toward Gerald. "Ollie, this man wants a tryout. You handle that, right?" Karl passes him off and fairly runs to the locker room, where safety and another cold one await.

FEBRUARY 21–22

An early departure to Charleston, for two games with the Gunners. Albany will play tonight and tomorrow night—three games in three days in two different cities, followed by another travel day, a game in Wichita Falls, then back home for one game against Rockford, then back on the road for one game in Topeka, then home for two . . . the CBA schedule is as interesting as everything else in the league. Luckily for the Patroons, a forty-plus point lead in the standings with only ten games left in the season makes these games important only as preparation for the playoffs.

Which does nothing to soften the pain of the worst loss of the season. Despite losing Michael Anderson to the San Antonio Spurs and Jamie Waller to Europe (and the peripatetic Ozell Jones, who has been traded once again, to La Crosse earlier in the week, his fifth CBA team in three years), Charleston takes six standings points and beats Albany by 14, 106–92, thus ending a seven-game winning streak. At one point the Patroons are down 22, and never get closer than 9. Only Stroeder, with 22 points and 15 rebounds, has a reasonable game. Charleston, struggling to make the final playoff spot, simply blows the Pats out.

The next night is a different story—although it almost isn't. At the half it's 58–48 Albany, and that advantage grows to 16 points by the fourth quarter. Then the lead falls away, nearly for good. The Patroons are up by 4 with just over a minute to go when Charleston's Keith Tyler fouls Clint Smith. Dan Levy announces to his radio audience that it's Tyler's seventh foul; since Levy is situated right next to the Albany bench, he also flags Karl and flashes seven fingers. Karl jumps onto the court.

"That's seven on Tyler. Technical," Karl shouts to the ref. The officials ask the scorer, and find it's Tyler's fifth foul, not his seventh. Delay of game, Albany, the second of the night—so it's a technical, all right, but against the Patroons.

"Well, there's egg on my face," Levy announces. "I had Tyler for seven." Karl seethes. Tyler makes the technical free throw, and cuts the lead to 3, 109–106.

Luckily for Levy, Albany holds on to win by 3. The victory raises Albany's record to 32–14, and with 205 points the Patroons officially qualify for the playoffs; with nine games left, the worst Albany can finish is fourth (even though first is a virtual lock).

At dinner afterwards, Karl says to Levy, "If we had lost I would have ripped your heart out."

FEBRUARY 23–24

From West Virginia to Texas—via Chicago. The Crazy Basketball Association's crazy flight plans.

At O'Hare, who should the Patroons run into this time? On earlier trips it's been the De Paul team and the WWF and Cazzie Russell; today, it's the Chicago Bulls. Clint spots his boy Michael Jordan on one of O'Hare's moving walkways, surrounded by kids, signing autographs. Clint pushes through, not to be outmaneuvered by mere children.

"Noooooooobody . . . nooooobody," Clint says in his best Mars Blackmanese. "My boy Mike, when you gonna set me up with some Nikes? You said you'd send me some in the mail. What's up?"

○ ○ ○

The next night, back at D.L. Ligon Coliseum for the first time since the ball-raining incident, the Patroons want to hurt the Texans again. It's looking more and more likely that Wichita Falls will finish fourth, and therefore be Albany's opening-round playoff opponent.

They are also looking for a way out of the recent stretch of poor play. Kelvin and Stroeder, in particular, are of concern to Karl. The team's overall attitude is poor. There is little leadership, either on the court or off. The chemistry has soured some, and Karl isn't sure why.

It gets worse. With a 17-point lead in the final quarter, Albany's lack of direction explodes into a horrific defeat. Wichita Falls scores 26 of the final 32 points, including the last 13 of the game. Kelvin's play infuriates Karl; Upshaw's defense is nonexistent, as Ennis Whatley scores all 7 of his points in the last quarter—all on free throws when Kelvin commits lazy fouls. Upshaw fails to direct the offense as well. As difficult as it is to pin a loss like this on one man's shoulders, everyone on the floor, from Karl to Dan Levy, is inclined to point fingers in one direction.

Losing two of three on the road is less distressing than how the games were lost. Kelvin is simply not responding. Stroeder is putting up decent numbers, but for unknown reasons (perhaps he feels he should be back in the NBA, and isn't coping well with that disappointment) is still in a funk. Steve Harris, the newest Patroon, is out of shape and not thrilled at being in the CBA. There is some lingering resentment at the treatment Shurina received as well; despite his physical limitations (no one thinks he is the best guard on the team), he did offer a positive attitude and gave fully of himself on the court and off. He took the lumps, did the grunt work—he offered some of the glue Karl needs.

Everyone is confused, in fact. All the recent changes—Popson and Minniefield and Harris in, Upshaw back, Ballard and Johnson and Shurina out—have forced Karl to juggle playing times and player rotations; that, more than anything, is causing the problem. Former starters aren't starting, minutes are being reduced for players like Lee and Rowland as Karl tries to get Popson and Harris and Minniefield in shape, and Karl isn't being as clear as he should in letting the players understand his reasons. Just when things were starting to roll, everything changed—perhaps too much. The result is grumbling on the bench, frustration for the coaches, and losses in games that should be easy wins.

All in all, the Patroons are a grumpy, disparate group. Bad attitude is rampant. And the playoffs start in two weeks.

Before leaving, though, the Texas police make another collar. The player van, this time with Minniefield driving, gets pulled over once more for speeding. Just to end things on the proper note.

FEBRUARY 26

Back at the Armory, Sunday afternoon; cranky moods all around. Karl bitches at Gerald, the two sounding like a not-too-happily married couple bickering about their children, their shared duties, and the never-ending complications of their daily lives.

"Gerald, why can't we leave Tuesday instead of tomorrow, so I can practice these fuckers."

"Coach, we just cain't."

"Then when do we leave tomorrow?"

"We leave at eleven oh three. Unless we leave later."

"When is Doc Nunnally coming in? I thought you made that call?"

"Well, Coach, I thought you wanted to wait till Wednesday. That's what I'm doing."

"What are we gonna do with Upshaw? He just doesn't get it. He doesn't appreciate his grace period is over."

"I know it, Coach, but he don't."

"Gerald, who are these new guys Rockford has? I've never seen these guys before in my life."

"That there is Darryl Gadsden, and that is Anthony Simms, and Mike Richmond, and—"

"Who?"

Just the tonic for the struggling Patroons: In comes the dismantled Rockford Lightning for a Sunday afternoon game. Pace Mannion is back in the NBA, this time with Atlanta; Fred Cofield, their three-point ace, has left for Europe; and Jim Lampley and Kenny Natt are injured. Other new additions are Ken Bannister (in a trade), Dwayne McClain, David Wood, and Jose Slaughter, along with Dominic Pressley, who in the rapid change of the CBA world is not so new anymore. They have lost four of their last five, and have slipped to third place in the Western Division.

And they blow the Patroons out of the gym.

The final is 114–101, but, as the cliché goes, it isn't that close. Pressley and McClain hit for 30 each. Six of seven points go to Rockford. The score doesn't tell the full story. It is only Albany's third loss at home this season and certainly the most thorough. Down by as many as 21 in the third quarter, Albany's only burst of competence narrows the gap to 7. But Rockford then opens the fourth quarter with 13 straight points—Albany doesn't score for over five minutes—and the Patroons limp down to the locker room.

Kelvin has been benched the entire second half. Although he didn't pout overtly, he is surly inside. Others have pouted, though, namely Stroeder and Rowland. (Stroeder's inept and almost embarrassing play, in fact—missed layups, silly turnovers, getting his shots blocked—has been noticed by the crowd, and boos and calls for his removal begin filtering toward the Albany bench. Rowland wants more minutes, he wants to score more points.) Steve Harris, the scoring machine, nets 6 points in 19 minutes. There is grumbling on the bench and on the court all afternoon.

Karl has been talking about these things, in bits and pieces, for days now. This afternoon's performance, however, brings it all out of him. He has found times, during the season, that demand strong words, long speeches, an overall accounting of where things stand in his eyes. He has a remarkable ability to speak, extemporaneously, about a number of things without losing either his points or his audience. Right now, he begins one of his longer and stronger talks. As is his style, he starts slowly and quietly, then grows more forceful and louder, then quiets again, like a storm that starts innocently, only to turn violent before it moves out to sea.

He says:

"To win basketball games, especially on the pro level, there's a word I'm sure you've heard a hundred times: fundamentals. Now there are certain nights you can shoot well, nights you cannot play very well and still win some games. But the best basketball teams, the toughest basketball teams, are the teams that are fundamental.

"I'll give you credit, you guys all season long have been fundamental. And good in your professionalism. That's what bothers me about what's happened here in the last week or so. There's a saying I know: the most disgraceful thing you can be to yourselves is never to live up to what you can be. That's the most disappointing thing you can be. A long time ago that's what my dad told me. My dad knew nothing about athletics. Nothing. He didn't know how to catch a baseball. But that's what my dad told me. He said, 'I don't know anything about it, but if you work your ass off and be the best you can be I'll give you everything I can give you.'

"Now, a lot of pro basketball is that way: consistency, fundamentals, mental attitude, preparation. The things that get real boring after fifty games. The things that get real frustrating. The little attitudes between one another in a locker room, the attitude between coaches and players over fifty, eighty games. You know who don't make The League? The ones who those things bother. The ones who don't have their heads on right every game.

"We just got our ass kicked. Badly. I don't know if it's because of talent; it might be, they played well, they shot the shit out of it. But we lost because of fundamentals. Part of fundamentals—I should bring in a scouting sheet. When we scout players in college, part of the fundamentals—we have a list: ball handling, passing, defense . . . You know what also falls under fundamentals? Attitude. How does he relate with the coach? How does he relate with other players? How does he relate with referees? All of those things are judged by NBA scouts. In fact, they're not only judged, they go on the fucking computer. Some of you guys were judged when you were back in college—six years ago—on your attitude all around.

"The NBA is a multimillion-dollar business. And they don't fuck around. *They don't fuck around, guys.* And I'll tell you something, you're fuckin' around. That's basically what we're going through. We're fuckin' around.

"I'll be honest with you. I have all the confidence in the world that you're gonna be able to turn that switch on. It might be in Topeka Tuesday night, it might not be till March eighth. I have all the confidence that we're gonna kick ass. But the way you're fuckin' around is not hurtin' anyone except you guys that have to look yourself in the mirror. And there's four or five guys in here that shouldn't be able to look yourself in the fuckin' mirror. The little games you're playing, the little tricks, the individualism . . . *I don't know what the fuck you're trying to do.* You're hurting the team, you're hurting the organization, you're hurting a lot of people today. *Throw it all out the fucking window! It doesn't matter!* The thing it's hurting is you.

"And that makes no fuckin' sense. If you don't try and be the best you can be for two hours of every day . . . do you realize how fortunate you all are? I know you all got a lot of bitches, a lot of you got screwed by the NBA, but you're making five hundred dollars a week to work two hours a day.

"Some of you are gonna make a lot more money. But letting yourselves down, that's something . . . number one, I'm not gonna play you if you do. I think you're embarrassing yourselves. Along with embarrassing the team and me. We've talked about those words, but maybe you don't understand: Professionalism. Mental intensity. Concentration. Focus. Those are things that win basketball games.

"Now we're in the CBA and we've won thirty-three, thirty-four games. I don't know what we've won. But check the record, gentlemen: we haven't beaten a good team lately. Our record the last twenty games is only 11–9, 10–10. Are you guys playing to the best ability you can? *Are you guys handling all the peripheral things?* Guys going up, going to Europe, new guys coming in . . . are you handling it as best as you can?

"I don't give a fuck if you go off the court and bitch about me and everything else, that's your prerogative. But if this stuff is bothering your attitude on the court, then you're hurting yourself. You should try to remedy that. I don't know how you do that. You might wanna come talk to me; my door has never been closed to anyone in this room. If you wanna talk to a psychologist, a counselor, we'll get that for you. But if you have a problem with your attitude . . . y'know, I've seen great players in the NBA with bad attitudes who can walk on the court and play. But there are not many, not many *in the NBA* who can have a bad attitude and play. I know one guy, fuckin' mopey bastard off the court, doesn't like to practice, tells his teammates to get fucked all the time, then he goes and plays. That's one. There's not many, anywhere. *And some of you guys are trying to do the same thing. You gotta be shittin' me.* You gotta be shittin' me.

"And just because you're in first place, and just because you're forty points ahead, to deteriorate what we've gained . . . is *stupid!* It's fuckin' *stupid!* That's what bothers me, *I don't like to be stupid! I don't like to waste work! I don't like to waste what you fuckers have built! And I definitely don't like to not be what we can be!* That's what I don't like.

"Now if you guys have any problems with what I'm saying, talk to me. 'Cause I'm not gonna put up with it. I'll lose every fuckin' game playing hard and playing with people who are trying to be what they can be. You can ask Clint Smith, *I did it in the fuckin' NBA, and I'll do it here.* I'm not gonna put up with bullshit.

"I don't know how you guys feel about their cuteness after they kicked our ass . . . *that shit is for losers, and a lot of the fuckin' attitudes in this locker room the last couple weeks are for losers. And excuses are for losers.* That's the one thing I love about the Boston Celtics. When they get their ass kicked you never hear about a mismatch or a rotation, they come out and say, 'We just got our ass kicked.' The Lakers say the same fuckin' thing. They don't blame it on playing time or rotations or 'I didn't get enough shots' . . . the fuckin' winners *don't make excuses!* Now the CBA is excuse-oriented. It might be that way because it's full of fuckin' losers.

"Think about what I'm saying. Think about it. And think about what we've been the last four weeks. Learn one thing if you learn any fucking thing: Don't ever let yourself be something you don't want to be. If you can't do that you shouldn't be here. *If you can't do that for two hours of practice and games, and not bitch about being there or have excuses, then maybe you shouldn't be here.* Maybe you shouldn't be here. And there's no one in this room that I'll say don't go home. Just come and ask me. I'll let you go.

"It's time to get it screwed on right."

○   ○   ○

At Thirsty's, Karl's dark mood continues. This loss—as well, indeed, as the last several losses—will take a while to work itself out; it might be a long night. Cathy Karl, knowing better than anyone how George gets at times like this, packs the kids home early.

Steve Shurina walks into the bar and, spotting Karl by the pinball machine, goes over to shake his hand.

"Where *you* been?" Karl says, partly snapping at Shurina, but also fond of seeing him.

"I had no idea it was an afternoon game, George, I swear to God," Shurina says. "Gerald never told me. I was driving up and flippin' through the radio, and when the game came on I couldn't believe it."

"Let me think about things for a while and then I'll talk to you. Don't leave."

"All right," Shurina says, and takes a seat with Grissom and Popson, to catch up on things. He tells of how depressed he's been; a devoted New York Rangers fan—like all true New York fans, he calls them by their real name: Duh Fuckin' Raynjuhs—he reports that, even with a week at home, "I didn't even go to duh fuckin' Raynjuhs game. I was so bummed. I just sat around like a load." Karl meanwhile tells Wilkin he may have made a mistake putting Shurina on IR. Later tonight, Karl will promise Shurina he'll be in the lineup Thursday night, for the Patroons' next home game. Who he will replace has yet to be determined. His spirits raised, Shurina decides to stay in Albany while the team is in Topeka, rather than drive back to New York. Duh Fuckin' Raynjuhs will have to survive a little longer without him.

Ken Johnson also walks in. He arrived back in Albany last night and was at the game this afternoon, sitting on the bench in street clothes next to Keith Smith. He says he is ready to play again. When he will play again is now up to Karl.

Keith Smith walks in, with yet another in an ever-changing series of ladyfriends on his arm, and gets cozy at the bar. Injured reserve seems to be suiting him well.

Greg Ballard doesn't walk in, but he may any day. Surprisingly, the SuperSonics have cut Ballard after his first ten-day contract. He'll be back in Albany, probably just to coach, but perhaps to play if needed.

And Kelvin Upshaw walks in. He takes a seat with Johnson and orders dinner.

Karl is at a table close by Kelvin's, separated only by a half wall. Karl sits with Gerald and Wilkin and Jim Laverty, drinking beers and dismantling his team. Dan Levy walks up to the table.

"Fuck you," Karl greets him in a not-untypical and mostly harmless cranky-Karl salute.

"I see you're in a better mood." Levy smiles back.

"When's Ballard coming in?" Wilkin asks.

"Fuck you, too." Karl orders another round. "I'm gonna waive Kelvin Upshaw. That'll get the message through to him."

"Now, Coach," Gerald says, "do you really want to do that?"

"Fuck you, Gerald."

"All right, fuck you Gerald," says Gerald.

Wilkin bursts out laughing.

"George is in a great fuckin' mood, isn't he?" Laverty laughs along.

"Fuck you, too. You watch. I'm gonna waive him."

"Now, Coach, is that the right thing to do . . ."

"Fuck you, Gerald."

"All right, fuck you Gerald, but maybe you should wait and see how he plays in Topeka."

"What time do we leave?"

"We leave tomorrow morning at eleven oh three. The van will be at the Quality Inn at—"

"Fuck the van."

"All right, Coach, fuck the van."

"And fuck you, Gerald."

"All right, fuck you Gerald . . ."

FEBRUARY 27–28

At eleven oh three, the van leaves the Quality Inn; at the airport, all meet for the flight to Topeka. All except Derrick Rowland. Without warning, the Patroons are now down their top scorer. The rumor is that Derrick is sick, but no one hears anything from him for two days.

So nine less than happy players and two desperately concerned coaches make the trip to Kansas for one game with the Topeka Sizzlers. The worst team in the CBA, winners of only ten of forty-seven games and already eliminated from postseason play, Topeka has recently suffered further distress. Lost within the past two weeks have been guard Carlton McKinney and his 23 ppg average to Europe, and forward Jim Rowinski, who has taken his 20 points per game to the Detroit Pistons. Only eight players dress for the game on the twenty-eighth, and only seven see action.

And once again, the Patroons blow a big lead and lose in embarrassing fashion. And once again, Kelvin Upshaw loses control.

Upshaw isn't the only culprit when a second half 15-point lead melts down to a 75-all tie after three quarters. Nor is he solely responsible when the Patroons watch a rebuilt 8-point fourth quarter lead slip to a 2-point deficit with 1:02 left. But when the clock runs down to 15 seconds, and the Sizzlers are still up by two, and Kelvin brings the ball upcourt, and is surrounded by three defenders but forces up an unlikely shot that of course misses, and a chance to tie the game is ruined before it can ever develop, Upshaw can be blamed.

And with that, a month that had started so promisingly, with a road trip that produced three wins in four games and a four-game sweep at home and a seven-game winning streak and an apparent roll into the playoffs, has instead collapsed into four losses in five games, disunity, unhappiness, ego clashing, confusion, dissension, and fatigue—mental, physical, spiritual. Only five games remain in which to get playoff-ready.

Now is not the time for the CBA Blues.

6

MARCH

MARCH 1

Coach Karl calls for an afternoon practice upon returning to Albany. Waiting at the Armory is Derrick Rowland. He apologizes to everyone for missing the game—he really was sick, but made the mistake of trying to communicate to the coaches on the road through the front office in Albany, so the messages were of course never delivered. With that cleared up, he talks to Grissom about the most recent loss, the team's overall slump, and the two captains decide to call a players-only meeting. Once everyone arrives, Rowland assembles the troops in the locker room and shuts the door. For fifteen minutes they talk—Rowland mostly, with help from Grissom and Lee, and others chirping in, about their recent frustrations, the disruption caused by the new arrivals (nothing personal, guys) just when things seemed to be going so well. They talk about the changes in the rotations, about being mad at having their minutes reduced and roles changed. But they also talk about accepting and understanding these changes. This is the CBA, and it goes with the territory, like it or not. Winning the championship is what matters now; George knows what he's doing (at least most think he knows what he's doing) and it's time to stop the bitching and pull together.

The meeting seems to help. A spirited practice follows, ending in Rowland accepting his "fine" for missing the Topeka game: Anyone makes a half-court shot, Derrick owes him $20; if Rowland hits one first, no fine. Karl adds that he gets $20 if he makes his patented back-to-the-basket half-court shot, and goes first. And connects. He pumps his fist in victory. Upshaw also makes one. Rowland is out $40.

Today is Wednesday, March 1. A week from today, on March 8, the Patroons will play their last regular season game. Included in the five games over the next seven nights will be several roster changes and a number of major considerations. Karl and Oliver are planning already.

The first move is to get Shurina back in the lineup—"Steve, you're playing tomorrow," Karl tells him after practice. His spot on IR will now be filled by Danny Pearson. Pearson is flying home for his grandfather's funeral; Karl also announces to Tim Wilkin that Pearson "hurt his knee, too."

Hearing this, Gerald waves his hands and limps away. "Oh Coach, Ah don't want to hear it. Don't get me involved. Ah just got finished gettin' the league office happy with us, which they weren't before."

"Why weren't they happy?" Wilkin asks.

"Because we got all these miracle cures. All our guys keep coming back after five games. We got the best trainer in the world, an' we don't even *have* a trainer." It seems the league is getting upset over all the Patroons' player jockeying; while not illegal, the moves do stretch the rules some, and Gerald has to smooth all the feathers George continually ruffles.

Gerald is prepared for more ruffling, though. Other moves are being considered. Ken Johnson may play Saturday. Will Clint Smith sustain a surprise injury soon? That's one possibility. Another is that someone may be off to Europe; Karl is trying to sell Clint, as well as Doug Lee. That would open a spot.

Still another spot might be needed for Greg Ballard. League rules require that a player dress for eight regular season games to be eligible for the playoffs, and Ballard played in only seven in his short CBA stay. Karl would certainly like the option of having Ballard available, so he somehow has to squeeze Greg into another game.

To do that, someone else would have to be waived, or lost to Europe or the NBA.

A lot could happen in the next week.

MARCH 2

At shootaround in the morning, the discussion continues. Italy and the Philippines are looking for a forward. Will it be Lee? Will it be Rowland? Will it be both?

"That would solve my problem with Ken Johnson," Karl says with a smile, until it is pointed out that it would also open up another one—that of entering the playoffs without a scorer. Rowland and Lee are the top two scorers on the team. "I guess you kind of want that in the playoffs, don't you," Karl says.

Yes, you kind of do.

"Switch ends, guys!" Karl shouts through the chill air. "Five bucks for half-court shots!" Pearson, who leaves for Florida tonight, swishes.

"That can't count! You're injured!"

Clint Smith banks one in off the glass.

"No way, Chuckie Brown! I saw you miss one already going at the other basket!"

"I didn't do no such thing, G.K.," Clint protests. "Five bucks, you owe me."

"No fuckin' way, Chuckie Brown."

"Aw, George."

Shurina, meanwhile, searches for Gerald. "He owes me my last two checks. I gotta pay rent, gotta pay my furniture rental, and Ollie says he lost my last paycheck. I can't believe it. I'm fucked."

○ ○ ○

The struggling Cedar Rapids Silver Bullets, losers of ten of their last eleven games, are in for two games, tonight (Thursday) and Saturday night.

"Hey! Ronny Rowan! C'mere," Gerald yells at the Bullets' star, who is over by one of the basket standards talking with Shurina, his former St. John's teammate. "We got a bet here, an' I can win it."

Rowan walks up and shakes Gerald's and George's hands. "The rumor is," Karl says, "that you're flying to Venice tomorrow."

"Are you flyin' outta here tomorrow?" Gerald says. "'Cause if you are, I win the bet."

Rowan looks as if he's been caught with his hand in the cookie jar. "I don't know if I want to go. You think I should, George?"

Karl and Rowan chat awhile, George telling him the pros and cons. "A lot of guys hate it in Europe, really hate it. But you seem like a bright guy, you can be miserable for two months."

"I guess I can, for that money," Rowan says, then leaves for warmups.

Karl spots a piece of paper on the scorer's table, listing the tentative playoff dates. Depending on the opponent, Albany won't begin the first round until either March 15, 16, or (most likely, versus Wichita Falls) on the seventeenth, a full nine days after the last game. And that gets Karl all hopped up once again. The CBA continues to baffle, and Karl vents some. "And I'm gonna tell Jay Ramsdell I'm not paying my fine, either," Karl promises, alluding to his recently incurred punishment for criticizing the officiating in the newspaper. "He can't take away my freedom of speech," Karl says. "Nine fucking days? What are we gonna do with these guys that long?"

Lightheartedness masks the importance of this game. A win is desperately needed to get things back on track. Karl decides to start Clint Smith. "Good or bad, things happen when he's in there," Karl says, and Chuckie Brown does stir things up from the start, hitting for 7 first-quarter points and leading the way to a 30–25 lead after one period. Derrick Rowland is also in the groove; he has 12 at the half, and contributes on defense—which is not his specialty—on the way to his best game in a while. Shurina comes off the bench and adds 8 points in only 7 minutes, and at the half Albany leads by 18. During the intermission Karl almost pleads: "Please don't let them come back; this team is ready to lose by 30." He also adds, "Please, let's use this half to make ourselves better."

Albany wins the third by 1 to take a 19-point lead into the final period. And within just over 6 minutes that lead is down to 8. Visions of the recent disasters, of the 17-point lead lost in Charleston and the 15-point advantage blown in Topeka, begin to circulate.

Then Doug Lee buries a three from the wing, and the lead is back to 11 and the Patroons seem infused with renewed confidence. The Bullets win the quarter, but Albany wins the game, and six standings points. More important, perhaps, is the fact that the lead is not wasted, and that nearly every Patroon contributes, and no one complains much about anything. Clint Smith scores 17 and adds 9 rebounds and 7 assists. Derrick scores 20, Dave Popson adds 12, plus 11 rebounds—in fact, seven of nine Patroons score in double figures. Only Steve Harris (who suffers from a stomach virus and doesn't play) and Upshaw (who doesn't play much when Dirk Minniefield and Clint perform so well) and Grissom (who simply has an off night) don't figure prominently.

"The monkey's off our back, guys," Karl says. "Nice job. Nice win."

MARCH 3–4

Practice on Thursday, the third: Clint Smith, reading the Albany *Times Union* sports section, sees that a Siena College basketball player (Siena is located just north of Albany, in Loudonville) has been referred to as Robocop. "Yo Timmy Wilkin," Clint calls out, "why they callin' this guy that? I thought you called *me* Robocop."

"I did, Clint," Wilkin explains, "but it got cut out by my editor. It never ran in the paper."

"Well, why they callin' this fella Robocop, and not me?"

"I dunno. Maybe because he's white, and Robocop was white."

Clint nods his head. "Oh, he's a big white kid, huh? I understand things now. In that case I better change my name to Bro-bro-cop."

○   ○   ○

Ron Rowan, the CBA's second-leading scorer, flies to Europe. Lee and Rowland, the Patroons' leading scorers, do not. Karl will have to make roster decisions himself. On Saturday the fourth, prior to tonight's game, he tells Clint his back has been injured. Ken Johnson plays tonight.

In fact, Clint has practically offered to go on IR. Karl has been considering Grissom as well, but Clint says he'll go on the injured list. "I can handle it better," he says, and he's right. Of all the attitudes infecting the Patroons lately, Smith's has been among the most stable on the court. He'd like to play more, of course, but he accepts what happens and plays his best when given the chance. And he knows his minimum ten-day injury period will expire before the playoffs begin, so he'll be eligible for postseason play from the first game. He probably *can* handle it best.

Even if some others can't. Cedar Rapids coach Gary Yeomans, spotting Clint in street clothes, asks Tim Wilkin what the deal is. When told, he smiles. "He looks pretty healthy to me," Yeomans says. And Jack Moser, watching Clint sashay in and out of the locker room with pilfered boxes of cookies, gives him some medical advice: "Hey, Clint, limp a little, will ya?"

The continuing lineup changes would seem of little concern tonight. After Thursday's loss, Cedar Rapids has gone through some convulsions of its own. "I don't know if you know what's happened," Karl addresses the troops before the game, "but they've had kind of a major shake-up over there. Rowan's gone to Europe, Randy Allen went up to The League [the Sacramento Kings signed Allen to a ten-day] and Lewis Lloyd was waived." Lloyd, according to Yeomans, didn't fit in well with the team, and had been benched the second half of the previous game. One of the open roster spots has been filled by Steve Hayes; "he's about forty-eight years old," Karl reports, and everyone laughs. Karl laughs, too. "Hey, Stroeds, he's even older than you. I coached against him in Montana, even before I had you. He beat us a couple times, too. I have no idea what kind of shape he's in." Hayes had been something of an assistant in Cedar Rapids, serving as, among other things, van driver for visiting teams. He is in no shape at all, and Yeomans will play only six of the nine uniformed players he has available tonight.

And that's why the loss is so devastating. Karl calls for a fast tempo; score 120 points and you'll win, he says. If it's in the 90s, they have a chance. The final is 94–91 against. A win would have clinched first place. This loss may have clinched impending disaster.

The team's chemistry is further dislocated. Clint's energy is missed, and any lasting effects from the team meeting a few days earlier seem diffused. Some players openly grumble that Karl has ruined the team (outside of Karl's earshot, of course). Everyone grumbles about the lack of a set rotation and the loose definitions of the roles. In the locker room after the game, Karl explodes in a rush of frustration and anger. After cursing out the referees as they are escorted into their dressing room, Karl storms into the Patroons' room and unleashes a hurricane of invective. His body shakes and his voice quivers during a lecture that is more profane than it is lucid. Karl is clearly at a loss, at least for these first ten postgame minutes, and his rantings can be heard throughout the Armory basement. A voice on the other side of the locker room door, during one momentary lull in the storm, drifts across the transom, announcing that, "this might not be a good night to get autographs."

When Karl's spent, when it's all unleashed, he turns it over to Gerald: "Tell 'em when we leave tomorrow." Gerald, however, has a few things on his mind as well, and gives his own five-minute version of hellfire. Sweating profusely, banging the table, and cussing as if he never promised not to cuss again, Gerald lets out his own hot views of things.

Then he segues right into the travel plans; a snowstorm has caused problems in the midwest, and the league, fearful that the Patroons won't get in to Tulsa in time, has postponed tomorrow's game. Instead of playing Sunday and Monday, the games will be held Monday and Tuesday. Gerald is trying to get a later flight tomorrow but hasn't heard from the league travel agent if that has been arranged. "Y'all have to call me tonight an' I'll know when we leave tomorrow. Call me at the Howard Johnson's. If you don't hear from me, we leave the Quality Inn at six forty-five."

Karl, humorless, leaves to talk to the media—all three of them—then looks over the final box score, sitting alone with a beer and his thoughts on a folding chair. His daughter, Kelci, calls down to him from the top of the stairs, "Daddy, are we going to Thirsty's?" He shakes his head no. That will be a first, and a signal of how deep his concern is. Not even Thirsty's can help him tonight.

Gerald, though, does appear at the eatery, to distribute meal coupons to the few players who come to chow (including John Stroeder and his wife, fresh from shuttling the Bullets to the Howard Johnson's Motel). Gerald makes the rounds, talks to all, tries to raise spirits. He even approaches Tim Wilkin and offers him something of an Oliverian scoop. In all seriousness, he says to Wilkin, "You can quote me on this, so long as you don't put it in the paper."

MARCH 5–7

An afternoon flight is secured; the team leaves around 5 P.M., and flies through the worst snowstorm the Oklahoma-Missouri area has seen in many years. A choppy approach, a frightening landing, a tow truck–led taxi to the terminal, a foot or so of new and still-piling-up snow on the ground, and welcome to Tulsa.

The first game starts out as a continuation of the previous week's nightmare. Tulsa breaks out with a 14–2 run and builds a 19-point lead midway through the first quarter. But Karl keeps the team's collective head together. And when Tulsa tries to play rough, Karl gets his chance to reestablish Albany's toughness. Wes Matthews, now playing for the Fast Breakers, throws a flagrant elbow at the head of Derrick Rowland. Rowland throws a punch at the offender, but gets spotted for it by the official, and is called for the foul. Karl is no fan of dirty play, but he decides to send a message to his opponents. During the next time-out he calls a huddle. "OK, guys, we're gonna run 20-G. Kenny Johnson, when you set the pick, I want you to knock Matthews on his ass." Johnson understands his mission and accomplishes it with gusto. As Matthews chases his man across the lane, he runs headfirst into the massiveness that is Kenny; Johnson, for his part, gets a little action of his own into the pick, and sends Matthews flying. The referee calls Johnson for an illegal screen. "You're right, ref," Karl says, smiling, "it was illegal. Good call." The message is clear, to Matthews and Tulsa coach Henry Bibby: You want to play that way, we'll play that way. Tulsa relents, and Matthews is quiet the rest of the game.

The aggressiveness also seems to charge Albany up. After one the Tulsa lead is down to 15. Albany holds on to win the second quarter by 3, which cuts the lead to 12. (It also gives the Patroons one standings point, which is all that is needed to clinch first place in the division. Almost lost in the recent troubles of the Patroons was the fact that they would eventually repeat as the regular season's Eastern Division champions. And if it came a few games later than expected, it has come now.)

The second half features the Patroons of a few weeks ago; they dominate the Fast Breakers as thoroughly as they were dominated earlier in this game. Albany wins the third Q by 20 (37–17), and builds that 8-point lead to as many as 14—a remarkable swing of 33 points overall from their largest deficit to their largest advantage. The final score has Albany up by 7. Rowland and Stroeder hit for 22 (Stroeder adds 10 rebounds). Kelvin plays a solid game and scores 17. Steve Harris, playing in his college town for the first time since graduating from the University of Tulsa in '85, plays his best all-around game to date: 14 points and 6 assists.

The following night, the Patroons revival continues. Tied at the half, the Pats go on a tear late in the third, and finish the Q with 38 points (to Tulsa's 24). They hold on for another seven-point win—118–111—and, as quickly as that, the Patroons seem back on course for a strong playoff run. Kelvin follows last night's strong showing with an even better performance, scoring a team-high 23 points, plus 6 assists. Rowland scores 20 and Popson nets 19. Doug Lee hits two three-pointers, giving him 93 for the season—one under the CBA single season record, set earlier this week by the now-injured Kenny Natt of Rockford. But Lee is outshot by Dirk Minniefield, who hits four long-rangers, including two important bombs late in the fourth quarter to quash a Tulsa charge.

These two games, nearly meaningless in terms of standings, have been crucial in turning around the Pats' foundering fortunes. Another win, at home tomorrow against last-place Topeka, and Albany will close out the season with three victories in a row. Perhaps then, the recent squabbles can be put aside.

The heavy snows have closed Tulsa down, so it's back to the hotel for dinner and rest. Karl checks in at the front desk for messages. He always has several stacked up, and as he flips through this pile he comes across one from Kelvin Upshaw's agent. He makes the call and hears some surprising news: The Boston Celtics want Kelvin for a ten-day.

MARCH 8

"You heard about Kelvin goin' to the Celtics, right?" Gerald tells everyone within reach at the Armory before the game. "Isn't that great?"

"Were you surprised, George?" Wilkin asks.

"Shocked. The Celtics had a scout here a couple weeks ago, supposedly looking Minniefield over. I think they realize Minny isn't playing too well yet. So they wanna give Kelvin a look." Speculation is that the Celtics will keep Kelvin for ten days, and then, if Minniefield is in shape, call up Dirk. That's what Dirk's hoping, anyway. Kelvin is just happy for another shot. When Karl told him, earlier in the day, the two had another emotional encounter. "Kelvin almost had tears in his eyes," George says softly. "I almost did, too."

Of course, it's not so emotional that Karl can't get on Kelvin a little more. When Upshaw arrives for tonight's game in black sweats and sneakers (the Celtics don't want him playing) Karl looks him over and snaps, "What's that?"

"I didn't know if I was coming tonight," Kelvin explains lamely.

"You better not show up for a Celtics game dressed like that," Karl answers.

"I wouldn't dress like this in Boston."

"Oh, that shows a lot of respect for me. Gerald, take twenty dollars out of his last paycheck."

The pregame mood throughout is light; the season ends tonight with a mostly meaningless game against Topeka. On the blackboard, which is usually filled with play diagrams, notes, matchups, thoughts on the game, and overall instructions, tonight has only PLAY HARD AND TOGETHER scratched across it. Clint Smith walks in and hands Gerald three parking tickets—he had the team van while the team was in Tulsa—and Gerald stuffs them into his notebook. Clint also reports to Jack Moser that the league office called to confirm his injury. "Yo Jack, that guy called from the league," Clint says. "He asked me what's wrong. I said my back is hurt. He said, 'You sure?' I said, 'Get outta here, who are you to be tellin' me my back don't hurt?' Argued with the guy for two hours."

"The league should install a WATS line to my house," Jack says. "I talk to that guy every day."

The locker room fills with more strays: Greg Ballard is in town, ready to go. Although he needs one more game to qualify for the playoffs, Karl has convinced the league to waive that requirement since Ballard is still recovering from a sprained ankle (that was the reason he was released by Seattle). Keith Smith also comes in, begging to be allowed to play—or at least warm up. "Let me into the layup line, man. Or just stand in the corner and shoot. I'm ready. I'm going crazy, George. Gotta play. What's up."

"When the doctor tells me you can play, then you'll play. Gerald, get everyone in here. Where's Derrick Rowland?"

"Probably in the bathroom combing his hair again," Grissom rags, just as Rowland walks in.

"OK gentlemen, let's go," Karl starts. Only two missions tonight; to continue the improved play established in Tulsa—"We were good because we were making the extra pass, and using our defense to generate our offense. That's where we excel"—and to get Doug Lee the three-pointer record. "Look for Doug, everyone, we want to get that record for him, early in the game if possible." Lee hardly listens; a stomach flu has attacked him, and he's not sure he'll make it through the game.

The game starts with a crowded bench—Clint, Keith, and Greg Ballard, all in street clothes, fill the end to capacity. Kelvin has to sit in the stands.

Doug Lee starts the game, and misses the first shot—a three, naturally. He misses two more (by a wide margin; it's clear Lee is off his game) and sits down, green about the gills and breathing hard. Later in the quarter he makes a layup, but in the second he misses three more three-point attempts, putting him 0-for-6. Not the best time for his worst shooting of the season.

During halftime, Lee bolts out of the room to throw up. He reports he missed that shot, too. Karl asks him if he can play. He'd like to, he says, as long as he doesn't hurt the team. Then he swallows a capful of medicine from Moser, and files out with his teammates, who offer encouragement and a steadying hand.

Kelvin stays behind, and starts crawling around the floor, looking for something underneath the chairs and table in the locker room. "What's the problem?" Karl asks.

"Lookin' for my earring," Kelvin says. "Lost it after the last game."

"Lose it! Keep it lost!" Karl and Moser chime in together. And Karl adds, "I hope you have enough sense not to wear an earring in front of Red Auerbach!"

Doug Lee, somewhat steadier, starts the third quarter and, with fortitude and luck, he hits his first two attempts to set the CBA single season three-point record. Lee immediately takes a seat on the bench, accepts some congratulations from his teammates and, within five minutes, wobbles downstairs, his work for the night done.

The game itself is a fairly easy win, uninspired and unemotional. Thoughts, of course, are already geared toward the playoffs. In the room Karl calls for attention. "Guys, thanks for a great season. For you rookies, I just want to let you know, pro basketball starts right now. This is the fun part. Playoff basketball is great. I hope you're surprised—I hope *I'm* surprised—at how intense and fun it really is." He goes over the coming week's schedule: day off tomorrow, optional practice Friday, some hard work over the weekend and all next week, including some film study. First game is Friday the seventeenth.

"Be proud of what you've done," Karl continues. "No matter what league you're in, winning a championship is an accomplishment. You earned the division championship, and you had a great year. You surprised a lot of people—including me—who thought you weren't a championship team, and you embarrassed a lot of people along the way. Thank you, really. I rode your asses hard, maybe too hard . . ."

"Lighten up, G.K.," Grissom yelps, and everyone laughs.

"All right. Thanks guys. Really. Great season."

Kelvin circles the room, shaking hands good-bye. "Hope we don't see you again," Stroeder barks at Upshaw with a smile. "Yeah you do," Kelvin answers. "I'll see you at Thirsty's."

Grissom, already three beers down, plans on a night of revelry. He gives his car keys to Keith Marder, the *Times Union* reporter, and recruits him as his designated driver. "I'm gettin' blasted tonight," Gris announces, and no one doubts it.

Karl asks Gerald to get him all the Wichita Falls films he can —"our games and anyone else's," Karl asks. "Ah am workin' on it," Gerald says. "First, ah gotta get Gene."

Gene Espeland is returning to help out for the playoffs, as Karl mobilizes his reserves.

Finally, Jerome Henderson, the Sizzlers' starting center, walks into the room and collars a beer. Henderson started the season in

Pensacola, prompting Stroeder to ask, "Jerome, what are you doing in Topeka?"

Henderson shrugs. "Long story, but that's where I am," he says. "Be on vacation starting Sunday." The Sizzlers are playing out the CBA string. The Patroons are just getting started.

And immediately, the guessing game begins. Only ten players can make up a playoff roster, and Karl has over a dozen to choose from. At Thirsty's, Wilkin and Karl take a stroll through the names, Karl making him guess who will stay and who will go. Wilkin figures the sure bets are Lee, Rowland, Stroeder, Minniefield, and Popson. Of those in IR, Pearson figures to be activated. That's six who make it on talent alone. Karl believes that character wins in the playoffs; Grissom, Shurina, and Clint Smith add that. Figure at least two of those three make the playoff squad. (Several players, in fact, have already gone up to Karl and told him not to cut Clint.) That leaves Ken Johnson, Steve Harris, and Greg Ballard. Wilkin argues that Harris hasn't shown anything yet, and he's expendable. Johnson gives rebounds—a playoff necessity—and his attitude is much improved. Ballard, of course, has an NBA championship ring and more experience than the rest of the team combined. He'll certainly be needed, especially in later rounds. And what happens if Upshaw comes back? And what about Lowes Moore, who could un-un-retire (as a retiree, he is a free agent and not restricted by the eight-game rule) and add quickness at the point, something Albany still lacks? The permutations are endless, and Karl is giving no indication which way he'll go. If he knows, he's not telling. More likely, he doesn't know. A week of practices will result in ten Patroons, several hurt and disappointed players, and one anxious coaching staff.

But that starts tomorrow. Tonight, there is some minor celebrating at Thirsty's. The 1988–89 Albany Patroons have ended their regular season with a record of 36–18, 233½ standings points, and first place in the CBA's Eastern Division. George Karl begins the postseason by hugging Gene Espeland, whom Gerald delivers to the bar. The three coaches huddle and plan the week's attack.

Grissom stands by his vow, wandering the floor with a glassy-eyed squint and a pitcher of beer in hand. His driver Keith is at the ready. The fellas grab a bite to eat, then leave together, off to their own brand of celebration. Shurina quenches his thirst, though not to excess. Even Stroeder hangs out, as does his wife, Nancy, who, encouraged by a few drinks of her own, offers her special theory of basketball. "John and I have a deal," she tells the table. "No layups, no lays."

"He misses layups all the time," Karl laughs. "Hell, he missed two or three tonight."

"I know," says Mrs. Stroeder. "Nothing doing tonight."

"Jeez, Nance," John howls. "Ya don't have to tell everyone."

"Hey, that's the deal. No layups, no lays." And out the door they walk, Mrs. Stroeder holding her head high, Mr. Stroeder sheepishly in tow. Some season-ending celebrations, it appears, will be more sensual than others.

7

$$\boxed{\text{THE PLAYOFFS}}$$

MARCH 9–10

A day off for the players, who scatter—Clint home to Cleveland, Minniefield to Boston, Grissom (and his hangover) to Atlantic City. (Before leaving, Gris has lunch with Keith Marder, his chauffeur. "I know I talked a while to George last night," Gris says. "What did we talk about?") The coaches confer at the Patroons office, borrow a VCR from another office—the Driving While Intoxicated Bureau—upstairs, and watch some film. Gerald begins new lists. He writes the names of the nine who dressed for the last game on the blackboard: Harris, Minniefield, Shurina, Lee, Rowland, Popson, Grissom, Johnson, Stroeder. Below them he writes the names of the three would-be Patroons: Clint Smith, Pearson, Ballard. And next to them all he draws a box: The window. One name will fill in the window, and those will be the ten playoff Patroons.

On the ninth, Thursday, the discussion centers on Harris, and Karl is surprised to hear that his staff wants Harris to play, at least in the first round. They feel that Harris's poor play has been due to illness, which has prevented him from getting in game shape. Work him hard this week and see how he performs against Wichita Falls, they say. If he's on, Harris can give the Patroons a dimension they don't have now—a true one-on-one scorer, a guy you can give the ball to and watch him create a shot. Rowland is a fine scorer off a set play, but not as good a creator. Although

Harris has done little since arriving, and has not shown much enthusiasm for being here, his special skills could be crucial in the playoffs.

So, the next day, at the optional practice graced only by Harris (dragged over by Gerald), along with Ballard and the rehabilitating Keith Smith, Karl offers a challenge: Lose a pound a day over the next week, work hard, and "show me that skinny ass I saw in Golden State." Karl suggests to Harris that his weight is affecting his game. Harris, a quiet, reserved man, smiles and nods slightly. He accepts the challenge and goes off to work out with Smith, Ballard, and Coach Gene.

Gerald, meanwhile, talks seriously with Tim Wilkin. Gerald is conflicted by two opposing requirements of his job—and, in fact, two opposing requirements of the CBA: winning a championship and helping those players he has right now further their careers. Choosing the final ten will mean releasing someone who has contributed all year, and Gerald feels real pain at having to do this. Additionally, Karl wants a player the Pats don't have right now, the kind of player he hasn't had since Vince Askew left; he still needs an athlete, a stud, a guy who can win the big game by himself if need be. Championship teams have them—a Larry Bird, a Magic Johnson—and Karl wants Gerald to look for one. Gerald is reluctant to bring anyone new in (unless the prospect is so much better than who is on the squad now that he instantly elevates the team's ability, and there aren't many players like that available right now), but he pleads with Wilkin not to write about this. He's a bit afraid it might be misconstrued, that the average fan, who cares only about winning, will think Gerald is shirking his duties by not assembling the best team possible. Gerald understands this—"all they care about are those flags," he says, pointing to the championship banners hanging from the Armory rafters, "and that's fine."

And as much as Gerald wants to win, he doesn't necessarily want to win at the expense of those players who have gotten the Patroons in *the position* to win. "If you ask me, am I motivated to call up the whole world and look for a player, the answer is no," he admits. Nevertheless, he prefers to keep the upcoming machinations private. Wilkin, while not following Gerald entirely, agrees not to write it. "When it happens," Gerald says, "then it's happened, and you can write it." Wilkin nods. Gerald seems pleased, until Karl comes over and begins talking.

Karl's plan, as of today (it will probably change tomorrow, and every day until the seventeenth, but that is yet to be played out) is this: Pearson plays immediately, as do Clint Smith and Shurina. Shurina plays until he "disappears"; it's Karl's belief that as the playoffs progress, some players become less and less effective. Not knowing how far Shurina can go, he plans to let the rookie, in effect, play himself out of the lineup. Popson plays until he gets a call from the NBA. Karl is trying hard to get Popson a ten-day. He feels Popson is the kind of player an NBA coach would at least want to look at, and he's mobilizing all his connections—including El Deano—to get Dave another NBA gig. There is no need for both Johnson and Grissom (both realize that Stroeder is better than each of them, or so Karl believes), so one will sit. He isn't sure who yet. There is a chance Minniefield will get a call-up later; if so, Lowes Moore is his ace in the hole. Should Kelvin stick in the NBA and Minny get a call, Lowes can be called in to take over at the point, with Shurina as the backup. Ballard? He's not sure when the big veteran plays, but it's certain that he will play at some point. Ballard's influence extends well off the court; simply having his presence around will help settle the skittish, bickering Patroons. But he will play, whether it's in the first round or the finals should they get that far.

That's the plan, anyway. But now there are more concrete problems to take care of. Gerald, back in the financial bidness, strolls across the street to the bank to get a cashier's check—he's got to pay a few Texas speeding tickets. Momentarily in the legal bidness, Gerald got the judge to lower the fines for himself and Doug Lee to $35 each; if he can do the same for Minniefield he'll be one happy coach/attorney/bail bondsman.

"Ollie, what about Doc Nunnally?" Karl asks for perhaps the tenth time.

"Ah'm callin' Doc tonight," Gerald reports, also for the tenth time. "He's workin' the Georgia Tech–Carolina game this afternoon. Maybe we can get him on a flight tonight."

"Ollie, you been saying that for a week. Just do it. I'm not gonna lose a playoff game because we don't have a trainer. I was willing to sacrifice one or two during the season, but not now."

Doc Nunnally has been working at Georgia Tech since leaving Pensacola, and when Jack Moser found he couldn't leave his job as a high school teacher and coach, he gave Karl his blessing to bring in a full-time trainer. As disappointed as Moser is (he'd rather train than teach, but the Patroons simply won't pay for a trainer), he understands. "I get the shaft every year in the playoffs," he says with resignation. And with Georgia Tech about to be eliminated from the SEC tournament, Nunnally will be available for the playoff run—as Moser's assistant at home, and as head trainer on the road. Which means that, aside from having a regular trainer to tape ankles and such, Gerald won't have to recruit Stroeder or Laverty—or himself—to drive the van anymore.

Ballard, Harris, and Smith finish their workout with some sprints, then change shoes to go. Ballard asks if the coaches are going to look at films. "I watched 'em yesterday," Karl says. "Do you realize how few plays Wichita Falls runs? I was all set, pad and pen, ready to write plays down—I had to wait a half hour before I spotted one." Karl says there will be no film study this afternoon.

"All right," Ballard says. "Just remember, we gotta get that tape machine back to the DWI people."

Such is the intensity of playoff basketball, CBA style.

MARCH 11

The first full preplayoff practice; only Dave Popson, who is home with his ailing father, and Danny Pearson, who is stranded by the untimely demise of Eastern Airlines, fail to show. Clint drives in from Cleveland and rushes straight to the Armory—only to find Karl ready to work the team out on the track that circles the court. Sprints and relay races get the team sweating; conditioning is one of Karl's main objectives this week. Which dismays Clint. "Thought I was coming back to play basketball," he mutters between gasps.

Running in the relay race—three-man teams attempt a mile under four minutes, with a reward of $5 a man for success—is Doc Nunnally. The diminutive trainer arrived this morning after getting Gerald's call last night, and is immediately hard at work (though running races wasn't in his job description). The races continue quickly—"Clint Smith, don't leave early!" Karl yells. "All right,

Coach," Clint promises, then leaves well before his teammate taps his hand. All four teams make the cutoff time; "I lost money on that deal," Karl says, happy to pay. Ken Johnson, however, wonders if it's worth accepting. "I hope he cuts my ass right away," Johnson pants. "Don't wanna have to go through this and then not play. Get my ass out now."

"Ollie, get 'em loose," Karl says. "I got a lot more games for 'em later." Doc takes Kenny aside and helps the big man stretch. "Nice to have him here, isn't it, big Ken," Gerald says. "Doc's my man," Johnson says smiling.

Jim Laverty, watching Karl prowl the court with a big smile, comments, "George is so happy to have a trainer here. It's better than sex for him." And as the players begin to jog the court, then take some shots, Laverty comments further. "You can see the attitude change already. Look at 'em. Stroeder's ready." "And Minny's ready," Gerald agrees. Indeed, the feeling that a new intensity has arrived is palpable, from Karl through Gerald and Gene, to the players, to the new trainer; the playoffs *are* different. And everyone is getting his game face ready.

Karl orders up a shooting drill, and to make it interesting continues his pattern of bribe-induced competitiveness: The players split into two teams, one at each basket, and rotate through shooting practice. First they run from the baseline to the top of the lane, taking a pass and shooting from both of those spots. Then they slide from one end of the free throw line to the other, receiving the ball and shooting from those locations. The team that makes the most collects $5 more per man. And quickly, the entire gym is captivated by the contest. The shot counting becomes hypnotic; first Karl's two kids chant along—15, 16, miss, 17, miss, miss, 18—caught up in the childlike pleasure of simple counting. Then Laverty and Tim Wilkin become transfixed, counting silently as their eyes turn toward one end, then the other—31, 32, miss, 33. Gene, under one of the baskets, and Gerald, under the other, keep official score, but the players not shooting score along—58, 59, 60, miss, miss, 61. At one end, Shurina races back and forth, and finds a rhythm—85, 86, 87, 88. "Yeah Steve," Minniefield encourages him on. "Stroke. Yeah. Stroke. Stroke. Stroke it like a nekkid woman." At the other end, Harris is in the groove—98, 99, 100, 101, 102. "Yeah, Lamar

Mundane, raining jump shots. Yeah," come the calls, Harris taking the nickname of the fictional playground legend in the Reebok television commercial. "Switch ends, guys," Karl interrupts. "Gene, Gerald, score?" Gene: "One oh eight." Gerald: "One oh seven." And again they go. Shot-swish, shot-swish, shot-clang-miss. More counting—185, miss, miss—"Shit!!"—186, 187, "Yeah, stroke it" —until Karl finally calls time. At one end, it's 201; the other announces 212. Players pant and grasp their knees, sweat dripping to the floor.

The spell of counting is broken, and normal activity returns: Kelci and Coby chase each other around the floor, Karl snaps open a diet Coke, Wilkin and Laverty talk about Bill Musselman, players call each other Lamar Mundane. But for a few moments, the pure, sweet pleasures of shooting a ball through a hoop and keeping a tally—basketball at its most basic and fundamental—had stopped time.

MARCH 12

Water jugs are filled and ready, ankles are taped, the court is clean and shiny. Three coaches sit on the scorer's table. Two trainers work the room. Is this the Albany Patroons? Is this the CBA?

"It's a good thing Gary Holle doesn't come to these practices." Laverty laughs. "He don't know what he's paying for. If he saw all these people getting paid he'd shit his pants."

It's Sunday. The talk is basketball, of course, first the various college conference championship games, which are being held today, and the NCAA tournament bids, to be announced tonight. Then, the NBA, and specifically the Celtics-Nuggets game, this afternoon's CBS telecast, which has featured the newest Celtic, Kelvin Upshaw. "Did you see Kelvin?" "He hit a three, and then a two, in the first quarter." "Looked good." "Got some serious camera time. Hubie Brown was talkin' about him a lot." "Did you see Michael Adams, he blew right by Kelvin. Just blew by him, and Kelvin fouled him as he went by." "Well, Adams blows by a lot of guys." "Yeah, 'Shaw."

Another serious practice, and the intensity level remains high. Minniefield in particular has a sparkle; the coaches fairly beam as Dirk works hard on a defensive drill and then leads the offense through some plays. "Dirk is on it," Gene says. "He gets right in the guy's jock on defense, the guy can't move. He's fired up. Now if we can only get Gerald fired up . . ." Gerald leaps out of his chair. "Ah am fahred up, dad gemit!" he shouts. Karl has a sprightly step of his own. He almost races from end to end, teaching, lecturing, coaxing, yelling, complimenting—coaching. As Clint Smith goes in for an easy layup during a scrimmage he jumps onto the court. "Hey, listen up, guys. We don't give up layups in the playoffs. No layups in playoff basketball; that's the way it's been for a long time. Foul him. Nothing dirty, I don't want anyone hurt. Just foul the guy. No layups in playoff basketball. Got it?"

Practice ends with another track meet, again with $5 rewards waiting at the finish line. As a former player, Karl knows that these are competitive people, and he is particularly adept at turning what is otherwise boring, tedious, and painful—but essential—conditioning work into challenges. The relay race goes two and a half miles this time, and as each player takes his third and fourth lap he hits his own personal wall. Bodies sprawl about the Armory. Greg Grissom lugs his big frame across the finish line, and collapses, toes up, in the corner. Laverty points him out to Wilkin and says, "Hey Tim, there's today's story. Gris's obituary."

"That's it," Gris moans, struggling to his feet. "Ah'm on the wagon for the rest of the playoffs." Wilkin says he doesn't believe it. "Well," Gris corrects, "mah own version of the wagon. No more'n two or three beers a night."

Karl pays off the winners. "All right, coaches. Let's get dinner, and look at some films. Coach Ballard, you're coming with us. Gonna teach you how to look at film like a coach."

MARCH 13–16

New sneakers—for some—on the thirteenth. Clint Smith, spying the stack of Converse shoe boxes, dashes in, lifts a pair, and dashes to a sideline seat. "Oooo-*weee*," he says, slipping on the left shoe. "Nice. Gonna take these out on the boulevard." With new shoes, and newly cleaned basketballs ("Hey guys, don't we love having Doc Nunnally here?" Karl shouts), and a disassembled Armory being reassembled (the seats have been taken down and are stacked along the sidelines—in some places actually edging onto the court) practice continues in earnest.

Having looked at game films of Wichita Falls, Karl begins coaching against specifics—how the Pats will defense the Texans' pick-and-roll plays, for example—and working against the tendencies of the individual players. "They are all predominantly righthanded," he coaches, "and they all look to drive the paint. They are a tremendously individual team; they don't run many plays at all. Stop their penetration, don't let 'em drive, and keep 'em using their left hand—move 'em left, and keep 'em left."

On Tuesday the fourteenth the morning is devoted to film study for the players. Karl divides the team in two. The first session is for the 1, 2, and 3 men—Pearson, Minniefield, Harris, Smith, Rowland, Lee, and Shurina—who take seats in the tiny locker room, where Gerald has set up a TV and VCR. Before starting the film, though, Karl wants to talk a bit about playoff basketball. First, he tells everyone not to worry about "the bubble," about whether they will be on the roster or not. "I think the NBA is gonna decide that for us, so just relax." Then he talks about attitude: "We are the best team, but the best team doesn't always win," he says, and cites several NBA examples of teams going through too many peripheral worries—contracts, feuds with coaches, and the like—to win. "If you lose your confidence, your attitude, your togetherness, you don't win in the playoffs.

"Now is not the time for attitudes," Karl continues. "You guys have to trust me. If I make choices, believe in me. If I play you 5 minutes, you have to like it. If you lose your confidence, I don't have time to get you up again. I have to bench you. So much in playoff basketball is confidence, and if I think one guy is the hot guy, I have to go with him. And if it means you sit, I don't have time to boost you up the next day in practice. You have to be ready. We need that togetherness. I can't give any grace periods anymore. If you run a play wrong once, I may tell you. Do it again, you might not play. In the playoffs, every possession is that important. *Every* possession; the game starts at the opening tip-off. You can't fall down by 17 and say, 'Time to go to work.' The playoffs don't work that way.

"You've heard me say this before, you play pro basketball with talent, heart, and brains. Sometimes you can win with just one working, you might be smart one night, maybe you hit some tough shots and talent wins it one night. In the playoffs, we need *all three*. *Every* night. Now Gerald tells me we might be the smartest CBA team ever. He says we're preparing harder than any CBA team ever has for the playoffs. I'm telling you, we're preparing about twenty percent of what we did in the NBA. Right, Greg Ballard? Up there, every play, every possession, every opponent is analyzed. You'd each get a film of your own on the guy you're guarding. You'd know everything, what time the guy gets up in the morning, everything.

"I'm telling you this, guys, this is the funnest time in basketball. This is why I coach. To win a seven-game series, go on, win another, and win a championship is a tremendous competitive challenge. It's like a war, a competitive war. And it's great. It's the most fun in the world."

In turn, Ballard, Gerald, and Gene express thoughts on the playoffs, about togetherness, staying prepared mentally and physically, not bitching. Minniefield then adds a story of his own, about being with the Celtics during the playoffs one year and not playing much, and of being angry at the Celtic coaches. When he did play, he says, he wasn't ready. He knows now that was wrong. "If you play 30 seconds, you gotta play hard as you can those 30 seconds," he says. "They might be real important 30 seconds, an' you gotta be ready."

Karl finishes up. "You guys have all had great years. You all helped your careers by being here. The only thing else you can do now is win the championship. Winning helps you, it helps me sell you a bit to the NBA, where I can say, 'This guy won me a championship.' I mean, I can sell you all now, you all did great, Danny Pearson, Doug Lee, Clint Smith, you guys been here all year, you been great. Steve Shurina, you surprised all of us, hell we had you cut about eight times"—everyone in the room laughs, including Steve—"we had you cut—"

"Before I even showed up," Shurina cuts in.

"The point is," Karl continues, "the only thing left to help your careers is winning. Now let's look at the films."

They go over the Texans' tendencies—"See how they all go right, all the time? They all drive, never look to pass. Never.

See?"—and all the while exercisers walk past the locker room door to change and run on the track upstairs. Water flushes through the pipes overhead, traffic honks outside the boarded windows, jogging feet pound on the ceiling, and the Patroons prepare for the opening round of the CBA playoffs.

Then the second shift—the big men—come in. Popson, Grissom, Johnson, and Stroeder hear the same discussion. The only change: Karl suggests, more for Grissom's benefit than anyone else's, watching the postgame activities. "You know I've never policed your nightlife, but now might not be the time to be staying up till six A.M." Karl smiles. "It'll get to you."

"We hear ya," Johnson says. "No booze, no broads."

"I didn't say *that*," Karl corrects, "just do it before midnight."

"I guess I gotta get started around eleven A.M., then," Gris plans.

Karl cues up a film concentrating on the Texans' big guys. Nothing much happens—Wichita Falls never uses its big men, they never get the ball, don't get plays called for them. "There's not much to tell you," Karl says. "Their big men don't touch it much, do they?"

Just then, on the film, Kelvin Upshaw throws up a wild left-handed hook shot that misses. "I should send this film to Boston," Karl says. "They won't be playing him so much after they see this shit."

Film study comes to an end. The players leave—"We go at three thirty this afternoon, not four," Karl says—and Gerald starts to go with them.

"Ollie, where you going?" Karl barks. "We got another film here to watch."

"Coach, I got problems. I gotta take care o' the players' money, it bein' payday," Gerald reports.

"Ollie, that's not important."

"It is to the players, Coach."

"Sit down. You can do that later."

"But Coach, Ah gotta—"

"*Ollie!*"

Ollie sits down, and the three coaches watch another film, as fat men with towels around their waists waddle past the door.

○ ○ ○

Practice that afternoon, featuring a full scrimmage. White beats green by 3, and the winners immediately surround Karl for the $5 prize. "I'll get you tomorrow," Karl promises. Finding no money here, the group descends upon Gerald, who has set up shop at the end of the scorer's table. His books are open—newly designed and coded, with color graphics and keys and charts that look to be more complicated than the problems they are supposed to be organizing.

Not to Gerald, though. "Gentlemen," he says confidently, looking up from his binders at the line of Patroons with their hands out, "I am about to straighten out the past."

○ ○ ○

The fifteenth and sixteenth provide more roster possibilities for Karl and Oliver. Practice on the fifteenth is still high-spirited as playoff intensity remains strong despite the now overlong wait for the first game. (This intensity is augmented by the players' knowledge that jobs are at stake; twelve athletes are competing for ten jerseys, and no one knows to whom those ten jerseys will be given.)

Gerald, surrounded by seven notebooks of various colors, sizes, thicknesses, and purposes—"This one here is my to-do book, this one here is my Wichita Falls book, this one here is my I'm not sure what"—is gettin' organized, and gettin' outta the business. "I don't know what I'm doin', but I'm gettin' something done," he announces.

"Ollie, call Stu Inman," Karl orders, striding up to Ollie's station courtside. Karl holds a message that Inman phoned earlier. "He doesn't usually call this time of day, so something must be up."

After much running around, Gerald eventually places the call from the closetlike room that serves as the Patroons' office at the Armory. Karl waits outside, listening as Gerald talks with the Miami GM's secretary. Gerald hangs up and says, "They want to talk about Popson. Also about Rob Rose and Winston Bennett."

"Rob Rose is pretty good," Karl announces with a laugh; Rose, one of Karl's favorite players in the CBA, is perhaps Wichita Falls's best performer, and Karl jokes that getting Rose to Miami helps both the Heat and the Patroons. But it's only a joke.

"I'm callin' Stu back later," Gerald says. "Who do I push?"

"You know perfectly well. We talked about it yesterday," Karl says.

"That's what I thought, Coach."

"You push Popson," Karl says. "And *then* you push Rose."

Popson is pushed well; he will probably be called up on Monday, when Miami returns from a road trip. Which presents more conundrums. Over drinks that night, the coaching staff, plus honorary coach Jim Laverty, meet to sort out the possibilities. Should Popson sit out the weekend games? How can the Patroons get Lowes Moore in when they already have excess players? Gerald explains the arcane CBA rules to Karl, and the plan is to bring Lowes in as a replacement for Kelvin Upshaw (who has not officially been replaced yet) and activate Pearson off the injured list. Either Grissom or Johnson sits, joining Clint Smith on IR. Ballard is not activated this round, until perhaps when Popson leaves. The only chore now is to get in touch with Lowes Moore.

At practice the next morning, Gerald reports failure at this mission. No one knows if Lowes is even available to play or interested in playing. Tim Wilkin, though, has talked to Lowes recently, and he reports to the coaches that Moore said he was interested. Another round of calls fails to find him, though. So as practice ends on Thursday the sixteenth, the day before the first game, Karl is no closer to his final ten.

Which pains Greg Grissom. As he pays his $10 to the NCAA Tournament pool and hands over his selections to Doc Nunnally, Grissom heaves a sigh. "I'm a nervous wreck," he says, as he looks across the court, where Karl and Popson are conferring. More than nervous though, Gris is feeling resigned. In his gut, he thinks he's the odd man out.

He'll have to wait till tomorrow to learn if his gut is right.

MARCH 17, GAME 1 OF THE PLAYOFFS

Lowes Moore is in and out of the Armory before any of the players spot him. He converses with Karl and Oliver, then leaves. He'll play on Tuesday, in Wichita Falls. But the word gets around anyway. And after shootaround, Grissom and Shurina talk. "Lowes is gonna play," Shurina says. "For who?" Grissom asks. Shurina doesn't know, but assumes it will be him. Both shake their heads. "He's fucking things up again," Shurina says softly, meaning Karl. "Remember what happened last time," he reminds Grissom, meaning the other roster shakeups.

Every move at this time of year carries added significance. Once out of the lineup, a player has no guarantee he'll ever play again. And that reality is eating Gris up. "I just know it's me," he says of the move scheduled for tonight. Karl talks with both Gris and Ken Johnson, and says he'll decide later today, but Gris can feel the decision already made. Still, he and Kenny slap hands on leaving the Armory. "You an' me, Kenny," Gris says. More like you *or* me.

A few hours later, Karl calls both players at home. When the early arrivals come into the Armory, they find Grissom in street clothes. He hides his disappointment pretty well; "Boy, my knee hurts," he says, smiling through clenched teeth. Still, he is naturally upset. He has no official comment for Tim Wilkin or the other writers, afraid he may say something that will jeopardize his return.

Karl's plan is to play Kenny tonight and tomorrow, then injure Johnson and replace him with Grissom. (Gris's injury had been incurred last week—as far as the league office will know—so his ten-day rest period started retroactively to make him eligible on Tuesday.) Lowes will replace Dave Popson, who will go to Miami following Saturday's game. Karl explains these moves to Jack Moser, who will then relay them to the team doctor, so that *he* may confirm them with the league. Gerald doesn't want to hear it. Karl says, "I don't know why you all think this is illegal. We did this all the time in the NBA. Players would come up to me and say, 'Injure me, coach, I'm pretty tired.' It isn't illegal at all." Moser gets the details down—"So Gris has a bad knee. What will Kenny's be? His back again? The doc's gonna love this." And the coaches dress for the game.

It's St. Patrick's Day, and Albany being a city heavily influenced by Irish immigrants, the crowd tonight is one of the smallest of the year, an unfortunate development for the first playoff game. Nevertheless, the coaching staff and players are generating their own intensity. Karl is as focused as he has been all year. Gerald's brow is permanently furrowed, beads of perspiration form on his round head as he wanders the Armory; "Ah jes' wanna win this basketball game," he repeats over and over. The locker room is suddenly filled to overflowing, with Jack Moser and Doc Nunnally, Gene Espeland and Greg Ballard and Gerald and George, Grissom and Keith Smith in street clothes.

Karl reiterates his week-long instructions for the game, sends his players to loosen up, and goes over the assistant coaches' stat-keeping requirements. For the first time this year, Karl has enough hands to chart things like fast-break points, offensive-rebound points, hustle points, all the little clues that help see the bigger picture. Greg Ballard explains Doc Nunnally's mission to him—Doc has never heard of some of these stats, much less kept track of them—while Karl changes into his suit, complete with green shirt and tie and green carnation. "I need all the luck I can get," he says. Then he sighs. "It was a hell of a lot easier playing in these things than coaching them."

An Armory worker pokes his head in the locker room. "We'll be underneath, Coach," he says. Armory staffers are planning to be under the court. They promise to hit the floor with poles and broomsticks and the like, to shake the baskets when the Texans are shooting foul shots. "That's what they call the home court advantage." Moser smiles. "Just make sure you're under the right basket," Gerald tells the ringleader. "Remember, this wasn't my idea," Karl warns as he laughs. "But then, I didn't say no to it, either."

And then the entourage walks upstairs. They fill two rows of seats; Ballard, Nunnally, Gene, and the assistant trainers sit just behind the bench. Rows of empty seats surround the court. The national anthem is skipped because the tape has broken. The quarter-point scoreboards have been removed—it's back to real basketball; only the final score matters. Doug Lee, Dave Popson, John Stroeder, Dirk Minniefield, and Danny Pearson take to the floor in near-library silence. Grissom, who has been pulling beers since arriving, sneaks a few onto the bench. And the second season gets under way.

The Patroons, from the outset, are flat. Minniefield, who has been so focused all week, is not into the game. Albany is losing the rebounds and the hustle points, failing to keep the Texans to the left, taking many and stupid fouls—doing nothing of what they have been training for all week. Even so, they stay on top of the Texans, holding anywhere from a 1- to a 6-point lead throughout the first two periods. At the half it's 55–54.

The coaches go over the stats in the hallway, a brain trust filling Karl with needed information. But for Karl the numbers only substantiate what he already knows. He marches in and gives a positive but stiff talk. No adjustments are needed; just do what we've been talking about all week, hustle after loose balls, get rebounds, stop the silly fouls. Don't put pressure on yourselves. Relax and play.

The Pats quickly lose the lead, and fall back by as many as 7 in the third quarter. Karl is juggling his lineup, looking for the connection. Minniefield doesn't have it tonight. Popson is playing soft, perhaps subconsciously laying back until he leaves for Miami. Steve Harris is ice cold. Stroeder is in foul trouble. Karl puts in Shurina, Lee, Rowland, Johnson, and Pearson. Down by 4 early in the fourth quarter, that combination will take the Pats to victory. Lee hits a 3, then Johnson grabs an offensive board and scores. It's 103–103. The crowd, quiet most of the night, comes alive. A happy Irishman in a green tam and cowboy boots stumbles through a dance on the court under one basket. A rotund Fritz wiggles to "Shout!" at the other.

Rowland hits a turnaround J with 2 minutes left to tie the game again at 107. At the other end, Johnson rejects a Derrick Taylor shot, Pearson collars the loose ball, feeds Lee for the layup, and the Pats lead by 2. Taylor ties it with a jumper. Under a minute left. Shurina takes the ball to half court, see an opening, and drives to the basket. As he's surrounded he spots Johnson; Shurina dishes, Kenny slams. Up by 2 again, 111–109. Taylor returns downcourt and buries a jumper; tied at 111, 34 seconds left. Albany time-out. Karl calls the play, but the Patroons foul it up and lose the ball. Derrick Taylor drives, lays it up for the hoop and the lead—but it's blocked, again by Johnson. Fourteen seconds left. Albany comes downcourt. Shurina stops at the top of the key. He spots Derrick Rowland in the left corner. Rowland has been the scorer all night. He takes Shurina's feed and lofts a rainbow from twenty feet. *Whap!* All net. Three seconds left, 113–111. The Texans inbound, lose the ball, and Albany squeaks out a victory.

"We dodged a bullet, guys," a relieved Karl says in the locker room. "Believe it or not, a win like this can make us a better team. Now we can win this in four or five games. They thought they had this one, and we didn't play well, and we still won. They gotta be discouraged." He pops two beers and empties one. Grissom follows suit, a bit less conscious than earlier in the night (at every time-out, as the players huddled around Karl, a wandering eye might spot Gris at the end of the bench surreptitiously sipping at a foam-filled plastic cup sent to him by his fans in the stands) but happy with the win. Jim Laverty, resplendent in a tuxedo (he missed the first half attending a formal dinner for an anachronistic Irish men's group dinner; Albany citizens still cling to several long-since scorned traditions like all-men, all-Irish formal dinners), congratulates the room. He reminds Karl of the team picture, rescheduled for tomorrow, and Karl tells everyone to be at the Armory a half-hour earlier than usual. "Coyne and Fernandez and them guys'll be here earlier than that," Laverty says. "Make 'em wait," Karl responds.

Karl fulfills his media obligations, talking with Wilkin and the suddenly expanded press corps covering the game. He has high praise for Lee (17 points, including three three-pointers) and John-son (6 rebounds and two blocks in only 18 minutes) and Pearson (15 points and 6 rebounds and his usual sound defense) and Row-land (a game-high 28, plus 8 boards, three blocks, and a strong defensive effort of his own) and Shurina (6 big assists, two important three's, and solid leadership from the point—in place of Minny—in a surprising 24 minutes of playing time, most of it down the stretch). "You can see who I had out there at the end," Karl says. "I had men. They were winners. That's what we needed; never mind the talent, you need the winners." He also makes a point of praising the crowd, which has been unresponsive all year and also for most of this game. It's false praise, but with a motive—in trying to get this mentioned in the paper, Karl hopes that it stirs greater participation by Albany's fans tomorrow, and throughout the play-offs.

"You think you come back with a win tomorrow?" Wilkin asks.

"I'm thinking by 20," Karl says.

And then it's time for food and drink. And, Jack Moser an-nounces, Gowdying, a sport widely practiced but, until now, un-named.

Moser explains the rules. "You ever watch the American Sportsman on TV? With Curt Gowdy? He'll be out on the boat, reeling in
these huge, beautiful fish. Throws his line in, fights 'em for an hour
or so, pulls 'em into the boat. What does he do? He holds it up,
smiles big, has his picture taken with a beautiful fish, and throws
it back.

"That's what us married guys do. Hook 'em, reel 'em in, put an
arm around 'em, get a picture taken, then throw 'em back. That's
Gowdying."

Gowdying it is, then. For the record, Moser lands three beauties.
Other Patroons pull in a few as well. Some less-married sportsmen,
going against everything that Gowdying stands for, decide that their
catches are keepers.

MARCH 18, GAME 2, ALBANY LEADS, 1–0

This time the team picture goes off without a hitch. Grissom
dons his uniform and smiles for the camera, then changes back to
street clothes. "I'm not drinking like last night again tonight," he
says. "The fans kept sending me beers. I must of had ten or eleven
during the game. Keith Smith couldn't keep up." Grissom is subdued
tonight, in more than just his thirst. Last night's too-close victory
was symptomatic of the problems facing the Patroons, problems
that have been addressed but not resolved. The team's chemistry
is still off.

Despite vows to the contrary, players are still unhappy with
their minutes, with the roles they are or are not playing, and with
the undecided nature of the lineup. The worries are off the court
—will I play? Will I be put on IR? Will he bring in other players?
—and they are affecting the play on the court.

The result is a 106–98 loss in tonight's match. In a game marked
by bad fouls (35 agains the Patroons as compared to 20 for Wichita
Falls), turnovers (26 to 11), and thoughtless shot selection (nine
blocked shots against), not to mention open grumbling and sniping
on the bench, Albany falls behind early, stays down by anywhere
from 5 to 10 for most of three quarters, pulls ahead by 1 with 5½
minutes left in the game, and then gives up 9 straight points to
lose.

Karl tries to pull the team back together afterwards. "In a way, I kind of like what's happened here. We haven't had a serious challenge in a long time. Probably since December. It's time for a gut check. They're *not* a better team. They have some good individuals, but they're *not a better team*. But you all realize *we* have to play together as a team. When we go individual, don't share the ball, don't make the extra pass, hey, we still win sometimes. But other times we get beat. We got our backs against the wall, and in a way that's the fun part of playoff basketball.

"It's time to be men. It's not time to blame. Not time to make excuses. You gotta hang together, you gotta fight together. I'm only gonna play the guys who play together. I think that's very, *very* important. You walk out of here with your heads high, and believing. If you can't do that we're in trouble. If you can, we'll win."

And then it's time for many small-group discussions. Karl pulls Lowes Moore into the men's room for a chat. Lowes arrived late in the game and took a seat behind the bench. He isn't sure he wants to un-retire again, and isn't sure he can help the team. He'll be at practice tomorrow and decide. Next, Dave Popson talks with Karl in the men's room. Popson is planning to drive home to Pennsylvania tomorrow, then leave for Miami. Next, Kelvin Upshaw says hello and good-bye. Kelvin, who has been playing well in Boston (he had 13 points last night), is being signed to another ten-day, and after that will probably be signed for the year. He's back in Albany on an off-day to pick up his things, and stops by the Armory in the second quarter. Decked out in a dark brown suede suit, black turtleneck, and three gold chains, Kelvin, too, sits behind the bench.

But now that he's a Celtic, and has played on national television, he is something more than he was a week ago. He is a star. Kids surround him for his autograph. Fans look and point, as if they had never seen him before, as if he had never played here, virtually anonymously, for five months. In the Armory basement, the scene of some harsher confrontations between the two, Karl gives some more advice: "Keep your mouth shut, play hard, you'll do fine."

"I'll call you, George," Kelvin says.

"Just play good," Karl answers.

Kelvin smiles and, shaking Karl's hand, says, "I'll still call you. You're my man."

Next, Karl orders Gerald to find a quiet spot to drink beer and figure out what to do. The coaching staff vetoes Thirsty's. T.G.I. Friday's is enlisted, where the fate of several players—and the fate of the team—will be determined.

○　○　○

Two blocks down Lark Street from the Armory is a smoky joint called the Sports Bar, a pre-Thirsty's hangout whose bartenders often offer free beers to Grissom and a select few—Shurina, Stroeder, Popson. Here, the players' side comes out. The talk starts out on the NCAA tournament pool and the upcoming games; there is a need to detox first, to think about things other than the loss. But in an instant, the mood changes. What's George doing? What's he *gonna* do? Is Lowes in? Is Shurina out? Is Ballard in? Is Gris out? What the hell is happening here? Grissom had said to Karl that this team is as close as any he's seen in the CBA, and that hasn't changed. Everyone gets along fine, for the most part. Around the CBA, you hear of teams fighting all the time. This is different. It's not personal. It's business. But Steve Harris has been a bust. Minniefield is not playing like an NBA veteran. Ballard and Lowes Moore don't know the plays. Karl doesn't think Shurina is quick enough; Shurina wonders what that means. He's doing the job, isn't he? Stroeder says he needs more than 27 minutes, like he was getting back when they were winning, when everyone was happy. Why did George need to play Popson so much? He said it was for Popson's confidence; well, what about Grissom's confidence? What about Shurina's confidence, injuring him before the ESPN game, after he played his two best games of the year? Why does George think Harris is worth it? Why does he need Lowes Moore?

It goes on like this for a while. It's not angry, not vindictive, not sniping. It's quiet, concerned. Their eyes wander the bar, looking for answers. Nothing is held against the players themselves. As they said, it's not personal. But quietly, over cold beers at a hole-in-the-wall down the street from the Armory, these Patroons try to get a grip on the forces that control their lives. And perhaps understandably, they subtly place the blame elsewhere.

George should have left well enough alone. He's screwing it

up. It's his fault. Maybe we're not playing as well as we can. That's true. But George has to take some of the blame as well.

"One more round, Frank. Then we gotta go."

MARCH 19

The changes are as follows: Dave Popson is signed by Miami; Steve Harris is cut; Clint Smith is injured (with a real injury, a bad back that he will later learn is being caused by kidney stones); Greg Grissom and Greg Ballard are activated; and Lowes Moore is re-signed. Meaning that three players—30 percent of the team—will be playing their first playoff games, and two of those will be virtual newcomers. This is a difficult time to be changing like that, and Karl looks drawn and tired as he arrives at the airport for the flight to Chicago and Dallas and the bus to Wichita Falls. Cutting Harris was especially hard—Karl had to take some heat from Harris's agent, though Harris himself, quiet and blasé his whole time here, said only, "You gotta do what you gotta do, Coach." Karl thinks Ballard and Moore can help; "I just don't know which plays they know, or which plays work for them anymore." The two will certainly help in the attitude department; Ballard's leadership has already been seen, and Lowes Moore is an especially classy, professional, and focused man. But Moore's addition further splits certain players. John Stroeder tells Tim Wilkin the Patroons don't need Lowes, and when the quote appears in the newspaper two days from now, Karl will have further problems to worry about.

(The only positive note is that the Texans have lost Ennis Whatley to the L.A. Clippers for ten days. Whatley, along with Rob Rose and Derrick Taylor, has been a principal player in giving Albany fits; his departure would seem to boost the Patroons' chances.)

With Doc Nunnally along to help, Gerald is less frazzled over travel arrangements. "Gerald, Jr.," as Gerald calls Doc, is taking care of business. The players meet at the airport and learn of the changes. Clint Smith, in sweats, howls at all the disruption. "This trip gonna be *wild*," he says. "Wish I could go." Then he asks Tim Wilkin to lend him some money: "Ten dollars would be nice, but twenty would be better."

At O'Hare, a stop at the bar for hotdogs and beers. Karl buys, and sighs. "This is the hardest team I have ever had to coach," he says. "I can't let up for a minute." Karl is not his usual self, less gregarious, less forceful in his personality, more withdrawn and reserved. He even laughs at one of Dan Levy's usually awful puns, something he would earlier in the year have smacked Levy in the head for. "You're so messed up you're even laughing at Levy," Wilkin points out. Karl giggles at the realization and recovers. "Levy, you buy the next round," he orders.

"I would, but Clint Smith hit me up for twenty dollars at the airport."

"He hit you too?" Wilkin laughs. "My boy, Clint Smith. Think we'll ever see that money again?"

"Not a chance."

On to Dallas, and a waiting coach for the bus trip north to Wichita Falls. A stop at Grandy's, for fried chicken. It's closed, but Gerald walks in anyway. Two minutes later he emerges with two boxes of chicken. "They said they were gonna throw it out, so I asked if there was any way they could sell it to feed some hungry basketball players, and they gave it up, free," Gerald says, thrilled at his acquisition. He wanders down the bus, offering sustenance. "Who wants a leg? Lowes, you want a leg?"

Grissom and Doug Lee play gin on a suitcase set up between their seats. The fellas stretch out in the back and Minniefield complains about the bus's musty smell. Ken Johnson reads a book. George Karl reads the paper up front, his reading light glaring off the newsprint. And the bus motors down the two-lane highway, into the Texas night.

MARCH 20

Everyone sleeps in. Doc and Wilkin taxi to the rental agency to pick up a van for the team and a car for Wilkin. On returning, Karl snatches the keys and orders a trip to the mall. "We gotta buy Ollie a sweater," he barks. "There's a big and tall store on the way."

First, the mall is scoped. And Doc Nunnally surprises one and all as the most determined scoper of the year. Doc, just five feet and change, heretofore known only as a hardworking, easygoing, exceedingly polite young man—everyone is "sir," and his Georgia drawl is steeped in southern charm—quickly reveals himself to be a relentless connoisseur of the fair sex. Like a bloodhound with his nose down and tail up, Doc darts this way and that, picking up his pace whenever he finds the scent, initiating the contact and, if no kill is made, moving on to the next. "You don't get chose if your mouth stays close," is how Doc explains his direct assaults on innocent mall women. Eventually, and with some effort, he is persuaded to leave. Karl takes the group to the big and tall shop. "We got a big, fat guy, needs a sweater," he says on entering. The clerk, a pretty woman who stands about Karl's height—6′ 2″—and weighs roughly as much as Karl does, stands up behind the desk. "How big is he?" she asks. "Big as me?" Karl quiets down. There are no sweaters; instead, Karl picks out two sport shirts, one blue and one pink.

Before practice, Ollie appears, wearing the pink one, most likely the first pink shirt he has ever worn, "happy as a pig in slop."

His happiness is lost when Dirk Minniefield comes down a few minutes late. Gerald berates him. "Just fine me," Dirk says distantly. "We don't make enough money to be fining you," Gerald says. "Show some responsibility."

They go at it a bit on the school bus that is hired to transport the visiting teams. Dirk stays distant. His play, and his mood, are distracted. Obviously, Dirk has gone through difficult times recently, and they are being compounded by new problems at home. In addition, his play is not up to his standards (his still-healing knee is certainly a factor) and the fact that Kelvin Upshaw is now a new star on his old team—which probably means he won't be called up—must be weighing heavily on his mind.

Practice ends at six. Dinner ensues, Karl telling NBA stories over steaks and beers, Doc Nunnally enthralled. It wasn't like this in Pensacola, and Doc is so happy to be a part of the Patroons— "they're the Lakers of the CBA," he says, "only cheaper"—he glows. His happiness continues at the hotel bar. Karl et al. pump at least ten dollars into the bar trivia machine trying to get enough points to register on the leader board. Doc works the room, Coca-Cola in hand, and manages to secure one phone number by offering tickets to tomorrow's game.

MARCH 21, GAME 3, SERIES TIED, 1–1

After breakfast, a team meeting is called in lieu of shootaround. Everyone gathers in Gerald's room. As the chambermaid wipes down the bathroom, Karl begins a quick talk. There is nothing new to say, but Karl says the old anyway, reiterating all the points he has been covering for almost two weeks. He adds only that they all should watch what they say to the press: "The writer down here seems to want to stir up some controversy, so be aware of what you tell him." And then he finishes, "Play better, and more intensely." Ken Johnson, sitting on the dresser, is flipping through a *USA Today*. Standing in a corner, John Stroeder lets his eyes wander around the room. Danny Pearson, stretched out on the bed, closes his eyelids for a few moments.

Karl needs to walk the mall, to relieve some tension. A fairly quick tour ensues, with Doc providing most of the amusement. By tour's end, he will have invited a half-dozen newly made female friends to the upcoming games. As Karl samples sunglasses at a mid-mall booth, Wilkin spots Doc climbing into the display window of a shoe store, helping the store's pretty manager arrange high heels and pumps.

○ ○ ○

At the game, Doc sits by Dan Levy. League rules allow only two nonplayers on the bench; with Karl and Oliver in charge, Doc is now officially the color commentator. More of what Karl calls organized stupidity, the silly little rules that are the CBA.

What isn't silly is the physical play that follows. Karl calls for a fast, physical pace: fast to take advantage of Albany's greater depth, physical to take the Texans' individual talents away. The game is not very fast, but it is physical, and the Wichita Falls crowd—loud, enthusiastic, boisterous, profane—gives this game the feel of playoff basketball that was not evident in Albany. The Texan players are getting boisterous as well, growing tired of Albany's clutching, bumping, and grabbing. Karl is playing NBA-style playoff basketball, but this is the CBA. When Greg Ballard grabs Mark Peterson's arm midway through the second quarter, Peterson heaves the ball at Ballard. Ballard, normally the most mild-mannered, controlled, and serene of men, charges and hits Peterson flush on the chin, and both benches empty. Neither of the main combatants is ejected, but they take their seats on their respective benches. Ballard sits down next to Shurina, who jokes, "Nice right hand."

"G-G-G-Gotta respect the old man," a serious Ballard stammers, adrenaline still coursing through him.

The game remains tight and rough as the two teams begin to develop a real dislike for each other. At the half Albany is trailing, 53–50. Karl's tie is already off.

Late in the third quarter, with the score tied at 72, the Patroons put together an 11–0 run that pushes the score to 83–72. The Texans' crowd stays in the game, getting so loud that the refs don't hear the buzzer go off on the 24-second clock before Danny Pearson hits a jump shot. Tom Schneeman, the Texans' coach, is furious, and the crowd is further incited, and the Texans fight to close the lead to 3 points, 92–89, and then 1, 96–95, with just over a minute left.

But Rowland hits a baseline J, and Ballard steals the inbounds pass and is fouled. He makes both free throws, and the victory is sealed when the Texans' Aaron Brandon misses a three-pointer. The final is 106–97. Eight Patroons score in double figures. Albany leads the series, two games to one.

The locker room is happy; Ballard is now known as Joe Louis, though Doug Lee, for one, is less impressed: "He can afford to fight. He's got all that NBA money. If I had the money I'd be right in there, too. I look at my check, and I gotta think about it. Can't afford the fines like he can."

Karl remembers an earlier incident. "Ballard did the same thing at Golden State. We were down 0–2, just lost the second game. I had no idea what to say to these guys. How do you motivate them now? They're one game from the golf course. But at the end of the game Karl Malone throws the ball at Ballard, everyone goes wild, a huge brawl. Then I knew I was fine. I had something to talk about."

The fight certainly helped tonight. Karl goes to dinner with his Dallas friends, relieved and more confident and planning to skip practice and play golf tomorrow. The players go back and rest, assured they can beat the Texans now, if not here, then back in Albany.

No one thinks this will be the last game the Patroons win this year. No one at all.

MARCH 22

Notes from an off day:

George Karl gets up early, drives to Dallas, and hits the links. Everyone else straggles down late, catches breakfast at the hotel, hangs around. Tim Wilkin works the lobby interviewing players for a story on the Albany fans; after hearing the Wichita Falls faithful, the players are not shy in letting their displeasure with the Albany rooters be known. The Armory has been quiet all year, and the players want and need support. But the story will cause more anger than it will stir the passions; this team has simply not gained the crowd's affection, and criticizing them in print won't help.

Doc Nunnally is worried. The league office called; they want Doc to go home. Three nonplayers on the road is one too many, and another team in the league—not the Texans, but another, more bitter rival of the Patroons—has apparently complained. Gerald says he will take care of it, but Doc is not optimistic; he knows how this league works. And he doesn't want to leave.

Wilkin takes Lowes Moore to lunch at Luby's, a chain of cafeterias popular in the South. Lowes looks smaller than his listed height of 6' 2", lighter than 190 pounds, and older than his thirty-one years. He has a mustache and goatee, a rounded face, calm eyes. Married, the father of two small girls, Moore is respected as a fine man of strong religious commitment, family orientation, and community service. He has made Albany his home—he's originally from South Carolina—and can add solid leadership and integrity to the team, if only the team will accept him.

He also adds good humor. "I think I'm the only brother here," he says, entering the cafeteria in his black sweat suit. "They're gonna make me clear tables." Over lunch, Lowes and Wilkin tell old stories. Now in his seventh CBA campaign (Moore also played parts of three seasons in the NBA, including 71 games with the New Jersey Nets in 1980–81), Lowes has plenty of stories. Many center on one Frankie J. Sanders, the Patroons' all-time character ("the J stands for jumpshot," he said) and a CBA legend. There was the time he was removed from a game by Phil Jackson, took his shoes off, and walked off the floor, only to be stopped by a retaining rope at the end of the court, forcing him to return to the bench, shoeless. And the time, during the playoffs, when Frankie J. received a death threat over the telephone (reportedly from Bill Musselman, who was then coaching against Albany), and was so shaken he'd spend hours in the bathroom smoking cigarettes, and when he woke up one night in his hotel room and saw the red message light blinking on the phone he jumped out of bed screaming, "What's that? What's that?" Lowes tells of the player who once told him, "I need drugs every day, man. I don't know how you do it, Lowes. You a better man than me." And of the time Phil Jackson and Charley Rosen (then Jackson's assistant) were both thrown out of a game, and Jim Coyne, obviously alcohol-impaired, stumbled onto the court and chased the referee around the gym. Lowes tells stories with a kind of detached bemusement, as if he himself can't quite believe he's been privy to such things. His inner strength is always apparent, though ("He's got some class, doesn't he?" Karl often asks, knowing the answer), and, clutching a book of inspirational verse, he leads the way out of the restaurant.

Wilkin stops off for a present for Gerald: a pint of ice cream. Waking Gerald from a deep sleep, Wilkin hands Gerald the gift, then notices a *Conan the Barbarian* comic book on his bed. "People might think I'm up here readin' *Playboy* or *Penthouse* or whatever," Gerald says. "I read *Conan*. There's some good coachin' philosophies in *Conan*."

"Like what?" Wilkin laughs.

"Like bein' physical. If Conan was a coach, he'd be preachin' all about physical basketball."

"Enjoy the ice cream, Gerald," Wilkin says.

"Ah will, buddy."

An afternoon practice, with Gerald in charge. The players wonder about the wisdom of Karl's taking the day off. Gerald runs a loose half-hour practice, then lets the team organize shooting contests while he lifts weights in the gym's weight room. Back to the hotel, where a few players congregate in the bar for the happy hour's free hors d'oeuvres. A quick stop turns into two hours of beers and chicken wings and spaghetti and nachos and bad jokes and anything that will help pass the time and alleviate the boredom.

"Let's go bowling tonight," Doug Lee suggests. "I gotta get out of here. I can't stand another night of cards."

MARCH 23, GAME 4, ALBANY LEADS, 2–1

Another pregame meeting in Gerald's room. "Hey, Minny, can you get me the Kentucky job?" Karl chirps. "I can get you an interview," Minniefield says. There are a lot of coaching jobs opening up now, in college and the pros, and even though it's the playoffs, everyone is thinking about next season and where they might work. Especially Gerald; the La Crosse Catbirds fired their coach, Ron Ekker, yesterday. Gerald will apply for that one.

The meeting is still more of the same, and ends quickly. Karl organizes another mall trip, careful to take the same people and park in the same spot as he did before the win two nights ago. Doc Nunnally is still afraid of losing his job, and when he shows no interest in pursuing his usual habits at the mall, instead shuffling slowly with head hanging and eyes downcast, Karl calls him over and tells him not to worry. "I'm the boss, I'll take care of it. You'll be an assistant coach. Or an assistant GM. We'll make Gerald the trainer. Or we'll buy you a ticket. They can't stop you from buying a ticket. This league tries to take away basic rights. So don't worry." It takes maybe three minutes, but soon Doc's old step is back, his eye is keen, and the game is afoot.

With two new phone numbers, he takes Karl home for his pregame rest, drives to the Econ-O-Wash to pick up the uniforms, stops at the Winn-Dixie for Karl's diet Cokes and orange juice and chewing gum for the players, flirts with two checkout girls, and returns to the hotel to hear Karl cursing out commissioner Jay Ramsdell about Doc's being with the team. Eventually, Ramsdell tells Karl he can officially request special arrangements for the playoffs. Karl officially requests. It has to come from your team office, Ramsdell says. Karl calls Gary Holle and has him fax a request to the league. The whole operation takes on a surreal, Catch-22 feeling. Karl, increasingly frustrated at the petty dealings the CBA demands, doesn't need this now. Doc, however, is just glad to be allowed to stay.

○ ○ ○

The PA announcer comes into the Albany locker room and asks Karl for his starters. Karl tells him, and asks who the Texans are starting. The announcer dips his head. "I'm sorry to show you this. This is really embarrassing. But this is what he said." Schneeman has announced his starters will include benchwarmers Aaron Brandon, Ervin Dillon, Henry James, and Martin Nessley, and not Derrick Taylor or Rob Rose or Cedric Jenkins.

"Was he being sarcastic?" Gerald asks.

"I asked him twice. He said those were his starters."

Karl shakes his head, incredulous. "Can you imagine doing that in the NBA?" he asks.

"I'm really sorry," the PA announcer says. "I'm embarrassed, but that's what he said."

Out on the floor, as the announcer names Brandon and Dillon and James to the cheering crowd, Rose and Taylor and Jenkins take the floor. The actual starters need not match the announced names, and Schneeman is trying to play some childish game. "Like that's gonna work," Grissom mutters. "Real class." Karl just stares ahead.

The crowd is a bit smaller but no less enthusiastic, and the contest is close and tough from the outset. Midway through the first quarter, Karl's tie is off, as the two teams trade leads. At the half Wichita Falls is up 1, 52–51, and in the locker room a feeling of confidence is evident. "We're all right. We're fine," Karl says. But the Patroons are not fine. Third-quarter lethargy, a bane all year, reappears; the hustle is gone, the turnovers are back, the rebounds are missed (the team's leading rebounder at game's end will be little Lowes Moore), the Texans rattle off a 14–2 run and open a 12-point advantage that Albany cannot overcome. They lose 106–97. All of Albany's ailments come to the fore: Minniefield is disconnected, and takes several bad fouls; Stroeder, also in foul trouble, looks unenthused as well; Doug Lee fails to stop Michael Tait and Rob Rose defensively, and his offense is off (just 10 points) when he feels his minutes aren't evenly distributed. The minutes problem, in fact, resurfaces with a vengeance, and Karl can't understand it.

After a serious tongue-lashing in the locker room—the main points include growing up, stopping the chirping at the refs and each other, and getting some rest—Karl looks over the final stat sheet. Except for Grissom, who played little because of a stomach virus, and Shurina, everyone got between 20 and 37 minutes. Lee had 32; Stroeder, 22, despite his foul trouble. The numbers don't lie.

(Well, they lie a little; Rob Rose is credited with 49 minutes of playing time, a remarkable figure considering regulation games run only 48 minutes. The stat keepers here, as well as at several other stops on the circuit, are not as proficient as they should be, often missing blocks, assists, and even occasionally—astonishingly —crediting free throws to the wrong man.)

As the players shower and dress and linger in the emptying gym, waiting for the entire group to convene and board the school bus back to the hotel, Karl ponders the stat sheet. What's their bitch? Everyone got minutes. Grissom, Lee, and Johnson are standing under one basket, and Karl walks over and asks them to explain. He's not angry or antagonistic; he's simply flabbergasted. As a former player, he knows what it's like not to get the minutes one wants —he rode the bench on plenty of occasions—but he can't figure out why Doug Lee should be angry with 32 minutes. The four talk for nearly a half hour. Johnson seems to understand Karl's points; Kenny has accepted that he will play only when Karl says he'll play, and though he wants to play more (and earlier in the year would have been more vocal about it), he is now better able to live with diminished time. Grissom also understands; Gris, in fact, might have the best understanding of basketball on the team. He disagrees with some of Karl's ideas, and believes that, even though the players must accept some of the blame for the team's poor performance, Karl has to accept some as well. Still, he respects Karl's decisions and lives with them. (Grissom has a sharp, quick mind for the game, for its subtleties, and might make a good coach someday, even if, as he puts it, he does look like "a slow, fat, white guy.")

But Lee and Karl never connect. Like two people describing the same car crash and coming to different conclusions as to who caused it, Karl and Lee simply aren't seeing the same game. Neither is necessarily more right than the other. Lee thinks he's playing well, and that the problem isn't the number of minutes, it's the flow in which they come. Karl thinks Lee is playing poorly, especially on defense, and that he needs to substitute often to minimize Lee's—and in fact every Patroon's—weaknesses. Some on the team will agree with Lee; Karl is jerking players in and out too much. Others side with Karl; this team isn't good enough simply to let play (individually, Wichita Falls has much better talent in Rose and Taylor and Jenkins) and Karl has to play a total team game.

The problem is, while the Texans' confidence is growing with each game, Albany's is decreasing. The players who've been there all season resent the newer ones. They think they are better than they really are, and deserve more time than they are getting. They have spent a long, difficult, frustrating winter in the CBA, watching other players get called to the NBA or to Europe, seeing people like Lowes Moore and Greg Ballard take spots on their roster, making just enough money to survive, living in cheap hotels and eating at bad restaurants and washing their own uniforms, and in their hearts they know they aren't going anywhere else this year. And maybe they are growing a little tired of it all. Maybe, deep down, where it won't show and where they won't have to admit it into the record, maybe they don't really care if they win or lose. Maybe, after five months of this CBA bullshit, they'd just as soon go home. Not all of them, to be sure. Maybe not even most of them. But some of them, if they are honest, if they could see how they carry themselves on and off the court, some of them would know it to be true.

And this team isn't good enough to let the CBA Blues take over now.

MARCH 24, GAME 5, SERIES TIED, 2–2

When the Texans' gym isn't made available early enough to suit the team (more silly games on the part of the Texans, perhaps, trying to throw Albany out of its usual game-day routine), Doc Nunnally locates a high school gym for shootaround at 11 A.M. The school bus travels north from Wichita Falls for twenty minutes, past lonely oil derricks and dry fields and crumbling shacks and tangled fences, under a deep blue and warming big sky, stopping in the town of Burkburnett, Texas. The Patroons are one mile from the Red River, one mile and the Red River from Oklahoma. The bus pulls up to an empty single-story brick and cinder block early six-ties/JFK-era school building, Burkburnett High. A custodian, roused out of bed on what is supposed to be her day off—the school is on Easter break—lets them into Bulldog Gym, donated by the Class of 1968, Home of the Fighting Bulldogs and the Lady Bulldogs.

Karl takes Minniefield outside for a one-on-one, concerned about Dirk's mental state and his lack of control on the court last night. Then he calls everyone into the lobby of the gym. A bulldog snarls on the wall, painted in orange and black. A bulldog statue, black as coal, stands sentry by one wall. Two trophy cases bookend a single table, under the fluorescent lights and the drop ceiling, on which the players sit. A long way from Golden State, a long way from the NBA, George Karl tries to salvage what is left of his team.

In an emotional, open, hurting voice that gets away from him, cracking once or twice, Karl wants to know what is on everyone's mind, why everyone is unhappy, and how to rectify it. He apologizes, even if he doesn't know what he is apologizing for. "I'm not trying to fuck you guys. I'm trying to win," he says at one point, and for one of the few times all year, he seems vulnerable. He hasn't completely lost control of the team or himself, but he knows things aren't right.

He talks awhile. Then he asks the players to talk, to get their problems off their chest. The minutes thing comes up; some players support Karl: "You gotta do what you gotta do, Coach," says Rowland. Others express their dissatisfaction. Still others keep quiet. Lowes Moore, showing more leadership in three days than perhaps anyone has all year—for this is a team that has lacked a leader all season long—implores everyone to accept his fate. "If you play a lot, or if you play not at all, you gotta be ready," he says. "If I don't play a minute, I still am in the game all the time, mentally."

"Well, you haven't been here all year, you're different," Stroeder says curtly, cutting him off. Lowes falls silent.

A few others say a few things, Karl standing in his usual way —feet wide, arms crossed—but without the essence that this pose needs. If only a bit, the confidence, the arrogance, the strength that normally radiates from Karl is softened.

"Gerald, have you got anything to say?" hc asks. And Gerald does. Loudly and profanely. His anger echoes through the lobby and into the empty gym, curses bouncing off the cinder block and shocking the unexpecting custodians alone on the court. Gerald is at once Knute Rockne, Bobby Knight, Richard Nixon at his most vulgar. "You act like this, you're fuckin' losers! *Losers!* You'll end up eatin' grass in a pasture all your life! You'll be a cow all your life! Now let's get together!"

The players slog back out to the court, run some plays, shoot a little, board the bus and return to the hotel.

Karl drives back to the hotel, too, goes up to his room, and stays there all afternoon.

○   ○   ○

In the pregame meeting, Karl is lively. He wants a physical game tonight, he says, pounding a fist into an open hand. The Texans have been killing the Patroons by driving to the basket; for the Patroons to win, that has to stop. The message imparted, Karl sends his team out and changes into his coat and tie. He paces the locker room, talking stream of consciousness. "I wish I was playing tonight. I'd be great. . . . I feel good about tonight, Gerald. . . . You think I'll ever coach a great team again, like in Montana that one year? . . . So Flip Saunders is CBA coach of the year, huh? . . . Well, let's go see what happens." The two coaches walk to the court.

What happens is rough. Grissom, starting, sends Michael Tait to the floor. Bodies are banging, and the calls are going against Albany. As the Texans drive for the basket, they get the fouls. It is not so at the other end when Lee and Shurina and Rowland drive. Halfway through the first quarter, Lee penetrates the lane, and Martin Nessley slams him with an elbow to the face. Lee hits the floor hard, and blood immediately gushes from his nose. "It's broke, I know it," he says, taking a seat on the bench. Doc Nunnally leaves his post as color commentator to administer to the wound.

Albany leads by 7 after one, and by 2—56–54—at the half. But the signs are not good. The fouls are adding up. Karl is playing an NBA style of playoff basketball—rough, physical, forcing the bad shots—but the refs are calling CBA ball—reward the offense, reward bad shots with fouls, reward the aggressor and not the defender.

In the third, the Texans take command by going to the foul

line fifteen times—and making fourteen—while Albany gets just two free throws. The Patroons also turn the ball over ten times, often in embarrassing fashion. Ken Johnson and John Stroeder grab the same rebound and wrestle it out of bounds. Shurina fires a lead pass to Minniefield, who isn't looking; the ball hits Dirk in the backside and bounces out of bounds. Four shots are blocked, three dribbles are stolen. Albany is outscored 31–16, to go down 13 after three quarters. Rose, Tait, and Taylor are having an easy time of it, scoring 23, 20, and 26 points respectively and being sent to the foul line thirty-four times for the game.

Albany chips back, though, and the lead shrinks to 10, and 7, and 5, and then 3 when Minniefield drives and scores. It is still at 3—93–90—with 3½ minutes left, when Rob Rose spots an open lane and drives the baseline toward an easy layup. Steve Shurina, as he has been instructed to do—no easy layups in playoff basketball, that's the way it is—grabs Rose's arm and is called for the foul. Rose feels he's been hacked all night, and thinks Shurina has given him a cheap shot. The film shows otherwise—it was a foul, but a clean foul, and it in no way was dangerous to Rose; Shurina in fact catches Rose to prevent his fall. But Rose approaches Shurina and shoves him. Shurina shoves back. As the players come together, Rose unleashes a punch to Shurina's head, just above the right eye. Shurina will say he never saw it coming; a sucker punch. The punch opens a gash on the eyebrow, and blood streams down his face. He charges at but is kept away from Rose, who has already backed away. The benches empty. The game is momentarily out of control.

Shurina and Rose are both ejected (though Shurina never threw a punch). The final 3-plus minutes are played out. The Texans' lead builds from 3 to 6, 100–94. Then it's 4. Then 5, 101–96, with 30 seconds remaining. Albany has the ball, and Stroeder drives, untouched, for a layup, cutting it to 101–98. The Texans bring it back, take time off the clock, but miss the shot, and Albany races downcourt. Minniefield takes a pass just inside the three-point line. He looks down, steps back, and lofts a three-pointer to tie the game—and hits! It's 101–101 ... and then, it's not. The ref, who has an excellent view of the play, calls a 2-point goal. Later, no one will agree whether it was or wasn't; Grissom thinks Dirk's foot was over the line, Schneeman thinks it was a viable three. But it hardly matters. Only three seconds remain.

Lowes Moore steals the inbound pass though, and Albany has one more chance. During their last time-out, Karl draws up the play, but the Patroons don't execute well. The play is designed for Doug Lee, but the ball ends up in Moore's hands, and from thirty-five feet he throws a desperation shot that is wide. And quickly, Albany is one game away from elimination.

"We're OK," Karl says in the locker room. "There's no reason we can't win two at home." But he knows there are plenty of reasons. His worst CBA nightmare is coming true. Bad refereeing —the Texans go to the line forty-eight times tonight, and score 36; the Patroons shoot just twenty free throws—refereeing that rewards individualized, CBA-style play gives the Texans a huge advantage. So does Albany's lack of quickness (where is Kelvin Upshaw? Where is Keith Smith?), and the team's disastrous penchant for turnovers (twenty-five tonight, to sixteen for Wichita Falls). Karl looks over the final stats, alone and subdued. "What did I say would beat us? Referees and quickness," he mutters. Twenty-nine fouls on Albany, eighteen on Wichita Falls. "There's no way the game could be that out of sync." His frustration forms a shield; usually surrounded after a game, he sits on the scorer's table by himself, and no one dares approach.

Back in the locker room, Shurina is taking the last of his six stitches. Tim Wilkin bustles in for a quote. Shurina tells him about the fight. "It was a foul, but it was a clean foul. It wasn't cheap or anything. I didn't do anything that would threaten his career. He threw a sucker punch. I never saw it coming. He's a fucking pussy."

"You know I can't use that in the paper, Steve," Wilkin says.

"Oh, yeah. All right, say he was a 'bleeping' pussy."

"I can't use pussy. They won't print it."

Doug Lee walks by, showered and dressed, with two blackening eyes and a bandage on his swollen nose. "Hey Doug," Shurina calls out, "Tim says I can't call Rose a fucking pussy. What should I call him?"

Lee stops, drops his shoulder bag to the floor, and thinks for a minute. He rubs his chin. Shurina ponders as well.

"How about 'chicken'?" Lee suggests.

Shurina shakes his head. "Nah. What else?"

"I'm on a deadline, guys," Wilkin prods. "I gotta go."

"What about 'baby'?" Shurina says.

Lee lets it sit a moment. "Yeah, that fits," he says. "That's pretty good."

"Make him a bleeping baby," Shurina says.

"Yeah, that sounds good," says Lee.

"Yeah, I like that," says Shurina.

"Thanks, guys," says Wilkin, and he dashes to his computer. And tomorrow, all of Albany will know that to Steve Shurina's way of thinking, Rob Rose, almost a fucking pussy, is instead a bleeping baby.

Back on the floor, Karl calls Doc over. "Find Gerald. Get the keys to the van. Let me get out of here." Doc finds Gerald, gets the keys, and Karl drives back to the hotel, leaving one and all behind.

MARCH 25

The bus to Dallas boards at 5:30 A.M. Kenny Johnson climbs in, leans over to Karl in the front seat and whispers, "We got a no-show. Dirk didn't come back last night."

Karl stays distant the entire trip home: Gerald works feverishly to find Minniefield, making phone calls from the Dallas airport and from O'Hare, to no avail.

Wilkin asks Karl for a few moments of time at O'Hare, and Karl gives them, in exchange for a diet Coke. He talks about frustration. Frustration on his part, with the officials who don't understand his way of thinking, don't understand the NBA way of thinking. Although he doesn't realize it, this may be his fatal flaw, his Achilles heel; all year long, NBA ball—defense, teamwork, execution—has beaten CBA ball—one-on-one, shake-and-bake, all three's and no d—but it has never been easy. And now, without the talent of the team earlier in the year, without Vince Askew and Keith Smith and Kelvin Upshaw, the Patroons don't seem to be good enough to play NBA ball consistently well. And the Texans are a better CBA team, with all that that implies.

He talks about frustration on the players' part. All year long, they've been reading *USA Today* and watching the NBA, and they're still here, and perhaps subconsciously they are thinking they're not NBA players. That has to affect them.

He talks about Minniefield, who has to be frustrated at watching Kelvin Upshaw go up to his former team and become a star. Kelvin is getting great press. They love him in Boston. And Dirk is still in Albany. Or was.

And then Karl walks off.

In an hour, they all meet at the gate and board the plane for the flight to their winter home. No one will say it, or even think it, but this looks and feels like the last flight they will take as the Albany Patroons.

MARCH 26, GAME 6, WICHITA FALLS LEADS 3-2

Easter Sunday.

"First of all, Happy Easter," Karl says at shootaround. "This is a special day, a positive day, a good day. A day of new beginnings." He has everyone stretch, run a little, shoot a little, and go. Stroeder complains in his barking bursts. "Making us play on Easter. That sucks. Made us play on Christmas and New Year's Eve, too. Shit. Don't make enough money for that. CBA sucks." Lowes Moore changes courtside from his sweats to a suit and tie, and leaves directly for church with one of his daughters.

Dirk Minniefield starts to leave the Armory for the last time.

Minniefield arrived in Albany late last night, and was met by Tim Wilkin. Minniefield says he's quitting, and Wilkin has filed the story in this morning's newspaper. Dirk has not had a drug relapse (that was the unavoidable question on everyone's mind, unfortunately, but no one thinks Dirk has slipped or doubts him when he says so now). He is simply tired of basketball, he says.

He comes to shootaround, though, and as he leaves Karl calls him over.

"You just gonna walk out?"

"Yup," Dirk says.

"Let's talk about it," Karl offers, and the two sit quietly on the visiting team's bench at the far end of the empty Armory, trying to sort it out. When they finish, Dirk leaves. Karl says he'll play tonight. Minniefield says he's gone.

Dan Levy and Keith Marder play one-on-one. Doug Lee talks about his nose, broken now for the seventh time. It needs plastic surgery, he says, but he'll need a month off to recover, and he can't afford to take the time right now. He wants to play in the WBL— the 6' 4"-and-under league—this summer. He can't afford not to play. The money is too good (about $25,000, far more than he's made in the CBA). Basketball is his profession, and he's got to keep working. Like everyone else in the CBA, Lee is here to do his job. When this job is finished, he'll get another. These men of the minor leagues are traveling salesmen, in a sense, selling their athletic talents, with dreams of making the big sale but selling nonetheless until no one wants their wares anymore. They are the Willy Lomans of professional basketball:

A salesman is got to dream, boy. It comes with the territory.

○   ○   ○

The end comes quickly; the Albany Patroons go gentle into that good night. They do not rage against the dying of the light.

The Texans do the raging. When it is learned that Rob Rose and Greg Ballard have been suspended for tonight's game, for throwing punches in the two separate incidents back in Wichita Falls, coach Tom Schneeman and GM John Treloar get into a shouting, raving, name-calling to-do with Albany's GM, Gary Holle. The Texans want Rose to play tonight (giving them a better chance of winning now), and take his suspension for the seventh game (knowing full well that Rose will sign a ten-day contract with the L.A. Clippers tomorrow, and be ineligible anyway). Holle says no; besides, there might not be a seventh game. Which gets them to calling each other assholes—"You're an asshole!" *"You're* an asshole!"— in the tiny office off the Armory lobby.

Karl hears about this in the locker room before the game, and shakes his head in further disbelief. "That's not all," Doc Nunnally reports. "Did you hear that they wouldn't give Dirk a ride from the hotel in Wichita Falls to the Dallas airport on their bus? They said,

'We have meetings on our bus. We can't have one of your guys on it.' "

"They only run about three plays," Karl says quietly. "What kind of meetings could they be having?"

"On the way over here, they were already telling me to pick them up at 5 A.M. tomorrow to take them to the airport, like they expect to end it tonight," Doc says.

"They really wouldn't give Dirk a ride?" Karl asks.

Gerald shrugs. "That's the CBA, Coach."

Minniefield plays, and starts. And the Patroons have some life. The crowd, spurred on by the criticism in the paper, is louder and more involved than all season. Albany even leads by 2 at the half.

As the second half begins, Greg Grissom and Lewis Jackson start pushing. A Texan holds back Grissom, and Karl runs out and grabs Jackson. When Tom Schneeman strides purposefully toward the group and tells Karl not to touch his players, George charges. All his frustration spews out; Schneeman, tall and thin, with a pinched face and nervous, uncomfortable, secretive manner, has come to personify for Karl all that is petty and cheap and unprofessional and without class—all that is the CBA—and only the intercession of several players and the referees keep Karl physically away from Schneeman. Karl's words are enough, though, as Schneeman, surprised and unsettled by Karl's blazing anger, steps back in fear.

Clint Smith, eating a cookie behind the bench, enjoys the show. "Look at G.K. This is great. Gary Holle and their guy are gonna go next."

Karl's alleged motive for his near attack on Schneeman is to fire his team up, and the altercation does seem to rev Albany's engines. A 20–11 run produces an 11-point lead midway through the third. But the Texans cut it to 1, 76–75, entering the last period, and immediately jump off to a 7–2 start. It is then that the Patroons seem ready to lose. There is some fight—Dirk Minniefield and Derrick Rowland cut the lead from 6 to 2—but then the calls go against them, and the Texans' lead builds back to 6, and the heads begin to droop. Wichita Falls turns the ball over on two straight possessions, but Albany cannot convert either into points.

With 3 minutes left, down by 7, the life is draining. Even when Rowland leads a charge, scoring 5 points in the next minute and closing the gap to just 1 with 1:30 left, the intensity is not there. Karl is trying, Jack Moser is trying. "C'mon guys! We're right there! Let's go!" Gerald is trying: "Forty-eight minutes! Forty-eight!" The players seem to be trying, but aren't. Cedric Jenkins's two free throws boost the lead to 3. Lowes Moore's jumper is in—and out, and Jenkins gets the rebound. He scores at the other end. The lead is 5. Forty-seven seconds left. Lowes Moore throws a pass away. Derrick Taylor is fouled; his two free throws push the margin to 7, 104–97. Another free throw; 105–97. Doug Lee misses a three.

The crowd begins to leave. "Go play golf," comes a cry from the stands.

Lowes hits a three, cutting it to 5, but two more free throws and it's back to 7, 8 seconds left. Karl calls a time-out, brings his team together in one last huddle, and draws the plays that will not take them to victory.

A few fans walk up to the bench and watch the huddle, like rubberneckers craning to get a look at a traffic accident, and then head out the door and onto Washington Avenue and into the mild spring night. They never see the final seconds of the 107–100 loss, the final seconds of the Patroons' season.

○   ○   ○

"What do we get paid for this, anyway?" someone asks quietly.

"A thousand bucks. First round is worth a thousand. Woulda been eleven hundred if we won."

"This *sucks!*" Grissom howls. "This fuckin' *sucks!* The refs suck! The Texans suck! It fuckin' *sucks!* Get me a fuckin' beer. I'm gettin' fucked up! Now I gotta go to fuckin' Nacog*doches* for the fuckin' summer! *Fuck!* It sucks! Got a keg at home, man, it's *gone* tonight. Fuckin' *gone! Fuck! Sucks!*"

Gris is the only howler. The others hang their heads quietly. Some have tears in their eyes. Many sit in their uniforms, not moving. Others are already getting undressed and preparing to shower. Gerald, looking old and tired, slumps into a folding chair, a blank stare on his face. Karl stands at the end of the table and, placing his hands at either end of its width, leans on it with the weight of unexpected loss. The room grows silent, the silence broken only by the happy whoops that filter over from the Texans' locker room next door. For a long moment, no one says anything. Then Karl lifts his head and addresses them for the last time.

"This is not the time, really, to say a lot of things. I'm a believer that all experiences are positive. I don't think any of us expected this to happen like it happened. But I think that what you all gotta do—what *we* all gotta do—is somehow, someway, when we walk out of this locker room be proud of what you did. We had a lot of bullshit in our year, maybe my inexperience in being in the CBA hurt us. I still believe if we would have won this series, we would have won the championship.

"What I'd like to do is meet tomorrow sometime, talk about your futures, what you guys wanna do. I need to get some things from you. Say around three o'clock, OK with everyone? I don't think any of us want to meet now."

Karl takes a breath, looks down at the table, and looks up again. "You guys have improved, and as I told you at the beginning, when you all came here, my desire was that when you leave here you're a better professional basketball player in some form, and also a better professional basketball player financially. That will be my goal the rest of the summer with you all.

"Sometimes it's very difficult to let losing ... I just know I have had a very good year. I'm proud of what you did, and a lot of you guys made me very, very happy, very, very successful. And I thank you for that. . . .

"It's a bitch losing, gentlemen. It's a bitch losing to some of this shit. But it happens. Let's bring it in one last time."

Slowly they encircle the table and put their hands together, and quietly they chant the chant that has sent them out the door before every game this year: "One-two-three ... together." They release, sit back down, each in his own mood. Sad, depressed, relieved, furious, preoccupied. Karl slowly circles the small room, shaking hands with each player, sometimes adding a pat on the head, a private remark, a joke, a smile. If he lingers just a moment with some of his players, if he smiles more supportively at Minnie-field, say, or looks a bit longer into Shurina's eyes and pats him twice on the cheek, no one notices. Grissom accepts his hand, then resumes his howling, draining beers as fast as they are given him. "This *sucks!*"

The room remains closed for a long while. No press is allowed in, and no one wants to leave the room and meet the public. The early dressers push quickly through the crowd to the showers, while the rest sit in various stages of undress. After several minutes, Karl walks out to talk with the reporters.

Slowly, the players collect themselves. Showered, dressed, they ascend to the upper level more in control, more accepting of the defeat. The jokes return, if somewhat forced, the smiles return, the hugs and kisses and handshakes are accepted. A last trip to the various bars and restaurants, and the night, and the season, will be gone.

For Karl, it won't be as easy. His eyes are rimmed with red. His voice is husky, humid. There is an emptiness, a hurting, that he does not try to cover. It is hard to think of anything that ends so suddenly and so thoroughly as a sports season. In a moment, where for six months an entire life existed, there is nothing left.

Karl lingers in the near-empty gym for a while, accepting pats on the back, talking quietly with the lingerers. Even learning that his wife's purse has been stolen during the game—it is recovered in the men's restroom, in a toilet, soaked through—fails to divert his mood.

Then, a last trip to Thirsty's, for several beers, and chats with some players. Keith Smith is going back to California, he says, to play in the L.A. summer league and rehab his knee and get ready for next year.

"You know," Karl says to Smith, "if we had had all of our best players at the end—you, Vince, Kelvin, Engelstad, Popson was coming around—we would have won, easy." Smith nods. In the CBA, it's not who has the best players all year; it's who has the best players at the end.

There is time for last chats with some of the friends that have been made over the past five months, friends that may or may not ever be seen again. Jim Laverty is at the bar, the Thirsty's waitresses are scurrying about taking orders, and they can be abused one last time.

Gerald and George sit at a table. Gerald says, "Coach, I'm sorry we didn't win. But I'm not sorry about the things we did. I'm sorry about the things we didn't get to do." George's eyes mist over once more.

George and Grissom meet. Gris is well into his yearly season-ending bender. "You ought to get in shape," George tells him.

"I know," Grissom says. "But right now I'm gonna get as fat as I can."

"Well, get fat for two weeks." Karl smiles. "Then take it off. Time is running out for you, Gris. You've got a good mind. You'd make a good assistant coach somewhere. But you gotta start taking care of yourself. You've only got about a year left."

"I know, Coach," Gris says. "But I can't think about that right now." He loads up several plates of chicken wings and returns to his apartment and his keg, followed by the Lees, the Stroeders, Shurina, and a few hangers-on.

Tim Wilkin walks up to Danny Pearson and offers a hand. Pearson hasn't talked to Wilkin since Wilkin's diary of the Dallas trip, in which he criticized Pearson's attitude and wrote about Pearson's run-in with Karl. "No hard feelings, Danny?" Wilkin asks. Pearson smiles. "Hey, man, no hard feelings. Just one of them things." They clasp hands. Then Wilkin and Dan Levy surround Clint Smith, wondering if they'll ever see the money they've lent. "Oh, yeah, no problem, you'll get it tomorrow," Clint promises.

A Patroons fan, in his cups, stumbles into Karl. "Thanks, man, thanks a lot," the fan says, shaking Karl's hand. "You're welcome," Karl says. "Sorry we couldn't have gone a bit longer."

"So, where you gonna be next year?" the fan asks. Karl says he really doesn't know.

Gerald tells Tim Wilkin the positives he has gotten out of the year; the sense of NBA-ness Karl has imparted that Gerald has never, really, experienced before in the CBA. Karl showed Gerald what the CBA could be. Wilkin asks Gerald where he'll be next year. Gerald says he really doesn't know.

Suddenly, it seems, 3 A.M. comes around, and the lights in Thirsty's come up over a nearly empty room, and the empties are collected and the plates are cleared and the glasses are washed, and it's time to go. Karl and Gerald are the last to leave, Karl pushing through the glass door first, Oliver trailing.

"Coach," Gerald calls to Karl, as the bartender locks the door behind him, "I got problems, an' I gotta ask you one thing ..."

○   ○   ○

It is 3 A.M., but the night is not yet over. The Grissom party goes for a while, until the married couples excuse themselves, leaving host Grissom and a ladyfriend over on the reclining chair, in close conversation. The other stragglers leave. Only Shurina remains, himself comfortably numb but more in control than Grissom (who tomorrow will not remember who stopped by). Shurina talks of his year here, of how he came as a nobody and leaves with a name— not a large name to be sure, but he is no longer the St. John's benchwarmer. He is now the CBA veteran, one-time starting point guard on the Eastern Division regular season champions. His basketball résumé has grown immeasurably. Next, perhaps, the WBL summer league. After that, maybe Europe, if he's lucky, and some real money—a nest egg to start a family and get on with life when basketball will carry him no further. Maybe even the NBA. One game, that would be all he'd want. That would show a few people who thought he couldn't play. But if not, if he can only make some money for a few years, then basketball will have served him well. Just as this season in Albany, despite its valleys, its disappointments and heartbreaks, has served him well.

But like every other member of the 1988–89 Albany Patroons, Shurina's basketball future is yet to be written. For now, as the late March sky begins to brighten and the birds begin to sing about a clear and warming day and the coming spring, Shurina climbs into his car and points it back to his apartment, his home for a few days more.

○   ○   ○

Over by the Hudson River, under the same brightening sky, George Karl sits on the sloppy banks, alone with a six-pack of beer, watching the sun rise and tossing empties into the muddy river.

8

THE POSTSEASON

Monday March 27 becomes a beautiful spring day. The sky is a clear summer's blue, deep and soothing, and fluffy clouds float lazily past an unexpectedly warm sun. By lunchtime the temperature is at seventy degrees, near-record warmth for a March day in Albany, and the long, cold winter is, for an afternoon, forgotten.

At 2:30, Karl and Oliver meet at the Armory. The folding chairs that only yesterday composed the Patroons' players bench are in disarray, the straight line now a jumble. Karl and Oliver pull two seats together and talk.

Both men look tired, drained. Karl hasn't slept much, if at all, and Gerald, his hair mussed and unruly, is in the same dark-eyed state. They want to get their stories straight before the players come in, in a half hour, for the final meeting.

"Now, are we required to fly these guys home?" Karl asks.

"No, we are not required," Gerald says. "But any organization with any integrity does it. You let me worry about the money and the arrangements and the things. I been doin' it all year, an' there's no reason for you to get involved now."

The players enter solo or in small groups and take seats on the bleachers behind one basket. Doug Lee, in shorts, comes with his wife, Becky, who has pulled baby-sitting duties and takes charge of Karl's two children. Dirk Minniefield never shows. Greg Grissom drags himself in precisely at three o'clock, his eyes hidden by a pair of midnight-black Ray-Ban Wayfarers, and announces brusquely, "I got up ten minutes ago."

There is a small classroom on the main floor of the Armory, across the running track, and Karl calls everyone in to it. The players squeeze themselves into the seats, plastic chairs with half-desk tops, like those found in high school. Karl stands at the front. Gerald takes a seat at his side, and spreads his notebooks in front of him.

First, Gerald passes out sheets of yellow legal paper. "We need addresses and phone numbers where we can reach you over the summer," he says. "Also, your agent's phone number," Karl adds. Everyone scribbles as Karl continues.

"The clutter of ending a season is always, you know, taking care of paying your bills ... please don't make any headaches for us. Please. You can keep all your practice gear, all your sweats, those are yours, but we need the uniforms back. They are more expensive; I don't think they want to have to replace them.

"We will be flying you home. Those that are driving, we'll reimburse your expenses there. I don't know if they did that in the past, but we'll take care of it."

Everyone is already restless; Clint Smith is giggling in the back, Grissom is mean and surly and hung with last night's demons, and he is snapping at everything that is said. Karl senses he's losing his audience. "Gerald, I'm gonna let you take over, 'cause they're ready for you. Go ahead, babe."

Gerald is mean and surly himself; he's got problems to clear up, and anticipates more problems ahead, and he's in no mood for any garbage. "OK, listen up," he says, all business. "I got shit to shovel right now, an' I don't need any more. If you'all got problems, you think somethin' is wrong, I will sit and listen to you, we'll work, and I'll fight, and do everything I can. I have written checks to players out of my own checking account, my players in Maine got paid when there weren't no money to pay 'em. Nothin'. Threw fifty-one dollars on the middle of the floor, that was all we had. So I don't mind if you come to me an' you're angry as hell an' all that. But don't be angry at me. If you're angry at me come tell me why you're angry at me. But don't be angry at me. You got the difference? Is there a difference?" More giggles erupt as the players try to follow

Gerald's reasoning. "We get the point," Grissom snaps, slumped low in his chair.

"I didn't get into some of the problems and I'd like to get into 'em. OK. We will take care of all that's due you, we will get you out of here. What I need is two things. I need to know when you want to go. Now, from the other side of the part of the thing is, some of you have your uniforms. Now, I have been told to get that uniform or there will be a hundred dollars taken outta your thing, your whatchacallit, your check. Now if you wanna pay a hundred dollars for your uniform, or fifty dollars for your pants, well then fine, just tell me you want 'em, an' then you ain't mad at me, I ain't mad at you and the world is beautiful. But if not . . . they ain't but uniforms, they ain't worth it."

"It's just me, it's mine, you can say my name," Grissom growls. "I'll get it to Doc later."

"I'm just sayin' to ya, hey, it's a two-way street. I got enough shit to eat from them other deals, so don't give me more. Unless you want it, then, hey put down the hundred. Any questions on that?

"I need to know when you wanna go home, if you're going home, how you wanna go home, and all that. I hope you can take care of your incidentals out there if you got incidentals an' things. When you get on that airplane at that airport, they are supposed to be at zero. If that's a problem, come an' see me." Clint Smith is convulsing, Grissom is sneering, everyone is getting antsy.

"OK? Is that fair enough? Hey, shit, I'm sick of it, I'm tired of it all too. But that's extra. I am tellin' you this. And I will live with this. I'm gonna say the thing: My integrity is on the line. If that's not enough for you, fuck you." Clint howls.

"Ain't that right, Danny?" Gerald asks.

"Right, Coach." Pearson laughs.

"If ain't that enough, ain't got nothin' else to say. Ain't got nothin' else to offer you 'cept money. An' I'm gonna get that to you. That's it. So let's handle this me-an'-you, together."

"Make sure you get mine, too, Gerald," Karl calls from the back, laughing.

"I'm gonna get that all done, whatever ways I can or can't. All right. Now. Coach, the only thing I know is I need to know . . ."

"Well, let's go over it," Karl jumps in. "Danny, when do you want to leave?"

"Uh, what's today, Tuesday?"

"It's Monday."

"Tuesday, I guess."

"OK," Gerald says. "Greg? Greg doesn't matter. Derrick doesn't leave. Lowes is here. Kenny . . . Wednesday? OK. Doug, you're driving, right? You're gonna be here a little while. Steve, you're going to New York. John, when do you want to leave?"

"Oh, probably Wednesday morning."

"OK. Doc, you'll be about next week. I'll put a big question mark there. Greg Ballard . . . driving. Clinton, you're driving?"

"Yup."

"Did you get your car out of the pound?" Karl asks.

"Yup." "Chuck-ee," Stroeder calls.

"Without being personal, anybody know where Dirk is? Know if he's here or not, or gone? He said he wanted to leave Tuesday afternoon. So I'll put down Wednesday morning. OK. Now. Danny, you're flyin' to . . ."

"North Carolina."

"Kenny?"

"San Francisco."

"OK. Coach, that's done. As soon as this meeting's over, I am going to the office, going to work, an' I'm not plannin' on leavin' there till I get everything straightened out. If you need to discuss anything with me, call me at the office, or talk to me here. Or if you want to call me at night . . ."

"Yeah, Gerald, where you staying now?" Stroeder asks.

"Buddy, if you find me you've found something. 'Cause I live in a little room with no phone and a heater they say if I turn it on it's gonna blow up. It gets cold out there, too. Does pro-plane blow up? It does, if it gets too hot?"

"Pro*pane*? It'll blow you clean out of there," Doug Lee tells him, chuckling.

"Well, I was forewarned. Now I'm freezin' my ass off."

"What about our checks?" several players chorus at once.

"That is what I'm working on today."

"What about the NCAA pool money?"

"Danny Pearson won. No one can catch him. He has three of the Final Four. He cain't lose."

The meeting starts to break down; Doc Nunnally collects the addresses and phone numbers, Gerald cools down, the players giggle even more among themselves. Then Karl steps back to the front of the room.

"OK, everybody, just to conclude all this," he says. "If anyone wants to spend some time, talk about your careers, I'll be glad to do whatever you want to do. I'd like to spend a half hour, forty-five minutes with all of you if you want. I'll be here probably till—"

"Pass them pens back," Gerald interrupts. "Gimme a phone number, at least your momma's phone number where we can get a message to ya."

"We'll talk about your careers, what your situation is, how you want me to help, what I think I can do, what I think you all should do. If it's important to you. We'll go to lunch, play golf. Gris, we can drink beer on the golf course. Ballard says he'll play. Shurina, Stroeder, you wanna play golf?"

"I won't be here," Stroeder says.

"Stay one more day," Grissom barks. "Shit. Wednesday, Tuesday, what's the difference?"

The golf date settled, Karl continues. "Are there any questions you all have for Gerald? Or myself?"

"What are we gonna do about the team van?"

"We're gonna drive it three more days, then we're gonna turn it in," Gerald says.

"Can I have it till then?" Stroeder asks.

"I'd recommend you get your checks as fast as possible," Karl advises, "because the league supposedly is gonna set some fines."

"Golf tomorrow?" Grissom yells. Stroeder stands up and starts to leave.

"Sit down, Stroeds, we're not done," Karl says. "Where you going?" Stroeder shrugs—"I dunno"—and takes his seat. Karl calls for attention.

"Guys," he says, "let me give you all one last lecture. It's been a strange year, but I think it's been a positive year. I'd like to talk to all of you individually, but if I don't I'd like to leave a couple of things with you. I think it's very important that you all have a certain professionalism. I think you all have it, but it's important to grow on. Some of you are younger than others, some of you have different directions you're going on in your careers, but there's three thoughts that I have that are very important in terms of professionalism, things I've learned, probably more so in the last two or three years than I thought I knew when I first got into coaching.

"The first one is, no matter how angry you get or how excited or happy you are, the most important thing in athletics is to communicate. Too many times when you get mad, you don't talk to each other. I think that's one thing I tried to do all year. Everyone here, I think we've had some tough talks, and I think we all feel better. Kenny, you and I have gone at it all year. Every time I've talked about a tough situation, I've felt better. Communication is very, very important. Too many times you guys shut up, don't ask questions, don't ask why. All you guys are intelligent, you all communicate well, but sometimes you're stopping yourselves from communicating. And sometimes that's hurting you.

"The second thing, and I really believe this a lot more now than ever, is that the professional athletes today take from the game. I know you all don't make much money, but we read about athletes in the papers all the time, guys getting paid ten thousand dollars to sign their names at autograph shows, speaking engagements for fifteen thousand dollars, and it seems like the athletes take . . . take . . . take. Now you're on a much smaller scale, but I really would recommend that, every year that you're in athletics, you give something back to the game. Give it back by talking to a community center, by running a camp for kids, by working for the Special Olympics, by going to schools. It takes some discipline on your part—you all would rather go play golf or see your girlfriend. Give something back. The game has given every one of us something. It's given a lot of us an education, given us a lot of friends, a lot of success. It's real important that you work on giving it back.

"The last thing, I think all of us need to set goals. I know it's not a good time to focus. I got a couple phone calls this morning, 'What are you gonna do? What are you thinking about?' I have no focus on my career right now. I don't know exactly what I'm gonna do or where I'm gonna go. I think it's important, a week from now, two weeks from now, that you all sit down with people that you respect and think about your careers. Think about what you have to do to reach those goals. It doesn't just happen. It doesn't just happen that you become an NBA player or a European player making a lot of money. You got to think about it. You got to discipline yourself, push yourself toward a goal. Whatever that is, if that means getting in the best shape of your life, if that means lifting weights, if that means Danny Pearson going on a nutritional diet, whatever it means. Goals are important. Focus on those goals and discipline yourself. Just saying 'I want to be an NBA player' without an intellectual push won't do it.

"Those are the three things. There have been enough lectures. Thank you for a very good year for me. Gerald Oliver, thank you for making my life a hell of a lot easier. Jack Moser, thank you for taking care of the health as well as you were allowed to. The only thing I can leave with is, have a great summer."

Stroeder shoots back up, followed by one and all out the classroom and onto the track. (Grissom stays down longest, then struggles with his equilibrium and takes his feet.) There are some more handshakes, some phone numbers exchanged. Tim Wilkin gets one last interview for his season wrap-up story, while Dan Levy helps some players filch a couple of the banners hanging from the balcony. Grissom leads a posse back to the Sports Bar, where Frank the owner has many bottles of champagne chilling. Gris, now in more comforting surroundings, removes his sunglasses for the first time and resumes his binge, with help from the coaches, Shurina, and a few others. The afternoon becomes the evening, as one by one the revelers leave. Gerald returns to the office. George retrieves his kids and meanders home. Greg Ballard makes plans for tomorrow's golf outing, then leaves by himself. Doc Nunnally, Tim Wilkin, Dan Levy . . . And as darkness falls, Shurina and Grissom are left, counting empty champagne bottles and planning the night's activities.

Over the next few days they scatter—Ken Johnson to California, Danny Pearson to North Carolina, Greg Ballard to Washington, D.C., John Stroeder and his wife to Washington state, Doug Lee and his wife to Illinois. Steve Shurina drives home to New York City. Their plans are mostly undefined, NBA summer camps in July, various summer leagues, time off.

Greg Grissom decides to stay in Albany for a while, at least until the NBA summer camps. He asks Jim Coyne for a job, and, as fate would have it, gets the one he is perhaps most suited for, the one Bill Musselman thought he did anyway; he drives a beer truck. Well, actually, he does promotion work for a Miller distributor, shaking hands and being a Patroon and encouraging consumption of Miller Lite. (And usually drinking more than his appearance fee will cover.) But he'll probably work a bit on a truck, too.

And Clinton Smith makes a dash for Cleveland. In his wake are numerous creditors, some friends (now former friends), some more officious types, all saying terrible things about him. The unofficial tally of Clint's great escape is $1,750 (not including the two twenties owed to Dan Levy and Tim Wilkin), plus some unauthorized electronic equipment and, possibly, a basketball (as yet unproven but highly likely).

Even without the Albany Patroons, the CBA continues and completes its '88–89 season. After beating Albany, Wichita Falls is swept out of the playoffs—4–0—by the Tulsa Fast Breakers in the Eastern Division finals. The Fast Breakers meet the Rockford Lightning (which beat Quad City and Rapid City, each by four games to two, to win the Western Division title) in the CBA finals. Tulsa takes both games in Rockford, then returns home to finish the Lightning off in four games and win the CBA championship.

When former Patroon/current Lightning Dominic Pressley is called up to the Chicago Bulls during the CBA finals, he becomes the twenty-eighth CBA player to move up this season, a CBA single-season record. In all, as of April 1989, fifty-four NBA players have CBA experience on their résumés. Among them is 1989 CBA All-League Second Team guard Kelvin Upshaw.

Two days after the Patroons' season ends, Upshaw calls George Karl from Boston. He's been signed for the rest of the season, and offered a two-year guaranteed contract, with the first year's salary at $150,000, about twenty times the $8,000 he made as an Albany Patroon. Kelvin, who almost didn't play here this year, almost quit, almost got cut, almost ended up working back at the UPS office in Chicago, calls Karl to say thank you.

George Karl stays in Albany while his kids finish school. For the first week he meets with his players individually, giving advice on the directions their careers might take and what they might do to improve their chances. In early April, he is honored with an invitation to sit on the dais of the Dapper Dan High School All Star Game's twenty-fifth anniversary dinner in Pittsburgh (in which he played back in the late sixties). He returns from Pittsburgh and plays some golf and takes a vacation with his family in Washington, D.C. And as spring makes its way into the Northeast, he ponders his future and wonders what he should do next, and waits for the phone to ring.

Gerald stays a couple more weeks, finally leaving in mid-April. He closes up all his bidnesses, gets everyone paid and sent home, and, when he's finally driven everyone crazy, Jim Laverty picks him up and deposits him at the Albany County Airport. And Gerald returns to West Virginia.

At this point it looks like Gerald will be back in Albany next year. He is retained as personnel director, to keep on top of the ever-changing professional basketball landscape and begin assembling the 1989–1990 Albany Patroons. He doesn't have a contract when he leaves, and there are a few sticky points yet to be resolved, but things look good. Gerald is happy. The past season has been a wonderful experience despite the unexpected early loss in the playoffs; Gerald has learned a lot, made new and lasting friends, gotten some things done. He's looking forward to building on that next season.

And he won't have to wait till August to get to work.

POSTSCRIPT—SUMMER, 1989

Over the summer, the CBA expands. Four new teams are added: the Grand Rapids (Michigan) Hoops, the Sioux Falls (South Dakota) Skyforce, the San Jose (California) Jammers, and the Santa Barbara (California) Islanders. Additionally, two of the less successful franchises relocate. The Charleston Gunners move to Columbus, Ohio, where they become the Columbus Horizon; and the Rochester Flyers find themselves in Omaha, Nebraska, as the Omaha Racers. To accommodate the new teams, the league realigns itself, dividing the sixteen teams into four geographical divisions.

Sadly, Jay Ramsdell is not around to see the league's continued success, tragically losing his life in the United Airlines crash in Sioux City, Iowa. The league owners appoint Deputy Commissioner Jerry Schemmel acting commissioner for the upcoming season.

The Patroons go through some changes of their own. Ben Fernandez sells his majority ownership to two local businessmen, who promptly announce that they intend to change the team's name to the New York Patroons—a move met with almost universal ridicule. Still, it might happen.

What won't happen is the return of George Karl. When the NBA fails to come calling, Karl accepts the head coaching job of Real Madrid, one of the top teams in Spain. Once again, Karl faces a dilemma. Spain is a long way from the NBA—longer, even, than the CBA. On the other hand, a reported two-year deal, at $250,000-per, plus all the usual Euro-perks, is hard to pass up. He goes, but with serious reservations.

And that leaves the door open in Albany. In July, Gerald Oliver is named the Patroons head coach for the 1989–90 season.

FINAL STATISTICS

Continental Basketball Association Standings (FINAL)

EASTERN DIVISION	W	L	QW*	Pts	Avg
Albany Patroons	36	18	125.5	233.5	4.3
Tulsa Fast Breakers	28	26	114.0	198.0	3.7
Pensacola Tornados	30	24	104.5	194.5	3.6
Wichita Falls Texans	23	31	104.5	173.5	3.2
Charleston Gunners	20	34	97.5	157.5	2.9
Topeka Sizzlers	14	40	83.0	125.0	2.3

WESTERN DIVISION	W	L	QW*	Pts	Avg
Rapid City Thrillers	38	16	131.5	245.5	4.5
Quad City Thunder	36	18	122.5	230.5	4.3
Rockford Lightning	34	20	121.5	223.5	4.1
Cedar Rapids S. Bullets	30	24	100.5	190.5	3.5
La Crosse Catbirds	19	35	103.0	160.0	3.0
Rochester Flyers	16	38	88.0	136.0	2.5

*Quarters won. Teams get 3 points for a win, 1 point for each quarter won, and ½ point for any quarter tied.

Avg = Average points per game played.

1988–1989 Albany Patroons
Final Regular Season Statistics

Player's Name	Games	MIN	AVG	FGM	FGA	PCT.	FTM	FTA	PCT.
Rowland	31	936	30.2	205	385	0.532	153	185	0.827
Askew	29	989	34.1	196	368	0.533	152	225	0.676
Lee	53	1682	31.7	220	482	0.456	245	285	0.860
K. Smith	16	523	32.7	99	184	0.538	34	62	0.548
Upshaw	40	1242	31.1	216	440	0.491	132	157	0.841
Stroeder	42	1326	31.6	225	469	0.480	160	197	0.812
Pearson	44	1250	28.4	195	397	0.491	139	172	0.808
Popson	14	300	21.4	69	127	0.543	16	28	0.571
Engelstad	13	338	26.0	51	126	0.405	29	35	0.829
Moore	2	40	20.0	9	11	0.818	3	5	0.600
C. Smith	43	845	19.7	161	316	0.509	61	103	0.592
Harris	10	211	21.1	37	83	0.446	11	16	0.688
Minniefield	15	334	22.3	33	66	0.500	22	26	0.846
Shurina	42	938	22.3	100	213	0.469	111	135	0.822
Ballard	7	125	17.9	20	41	0.488	17	19	0.895
Pressley	5	79	15.8	12	18	0.667	4	5	0.800
Johnson	44	948	21.5	111	212	0.524	57	121	0.471
Jones	11	138	12.5	22	40	0.550	12	20	0.600
Grissom	43	716	16.7	57	135	0.422	39	54	0.722
Albany Total	54	12960	240.0	2038	4113	0.496	1397	1850	0.755
Opponent Total	54	12960	240.0	1877	4074	0.461	1266	1680	0.754

Score by quarters

	1	2	3	4	OT	TOTAL
Albany	1482	1545	1487	1496	0	6010
Opponents	1434	1441	1388	1387	0	5650

Points by quarters

	1	2	3	4	TOTAL
Albany	31.5	34.5	30.0	29.5	125.5
Opponents	22.5	19.5	24.0	24.5	90.5

3PM	3PA	T-PTS	G-AVG	REBS	AVG	AST	AVG	BS	ST
16	50	611	19.7	120	3.9	80	2.6	20	39
0	4	544	18.8	267	9.2	76	2.6	24	41
95	220	970	18.3	174	3.3	138	2.6	4	58
9	20	259	16.2	55	3.4	77	4.8	2	27
12	31	600	15.0	105	2.6	238	6.0	10	62
4	21	622	14.8	429	10.2	107	2.5	36	33
10	32	559	12.7	210	4.8	87	2.0	12	39
0	0	154	11.0	85	6.1	13	0.9	12	3
3	9	140	10.8	82	6.3	19	1.5	1	9
0	0	21	10.5	3	1.5	7	3.5	0	1
1	5	386	9.0	176	4.1	86	2.0	2	30
0	0	85	8.5	39	3.9	15	1.5	1	8
13	30	127	8.5	42	2.8	66	4.4	1	15
13	37	350	8.3	126	3.0	134	3.2	2	35
0	2	57	8.1	37	5.3	10	1.4	2	3
2	5	34	6.8	5	1.0	12	2.4	0	7
0	1	279	6.3	421	9.6	27	0.6	39	13
0	1	56	5.1	38	3.5	6	0.5	2	4
1	4	156	3.6	222	5.2	46	1.1	43	15
179	471	6010	111.3	2636	48.8	1244	23.0	213	442
210	671	5650	104.6	2250	41.7	1091	20.2	315	537